MARXISM AND FILM ACTIVISM

Marxism and Film Activism

Screening Alternative Worlds

Edited by
Ewa Mazierska and Lars Kristensen

berghahn
NEW YORK · OXFORD
www.berghahnbooks.com

Published in 2015 by
Berghahn Books
www.berghahnbooks.com

© 2015, 2018 Ewa Mazierska and Lars Kristensen
First paperback edition published in 2018

All rights reserved. Except for the quotation of short passages
for the purposes of criticism and review, no part of this book
may be reproduced in any form or by any means, electronic or
mechanical, including photocopying, recording, or any information
storage and retrieval system now known or to be invented,
without written permission of the publisher.

Library of Congress Cataloging-in-Publication Data

Marxism and film activism : screening alternative worlds / edited by Ewa Mazierska and Lars Kristensen.
  pages cm
  Includes bibliographical references and index.
  ISBN 978-1-78238-642-1 (hardback) — ISBN 978-1-78238-643-8 (ebook)
 1. Motion pictures—Political aspects. 2. Motion pictures—Social aspects. 3. Communism and motion pictures. I. Mazierska, Ewa, editor. II. Kristensen, Lars Lyngsgaard Fjord, editor.
  PN1995.9.P6M39 2015
  791.43'658—dc23

2014033568

British Library Cataloguing in Publication Data

A catalogue record for this book is available from the British Library

ISBN: 978-1-78238-642-1 hardback
ISBN: 978-1-78533-762-8 paperback
ISBN: 978-1-78238-643-8 ebook

Contents

List of Figures   vii

Introduction   1
Ewa Mazierska and Lars Kristensen

Part I. Past Activism

Chapter 1. Between Socialist Modernization and Cinematic Modernism: the Revolutionary Politics of Aesthetics of Medvedkin's Cinema-Train   29
Gal Kirn

Chapter 2. Politics and Aesthetics within Godard's Cinema   58
Jeremy Spencer

Chapter 3. Marker, Activism and Melancholy: Reflections on the Radical '60s in the Later Films of Chris Marker   81
Jon Kear

Chapter 4. Marx Immemorial: Workers and Peasants in the Cinema of Jean-Marie Straub and Danièle Huillet   105
Manuel Ramos-Martinez

Chapter 5. In the Heat of the Factory: the Global Fires of *The Hour of the Furnaces*   124
Bruce Williams

Part II. Present Activism

Chapter 6. Contemporary Political Cinema: the Impossibility of Passivity   145
William Brown

Chapter 7. Cultural Resistance through Film: the Case of Palestinian Cinema   166
Haim Bresheeth

Chapter 8. The Contemporary Landscape of Video-Activism in Britain   186
Steve Presence

Chapter 9. Marxist Resistance at Bicycle Speed: Screening the Critical Mass Movement   213
Lars Kristensen

Chapter 10. Swallowing Time: On the Immaterial Labour of the Video Blogger   234
Michael Chanan

Chapter 11. Recovering the Future: Marxism and Film Audiences   253
Martin Barker

Notes on Contributors   272

Index   276

Figures

Figure 1.1. Agit-train 'Lenin'. Image from Red Files Website.   40

Figure 1.2. Camel of Shame, animated character from cinema-train films. Screen capture from Chris Marker's *Last Bolshevik* (1993).   45

Figure 2.1. Godard, *La Chinoise* (1967). Screen capture.   72

Figure 3.1. Cinema is not magic, it is a technique, a science born in the service of will: the will of workers to free themselves. Screen capture from Groupe Medvedkine de Besançon, *Classe de Lutte*, Société pour le Lancement des Oeuvres Nouvelles (1968).   87

Figure 3.2. Peace signs featured as part of the imagery of revolt. Screen capture from Chris Marker, *Le Fond de l'air est Rouge* (1977).   99

Figure 4.1. Group of peasants. Screen capture from a television broadcast of *Operai, Contadini* (*Workers, Peasants*, 2000) by Jean-Marie Straub and Danièle Huillet.   114

Figure 4.2. Group of workers. Screen capture from a television broadcast of *Operai, Contadini* (*Workers, Peasants*, 2000) by Jean-Marie Straub and Danièle Huillet.   115

Figure 5.1. Debunking the Good Life. Screen capture from *The Hour of the Furnaces* (1968), Grupo Cine Liberación.   129

Figure 5.2. Factory takeover. Screen capture from *The Hour of the Furnaces* (1968), Grupo Cine Liberación.   131

Figure 6.1. Under erasure: Deleuze's name is crossed through on a blackboard in *Elite Squad*. Screen capture from *Tropa de Elite*, or *Elite Squad* (José Padilha, 2007).   157

Figure 6.2. The window as cinema screen: Champion watches his son, Adam, being abducted by the army in *A Screaming Man*. Screen capture from *Un Homme qui Crie*, or *A Screaming Man* (Mahomet-Saleh Haroun, 2010).   162

Figure 7.1. The Palestinian girls' choir singing the nationalist Hebrew 'independence' song in Elia Suleiman's *The Time that Remains* (2009). No funding from the Palestine Authority was used, in a film financed by European TV channels and the MEDIA programme, in the main. The image is courtesy of the filmmaker. 179

Figure 7.2. Emad Burnat with his broken cameras in *Five Broken Cameras* (2011). The film received no support whatsoever from the Palestinian Authority, like most other films produced in Palestine. The image is courtesy of the film's co-producer, Guy Davidi. 181

Figure 8.1. *Globalisation and the Media* (2002). Screen capture from YouTube. 198

Figure 8.2. *SchNEWS at Ten* (2005). Screen capture from *SchNEWS at Ten* (SchNEWS, 2005). 202

Figure 9.1. Critical Mass Houston, United States. From YouTube, 'Houston Critical Mass – July 2013', uploaded by Abrahán Garza. 223

Figure 9.2. Critical Mass Hamburg, Germany. From YouTube, 'critical mass hamburg 24.06.2011', uploaded by Martin John. 224

Figure 9.3. Critical Mass Cluj-Napoca (Kolozsvár), Romania. From Vimeo, 'Critical Mass March 2013 Cluj-Napoca/Kolozsvár', uploaded by Torok Tihamer. 225

Figure 10.1. Image from *Chronicle of Protest* (Michael Chanan, 2011), a documentary compiled from the author's video blogs for the *New Statesman*. 239

Figure 10.2. Image from *Chronicle of Protest* (Michael Chanan, 2011), a documentary compiled from the author's video blogs for the *New Statesman*. 249

Introduction

Ewa Mazierska and Lars Kristensen

It is widely assumed that one of the main differences between Marxism and other types of philosophy is its practical orientation, most clearly revealed in Marx's 'Theses on Feuerbach' and *The Communist Manifesto*. Thesis 8 of 'Theses on Feuerbach' states: 'All social life is essentially *practical*. All the mysteries which urge theory into mysticism find their rational solution in human practice and in the comprehension of this practice' (Marx and Engels 1947: 199). This thesis suggests that practice tests the usefulness of theories, but equally theories reflect on practice. Theories and practices are thus dependent on each other, although the precise character of their connection is difficult to assess. Thesis 11, the best known of Marx's 'Theses on Feuerbach', states: 'The philosophers have only *interpreted* the world differently, the point is to change it' (ibid.: 199). This thesis represents Marx as diverting from a Hegelian version of history as a sequence of events, emerging as if on its own accord, or shaped solely by material forces. Instead, it evokes the idea of history as an arena, in which objective and subjective factors come together, producing results that cannot be predicted on the basis of what happened previously. This means that people striving for a specific state of affairs should not wait in a comfortable armchair for this state to occur, or resign in the conviction that it would not happen during their lifetime, but work towards its fulfilment. Among these people a privileged place is occupied by those, who thanks to their intellectual resources, are able to better understand the world in which they operate than the bulk of the population. As Marx writes in *The German Ideology*: 'Consciousness can sometimes appear further advanced than the contemporary empirical relationships, so that in the struggles of a later epoch one can refer to earlier theoreticians as authorities' (ibid.: 72). The moral duty of those with advanced consciousness is to work towards the change, bringing about the Communist revolution by means such as education, political activism and, when necessary, armed struggle. In *The Communist Manifesto* Marx labels this section of society 'Communists', saying that:

The Communists are distinguished from the other working-class parties by this only:

1. In the national struggles of the proletarians of the different countries, they point out and bring to the front the common interests of the entire proletariat, independently of all nationality.

2. In the various stages of development which the struggle of the working class against the bourgeoisie has to pass through, they always and everywhere represent the interests of the movement as a whole. (Marx and Engels 2008: 52)

In the twentieth century, when communism appeared to be winning in some parts of the world, the term 'Communists' was replaced by expressions such as 'revolutionary avant-garde' or 'engineers of human souls', the last term being applied specifically to artists. Terms like these gained negative connotations due to equating their referents with the cadres of the Communist parties in the Soviet Union and other countries of state socialism, so-called *nomenklatura*, which rather than leading the masses to achieve democratic socialism, used their power to advance their social position at the expense of the disadvantaged. However, the fact that this happened does not undermine a need for activism and political leadership to achieve or even approximate the Marxist ideal of a just and egalitarian society. On the contrary, against the background of the subsequent fall of state socialism and the successes of neoliberal capitalism, Marxist activism is needed more than ever. As Stuart Hall put it in the 1980s, we 'need a party' (Hall 1988: 180), namely a mass and well-organized left-wing movement able to overthrow the current capitalist regime. This movement would not happen, if not, initially, for a tiny minority, able to point out to the majority that the world needs a dramatic change and suggest how to accomplish it. The character and the role of this party and its leaders, however, keep changing in step with changing historical circumstances. In particular, the current speed of communication, the diminished role of direct censorship and with that the rise of a global flow of ideas, unimagined just decades ago, requires a different strategy from the activists than in the past. One goal of this book is to find out what was required of those with 'advanced consciousness' in the past and what is expected from them now, in order to approximate the ideal of creating an egalitarian and just society.

Marxist Theory, Marxist Practice

Let us begin with recollecting the past of Marx and Engels. The authors of *The Communist Manifesto* were, at the beginning of their careers, associated with the group of disciples of Hegel known as the Young Hegelians, which also included Bruno Bauer, Max Stirner and Ludwig Feuerbach. As R. Pascal notes, they had learnt from Hegel that the state is the embodiment of the absolute mind, of the ideas of freedom, justice etc., and they demanded that it should really be so. They therefore subjected the dominant conceptions of their times to a detailed criticism, and maintained that if true notions were substituted for the prevailing ones, society would be reformed. But, while going to all lengths in criticizing existing conceptions and conventions, the characteristic of the group was that it refused to take part in movements of reform, believing that ideas lose their purity in the hands of the masses. This antithesis between intellect and masses soon led to an antithesis between support of existing conditions and the movements of social reform, and many of this group ended up as ardent reactionaries. Only Marx and Engels accepted the challenge of the times. In 1842 Marx undertook the editorship of a newly funded progressive liberal radical newspaper, the *Rheinische Zeitung*, 'yet within a year Marx had turned his back on the entire movement of democratic and forward-looking burgers and had joined the sparser ranks of those opposed in principle to market economy, its system of money and its culture of economics' (Meikle 2009: 56). Forced by state censors to relinquish his post, he emigrated to Paris in 1848 and thus began his nomadic life. Engels had been wrenched out of the abstract world of the Young Hegelians by a business trip to Manchester, where he entered into relations with the working-class movement of Chartism (Pascal 1947: ix-xii). For the rest of their lives the two 'fathers of Marxism' fulfilled their own criterion of a Communist by engaging in political journalism, as opposed to devoting themselves merely to 'proper' philosophy, which was accessible only to an intellectual elite and leading political organizations: the Communist League and the First International. For his political activism Marx especially paid a heavy price, by entering into conflict with the political authorities and being continuously expelled from the countries where he engaged in such activities; Germany, France and Belgium, before dying on foreign soil in England. The multiple expulsions and continuous uprooting immensely affected his working schedule. One can speculate that if he had had a more stable life, he would have written more, including finishing his magnum opus, *Das Kapital*. Yet, it is political activism that provided Marx's writings with their deepest insights and furnished them with a specific aura. Many readers trust Marx's work because they know that there is no gap between the man and his teaching – he was the living embodiment of socialist praxis. For other, more conservative commentators, Marxist involvement in active politics renders him as a 'pseudo-philosopher', not fit for the pantheon of Western thought (Scruton 1995: 203).

Virtually all well known Marxist philosophers of the two generations following Marx were involved in active politics, to name just Karl Kautsky, Rosa Luxemburg, Karl Liebknecht, Antonio Gramsci, Karl Korsch and VI Lenin. However, the closer we come to contemporary times, the smaller is the proportion of Marxists thinkers involved in frontline politics. This situation can be attributed, among other factors, to the absorption of Marxists thinkers after the Second World War into (mostly) Western academia, especially in France and the United States. On the one hand, this situation allows Marxists a secure existence, which includes making their living from teaching and writing academic books, which their predecessors could not take for granted. On the other, however, it leads to a perception that theorizing Marxism is an art for art's sake. As Macdonald Daly observes in a book devoted to Marxist aesthetics, mentioning authors such as Jean-Paul Sartre, Lucian Goldmann, Louis Althusser, Pierre Macherey, Roland Barthes, Etienne Balibar and Pierre Bourdieu, the price paid for such academization and theoretical advancement of Marxist theory was not only neutralization of political activity, but also 'intensifying rebarbativeness and obfuscation in the discourse many of these scholars employed. The experience of reading any of the critics named above can hardly be said to be easy or straightforward. The level of education and degree of wider philosophical and theoretical knowledge required for their understanding are taxing' (Daly 2006: xxii–xxiii). No doubt the difficulty of some forms of Marxist discourse puts off prospective Marxist activists, or makes them think that their activism has little in common with Marx's and Engels's teaching.

The question of how 'practical' or 'praxis-oriented' a Marxist thinker, and by extension artist and critic, should be, became itself an issue widely debated in Marxist circles. Predictably, on this occasion, base strongly affects superstructure – a dividing line is between the 'armchair Marxists' and those who themselves are involved in active politics or at least in popularizing Marxism outside academia. We would like to draw attention to the arguments used by some of the most prominent Marxists of the twentieth century. One of them is a co-creator of the Frankfurt School, Theodor Adorno. The starting point of his short essay poignantly titled 'Resignation' is that a reproach of resignation was levelled against the members of this school for political passivity:

> *The objection raised against us can be stated approximately in these words: a person who in the present hour doubts the possibility of radical change in society and who for that reason neither takes part in nor recommends spectacular, violent action is guilty of resignation. He does not consider the vision of change which he once held capable of realization; indeed, he actually had no true desire to see it realized in the first place. In leaving conditions as they are, he offers his tacit approval of them. (Adorno 1991: 171)*

In response to the criticism of inactivity, Adorno claims that the request to act, as opposed to only talk (or write), hides a hostility towards theory or at least does not attribute to theory the importance it deserves. 'The often-evoked unity of theory and praxis has a tendency to give way to the predominance of praxis. Numerous views define theory itself as a form of repression – as though praxis did not stand in a far more direct relationship to repression' (ibid.: 172). Secondly, he condemns much of praxis as 'psuedo-activity',[1] which is in fact worse than a lack of activity. Thirdly, he argues that thinking is itself a form of action and even of revolutionary action:

> *In contrast [to psueudo-practitioner], the uncompromisingly critical thinker, who neither superscribes his conscience nor permits himself to be terrorized into action, is in truth the one who does not give up. Furthermore, thinking is not the spiritual reproduction of that which exists. As long as thinking is not interrupted, it has a firm grasp upon possibility. Its insatiable quality, the resistance against petty satiety, rejects the foolish wisdom of resignation. Open thinking points beyond itself. For its part, such thinking takes a position as a figuration of praxis which is more closely related to a praxis truly involved in change than in a position of mere obedience for the sake of praxis. (ibid.: 174–5)*

Slavoj Žižek, albeit in the context of the way U.S. politicians dealt with recent economic crises, echoes Adorno's argument, mocking those who engage in pseudo-activity, rather than thinking. 'The old saying "Don't just talk, do something!" is one of the most stupid things one can say, even measured by the low standards of common sense' (Žižek 2009: 11). Implicitly such comments privilege theory over praxis, both as preceding praxis chronologically and logically. Yet, despite Adorno's immense rhetorical skill, one can see that the author avoids rather than tackles head on the problem of Marxism as a form of activism.

On the other side of the barricade, so to speak, we find those who argue that a reliable theory (and not only a Marxist theory) is that which is created in conjunction with praxis. This requirement was recently proposed in an eloquent way by French philosopher Alain Badiou, who wrote:

> *I have suggested that a philosopher (and this neutral noun naturally encompasses both male and female varieties) must be an accomplished scientist, an amateur poet and a political activist, but also has to accept that the realm of thought is never sealed off from the violent onslaughts of love. Philosophy requires its practitioners of either gender to assume the roles of savant, artist, activist and lover. I have called them the four conditions of philosophy.* (Badiou 2012: 2)

Badiou's requirement that philosophers should be both political activists and lovers can be read metaphorically as a demand to be all-rounded individuals, whose identities are united rather than divided into separate functions. Such a demand, however, is not universally accepted, to a large extent due to great specialization of knowledge and a growing distance (physical and temporal) between work processes and their effects.

It is also worth mentioning in this context Michel Foucault, who in his talks with Duccio Trombadori, published as *Remarks on Marx,* draws connection between one's attitude to Marxism and one's living experience of political struggle. Foucault mentions that in Communist Poland Marxism meant something different than in the France of the 1960s, and this was still a different thing in Tunisia, where Foucault found himself in 1968. In Poland, for the majority of the population it was an object of total disgust; in France a matter of subtle theoretical discussions, which led to the fragmentation of Marxism into small bodies of doctrine that pronounced excommunication upon one another; in Tunisia a call to action, 'a kind of moral force, an existential act that left one stupefied' (Foucault 1991: 135). Foucault does not hide that it was a Tunisian version of Marxism that appealed to him most. Indeed, the national liberation of postcolonial countries seems to be a perfect example of Marxist theory merging with direct political action and cultural resistance, especially through cinema (Wayne 2001); a fact that this book attempts to reflect.

Post-May '68 Activism

Foucault and many philosophers of his generation, in one way or another at certain periods of their lives, became active in politics. Badiou is a founding member of the militant French political organization *L'Organisation Politique*, which was active from 1985 till 2007 and was concerned with direct intervention in issues such as immigration, labour and housing. Foucault was involved in the movement striving for prison reform in France. Antonio Negri was accused of supporting the Red Brigades, a Marxist paramilitary organization, which was responsible for the kidnap and murder of the Italian president Aldo Moro. As a result, he was sentenced to a long prison sentence and forced to flee to France. Although Foucault, Badiou and Negri's life trajectories are in many ways different, they are connected by the fact that their youth coincided with the political fervour of the late 1960s and 1970s, when the postwar consensus in Europe started to crumble and there was an expectation that around the corner awaited a new political order. Especially significant in this context is the year 1968, when there was a great political turmoil in many parts of the world, most importantly in France. This turmoil did not lead to the introduction of a worldwide or even pan-European socialism but, paradoxically, paved the way to a more ruthless version of capitalism, known as neoliberalism or late capitalism (Debray 1979),[2] and to a crisis in Marxist theory and praxis. This crisis resulted from the perception that Marxism, as practised before 1968, did not respond properly either to the changing composition of Western societies, such as the decline of the industrial working class, increase of migratory workers and the emancipatory ambitions of various marginalized groups, most importantly women (Boltanski and Chiapello 2005; Harvey 2006). Consequently, the year 1968 marks a shift to a different model of politics than traditional Marxist politics – postmodern politics. To understand this, it is worth again evoking Badiou, who argues that there were four different 'Mays'. One was marked by a revolt on the part of young university and school students. The second was the biggest general strike in the French history, whose point of reference was the Popular Front. This strike proved very heterogeneous, with workers showing insubordination to trade unions and the Communist Party. The effect of this May, as observed by Stuart Hall, is that since then being radical no longer meant identifying with radical party politics but being 'radically against all parties, party lines and party bureaucracies' (Hall 1988: 181). The third, no less complex, was the libertarian May, which concerned the question of changing moral climate, sexual relations and individual freedom. It gave rise to the women's and gay rights movements and had a significant impact on the cultural sphere.

The last May, which lasted from 1968 to 1978 and which is of special interest to us, was to do with the end of the old concept of politics and, consequently, redefinition of the political field. From the 1970s in the West, any social cause and struggle, any cultural activity, could be viewed as political. This had an effect of giving voice to the sections of society that were overlooked by politicians in the earlier periods, such as women and ethnic minorities, and causes that were previously deemed relatively unimportant within Marxist discourse, such as ecology. This development can be viewed positively, as leading to creating an egalitarian and just society, in which the interest of every disadvantaged group is properly looked after. However, as Badiou observes, with the widening spectrum of political voices came the loss of hierarchy of political agents and causes; they had all drowned in the cacophony of 'postmodern politics'. Badiou thus concludes that May resulted in the end of the idea that there is such a thing as an historical agent offering the possibility of emancipation: a notion at the heart of Marxism. It was variously known as the working class, the proletariat and sometimes the people, and though there were debates as to its position and its size, everyone agreed that it existed. The shared conviction that there is an 'objective' agent inscribed in social reality, and that it offers the possibility of emancipation, is probably the biggest difference between then and now (Badiou 2010: 43–100). Elsewhere, echoing Jean-François Lyotard's idea of postmodernism as the end of 'grand narratives' (1984), Badiou describes the 1970s as a watershed, which divides 'the final years of revolutionary fervour' from 'the triumph of minuscule ideas' (Badiou 2007: 3).

Iain Hamilton-Grant describes this situation in such terms: 'Where the political will of a people, a nation or a culture used to be harnessed to long-term general goals, now fragmented groups engage in short-term struggles. The spread of identity politics over the last twenty years is testimony to this, with its emphasis on ethnicity, class, gender and sexuality replacing political credo' (Hamilton-Grant 2001: 30). He further observes that the consequence of engaging in identity and micropolitics is leaving macro decisions to the enemy: 'By concentrating all the attention on "micro-political" issues, or on short-term single-issue politics, the very real large-scale political structures that govern our everyday lives are disregarded and left uncontested to the enemy, which simply translates into covert support for, or actual complicity with, the status quo' (ibid.: 31). If we accept this argument, then left-wing micro-activism (often undertaken by numerous NGOs) is open to the criticism of being in fact an obstacle to universal emancipation by acting as a means of diverting people's attention from the larger picture of politics or as a vent to their political frustration.

The overall lack of effectiveness of postmodern politics can also be seen in the context of the development of Western capitalism, as theorized by Herbert Marcuse, a member of the Frankfurt School, whose influence on the political ferment of the 1960s was probably greater than that of any other philosopher (Jameson 1990: 5). In his works, and most importantly in *One-Dimensional Man*, Marcuse pictures a flattened, 'one-dimensional world', populated by 'one-dimensional people', where there is no place for truly radical ideas. In such a world consensus reality is the only reality, dissent is commodified and absorbed by capitalism and radical ideas are rejected because they are rendered too difficult for the general population. Marcuse draws attention to the link between an advancement of technology and increased difficulty of breaking free of the capitalist shackles (Marcuse 1964) – a fact to which we return shortly.

The year 1968 is also an important date in the history of cinema, especially French and European cinema, because during this moment filmmakers became as politically active as never before, perhaps with the exception of the period following the October Revolution. However, the overall effect of May '68 on cinema is a subject of competing opinions, with some authors, such as Catherine Breillat, claiming that it was 'a micro-event of no importance', while others, such as Jean-Michel Frodon, argue that 'the direct effects of '68 were negligible but the underground effects were gigantic and mostly good' (quoted in Foucault 2008: 30). We lean towards the second opinion, believing that May '68 brought several ideas that till now have informed our thinking about left-wing cinema and even pertain more to contemporary times than to the late 1960s and 1970s. One concerns transcending or rather extending the idea of film authorship, resulting from a belief in collaboration, based on partnership between different people engaged in filmmaking, such as directors, actors and film technicians, as well as among filmmakers working in different countries and in different types of films. The cinema of '68 was to a large extent cinema of film collectives, of which the most famous is the Dziga Vertov Group, led by Godard (see the chapter by Jeremy Spencer in this collection) and of international and inter-continental solidarity, most importantly solidarity between filmmakers from the developed and developing world, as discussed in the chapter by Bruce Williams (see also Emmelhainz 2009: 650). Another important May idea concerned tearing down the division between the producers and consumers of films, in this way making cinema more democratic. Filmmakers of this movement wanted to make films for people who could see themselves on screen, often literally, by filming strikes and employing nonprofessional actors. Furthermore, May '68 demonstrated that great films can be made on a very low budget. Lastly and most importantly, however, during May '68, more than at any earlier moment of history, cinema became intermingled with political activism. Since then, it is difficult to imagine political activism shunning cinema or the moving image in a wider sense and, conversely, political cinema staying aloof from extracinematic political action.

Marxist Filmmakers between Irrelevance and Betrayal

And yet, the overall impression is that post-'68 Marxist or even more broadly understood left-wing cinematic activism is more on the periphery of cinema than ever before. Already the films made by Marker and Godard have a small audience in comparison with Hollywood blockbusters. Moreover, the gap between the success of films such as *The Matrix* (Andy and Lana Wachowski, 1999) in reaching an audience, in comparison with those made by British left-wing videoactivists, is growing rather than shrinking. Why is this the case and how to halt and reverse this process? How to be a successful Marxist film activist in the twenty-first century, one who manages to unite people for the common goal of a socialist revolution? To help answer this question, let's look at some theoretical positions regarding Marxist activism and political cinema at large.

Historically, we can identify several positions regarding Marxist film activism. Firstly, one can argue that making films containing Marxist ideas and motifs is itself a form of activism, because it requires more activity, including collaborating with other human beings, than producing other types of Marxist texts. Accordingly, all filmmakers are activists – and all filmmakers of Marxist persuasion are political activists. However, for many Marxist filmmakers, making films including Marxist motifs is not enough. This requirement was presented most famously by Jean-Luc Godard during his militant (post-'68) period, when he announced that he does not just want to make 'political films', but to make them 'politically' (see the chapter by Jeremy Spencer in this collection). Early Marxist filmmakers working in the Soviet Russia, such as Dziga Vertov and Aleksandr Medvedkin (the latter being the subject of the chapter by Gal Kirn), fulfilled this condition by making films not only about specific political problems, but together with those affected by these problems and showing them the fruit of their common work. They also put themselves into the task of reforming the film industry, so that it could serve Marxist purposes. Although technically and logistically it was an enormous task, it was made easier due to them having an ally in the country's political leader, Lenin, who proclaimed cinema as the best language to reach the masses. Lenin exalted cinema because, due to being silent and visual, it spoke even to the illiterate, an advantage particularly appreciated in a country with a high proportion of people unable to read or write. Even though Soviet Russia is nowadays regarded as falling short of the Marxist ideal of communism, everybody agrees that Marxist cinema had its heyday during the early Soviet period (Kleinhans 1998: 106–7).

According to Godard, making films politically in the Western context means using independent financial sources, rather than being backed by large companies, which are profit-oriented, in a self-reflexive way, revealing the means of their production, and directly engaging with the audience, for example by showing them in factories and during rallies, for the purpose of politicizing the viewers. By trying to fulfil these conditions Godard followed in the footsteps of earlier Marxist filmmakers, such as the previously mentioned Dziga Vertov and Aleksandr Medvedkin, as conveyed by naming his collective after the former. The requirement of producing political films politically results from the conviction that every film made within a capitalist framework ultimately serves capitalism, even if it encourages us to attack the very system that produced it, an idea shared by Godard with Marcuse, as already indicated. However, under the capitalist system, following this recipe brings a risk of reaching a very small audience because films of this sort are shunned by large television stations and multiplexes. To put it bluntly, it most likely leads to irrelevance. This was the case of Godard, whose 'militant films' are hardly known outside the circle of committed academics and such principled directors as Peter Watkins, who after leaving the BBC on the grounds of being a vehicle of the political establishment, practically lost contact with mass audiences and sentenced himself to working on the peripheries of cinema.

It is difficult to say whether a view that Marxist films should be made politically is concurrent with Marx's opinion. Marx, of course, did not comment on different ways of making films as there were no films in his time, but he praised such authors as Honorè de Balzac, who despite being conservative and royalist, was able to reveal the immortality of capitalism and hence, potentially, help to fight it (Prawer 1976: 318). Jacques Rancière develops Marx's line of thinking by pointing to the political significance of *Madame Bovary* by Gustave Flaubert. Despite Flaubert's aristocratic situation and political conformism (and, of course, using capitalist channels of communications with the readers, namely profit-oriented publishing houses), he regards *Madame Bovary* as a progressive work of art of great significance, helping in the emancipation of women (Rancière 2004: 12–19).

If we accept such a position, then mainstream, big budgeted, narrative films, produced in Hollywood as commodities by and for 'consumer society' and screened in multiplexes, should not be regarded by Marxists with hostility as being a product of political conformism, but as work that merely promotes and normalizes the capitalist status quo, or serves as proof of the great skill with which capitalist rulers are able to absorb and neutralize all possible dissent. A more productive approach is to assume that the relationship of them to the represented reality and to potential viewers is more ambiguous and complex, as argued by some chapters included in this collection. In particular, some films, sponsored by capitalists, might encourage viewers to think seriously about the injustice of the capitalist class system and in this way make a contribution to the struggle for human emancipation. This approach is reflected in recent scholarship focusing on Marxist motifs in the films of James Cameron (Kendrik 1999) and the Wachowski siblings (Burns 2015).

By and large, Marxist film activists face a dilemma: either shun the capitalist mode of production and distribution and risk becoming irrelevant, or try to address the global audience by preaching their sermon from pulpits controlled by the capitalist devil and risk that their sermon will serve furthering capitalist causes. Of course, between these two extreme positions there are many more moderate, which are explored in this volume.

Active Filmmaking, Active Viewing

Activist filmmaking is as much a matter of the behaviour of filmmakers as that of the audiences. Perhaps for our purpose the best starting point is to assume, as did Jacques Rancière, that the spectator is not passive, but already active and creative thanks to selecting, comparing and interpreting images, sounds and ideas (Rancière 2009: 11). The task of the Marxist filmmaker is thus not to 'wake up' the sleepy spectator, but to mobilize him or her in a way that would be most conducive to achieving Marxist ideals in specific historical circumstances. However, this is not a straightforward task – audience studies is still one of the most undeveloped branches of film studies.

What is, however, safe to assume is that the section of the potential audience who would most likely benefit from the transition to socialism is nowadays very heterogeneous and fragmented, both in terms of its external circumstances and consciousness, as Stuart Hall observed. For example, those who largely replaced the industrial working class, the proletariat, who constituted the core of the Communist movement in Marx's times and many decades after his death, are often unemployed or work in several part-time positions, isolated from each other and unaware of the existence of many in similar circumstances. The traditional Marxist hubs associated with the working class movement, such as political parties and trade unions, under the neoliberal regime became politically marginalized. In the West (or global North), showing films in factories is no longer a viable option, because very few factories are left. Moreover, potential recipients of Marxist films wear many 'hats', and have many conflicting identities. For example, a white female worker might be engaged in the feminist struggle, but equally be hostile to granting more rights to immigrant workers, irrespective of their gender.

The successful strategy appears to be to respond to the heterogeneity, to the plethora of seemingly different grievances of different groups by recognizing both their uniqueness and their common core, and trying to unite them by showing their common interest. This requires (re)creating a sense of historical agency, which was lost on the campus streets of Paris, London and Stockholm. For that we need theorizing and engaging the new subjects of socialist struggle, confirming the opinion of Gilles Deleuze, quoted by Manuel Ramos-Martinez in his chapter, that the task of modern political filmmaking is not to address itself to a predetermined people but to recognize its absence and contribute to its invention. Such attempts already exist; examples are concepts such as 'multitude' and 'precariat', which largely replaced the old term of 'working class'. It could be argued that a large proportion of contemporary political cinema addresses these new subjects rather than the proletariat in the old sense.

Marxist film activists shall also be aware that the reaction of the audience is time and culture specific. A given political film can activate the audience shortly after it was made, but usually not twenty or fifty years later, as demonstrated by Bruce Williams in his discussion of the reception of Fernando Solanas and Octavio Getino's *The Hours of Furnaces* (1968). Although the appreciation of its aesthetic value has increased greatly, its activist potentials have demised almost at the same rate. One even senses that the film's subversive nature is somehow tamed through the audience's heightened awareness of its beauty. Overtly political filmmakers therefore try to react to political events promptly, acting as journalists rather than auteurs who patiently wait for inspiration and take time to polish their works. This is one reason why documentary films are a privileged type of political or activist film (Waugh 1984; Torchin 2012: 2). The apparent roughness of Dziga Vertov's films, or those of Jean-Luc Godard from his militant period (although often concealing a meticulous attitude to structure behind the roughness), results from their understanding of this requirement. Another reason that documentaries occupy a privileged place among activist films is that, as Michael Chanan maintains in his chapter, documentary was born and remains relatively free, being filmed away from the studio by small crews on low budgets.

However, we believe the committed Marxist filmmakers should not be dogmatic about the formal qualities of Marxist films. A narrative and fiction film can make as much impact on the audience, if not more, as documentary and non-narrative; to use Deleuzian terms, films employing movement-image might be as effective as those adhering to time-image formula. This depends on the specific viewing habits of the given audience, which in turn depends on its level of film education and, in a wider sense, on what Pierre Bourdieu describes as 'habitus' (Bourdieu 1990), confirming Nelson Goodman and EH Gombrich's claim that every aesthetic experience is an epistemological experience. The more we know about a specific type of art, and the better we understand it, the more likely we are to like it (Goodman 1968: 258–65; Gombrich 2006: 22).

The Marxist activist needs not only to have important things to say, but to reach the adequate channels of communication. Not long ago there was a belief that the most important channel for this type of films was the internet. Indeed, the literature concerning online activism is large and fast growing. However, as Peter Dahlgren observes in his preface to the volume entitled *Cyberprotest*, published in 2004, 'after a few years of somewhat unfulfilled anticipation, the conventional wisdom has it that the internet, while certainly of political significance, is not about to engender major alterations in the overall way that democratic systems function. Even the results of ambitious experimentation where so-called edemocracy is inserted into the dynamics of the formal system have been modest' (Dahlgren 2004). Alexandra Juhasz, discussing documentaries posted on YouTube, argues that, although they 'could get a lot of hits, but will rarely be seen with the level of care and commitment that engenders connection. The viewing context of YouTube serves to quiet the radical potential of even the most repeatable and rousing of phrases' (Juhasz 2008: 303). Dahlgren's and Juhasz's diagnosis chimes with the views of Marcuse on the way the capitalist system operates, as already mentioned. This opinion is also largely corroborated by authors of several chapters included in this volume, such as Michael Chanan, Steve Presence and Lars Kristensen. However, although they agree that the internet is another capitalist instrument of commodification, including commodification of dissent, they argue that Marxist film activists cannot ignore this means, because there are few alternatives left.

Another channel of communication which recently attracted much attention is the space of film festivals (Iordanova and Torchin 2012). Unlike the audience of YouTube, which is dispersed and typically lacks deeper engagement with the films it is watching, festivals provide the films with context and community. However, there are at least two reasons to be sceptical about festivals' effectiveness to achieve Marxist goals: an egalitarian and emancipated society. Firstly, festivals tend to address very specialized and usually well-informed audiences. In other words, they preach to the converted rather than those who need persuasion. That said, as Leshu Torchin argues in her essay on film festivals and activism, 'if one stops preaching to the choir', they may stop singing (Torchin 2012: 6). The second argument to be wary of festivals is their usual focus on single issues and micropolitics. Film festivals are thus model vehicles of postmodern politics, which, as we argued earlier, might be seen as being ultimately anti-Marxist.

Structure and Chapter Outline

The scope and organization of this book reflects the fact that Marxist film activism is a question of the production, textual characteristics and reception of the films. Consequently, practically all the chapters in this collection deal with all three of these aspects, although they differ in that they emphasize different moments in a film's life cycle. Equally, when choosing the chapters we wanted to account for the fact that there is no fixed recipe for a Marxist film, namely a film that would make the spectator act towards introducing or strengthening socialism, not least because films, in common with other cultural artefacts, as Marx knew very well, exist in history. When historical circumstances change, the meaning of the film and its power to influence the audience changes too. However, rather than taking this fact for granted, the authors of this collection analyse case studies, trying to account for how the specific time and place affected film production, distribution and reception. It was our ambition to present as wide a spectrum of cases as possible, using examples from different periods of cinema's history and different locations. We were especially interested in contemporary film activism for two principal reasons: firstly, to fill a gap in research as this form of activism is barely covered in existing publications, and secondly, because we believe that there is a qualitative difference between the older and newer forms of film activism, resulting from the almost hegemonic position of the neoliberal version of capitalism, and an increased accessibility of digital technologies and growth of channels of distribution of films. One could expect that these two factors have a contrasting effect on Marxist film activism; the first reducing opportunities for independent production, distribution and exhibition of films, and the second increasing them. However, rather than assuming such a pattern, the authors try to find out if it can be detected in the specific cases they are investigating.

A need to account for the continuity and change in Marxist and left-wing activism in a wider sense affected the structure of this book. Its first part is devoted to accounts of past activism. It begins with a discussion of one of the first, and till now most radical, examples of cineactivism, Aleksandr Medvedkin's 'cine-train' (*kinopoezd*), operating in the years 1931–33. The author of this chapter, Gal Kirn, regards Medvedkin's experiment in activism as a particular form of novel political re-appropriation of technologies of motion (train) and vision (cinema), leading to the creation of a new space of art, which is literally and metaphorically dynamic and in which the boundaries between artistic creation and manual work, as well as between art production and consumption, are blurred. Cine-train is thus a perfect example of activist cinema in which the filmmaker is much more than a filmmaker, and the viewer much more than a viewer. By the same token, cine-train fulfils the Marxist ideal of 'amateurism', in which people perform different jobs for their own satisfaction and the benefit of the community. Kirn underscores that such a radical form of film activism was possible only because of the entirely new political situation in Russia following the October Revolution, and discusses in detail the conditions that have to be fulfilled for the cine-train to move at full speed, both literally and metaphorically.

The next three chapters look at the leading figures associated with the '68 movement: Jean-Luc Godard, Chris Marker and Jean-Marie Straub and Danièle Huillet. Jeremy Spencer, in the chapter 'Politics and Aesthetics within Godard's Cinema', discusses Godard's turn to political cinema or, as the director himself put it, to making political films politically, which happened around '68. Spencer observes that during this stage in his career Godard modelled himself on Dziga Vertov, as expressed in naming his project the 'Dziga Vertov group', as well as drawing on Bertolt Brecht's ideas of political art. Godard's main idea behind this decision was a desire to activate the viewer by eliciting in him a specific intellectual reaction, different to the reaction of watching an entertaining, mainstream Hollywood film. The key to creating such intellectually stimulating films was editing, understood as the organizing of sounds and images with the intention of presenting a concrete political situation and transforming it. In practice, it meant using the language, as Peter Wollen put it, of 'narrative intransitivity, estrangement, foregrounding, multiple diegesis, aperture, unpleasure, reality'. However, Spencer ultimately questions Godard's strategy as impractical and theoretically weak. Testimony to the former is the director's 'ghettoization' during the militant period, his loss of contact with the mass audience and rejection of his work by major distribution channels. Following Jacques Rancière and Fredric Jameson, Spencer also questions the political efficacy of the political art of the sort proposed by Godard. He argues that there is no guarantee that the typical juxtapositions of Godard's films will be put back together by the spectator in the form of a message, let alone the right message. On the contrary, there is a big danger that Godard's films would leave the viewer indifferent to the messages which they contain.

After Godard, Chris Marker is considered in the chapter 'Marker, Activism and Melancholy', authored by Jon Kear. Kear presents Marker as a model '68 intellectual, mentioning that after the war he was a writer and critic working on the journals *Travail et Culture, Cahiers du Cinéma* and the neo-catholic Marxist *Esprit*. These literary aspirations were to continue to guide Marker's work, even though later filmmaking took precedence over other forms of intellectual activities. Although Marker aligned himself with Marxism, he never joined the French Communist Party (PCF) and was critical of the legacy of Stalinism and the then contemporary Soviet model of communism. Like many left-wing intellectuals of his generation, he was increasingly drawn to the struggles in Latin America, Asia and Africa as holding the possibility of a New Left coalition. In a fashion typical of '68 movements, Marker became particularly interested in early Soviet filmmakers, especially Medvedkin, to whom he dedicated one of his most famous films, *The Last Bolshevik* (1993), and created a filmmaking collective, SLON, whose objective was to produce films and train industrial workers to establish filmmaking collectives of their own. Although the objective of Marker's cinema was, as with all Marxist filmmakers, a worldwide revolution, his films, as the title of Kear's chapter suggests, are imbued with melancholy, suggesting a missed chance of changing the world – an impression one also gets when watching Godard's films made after 1968.

If activist cinema is a communal cinema, then the films of Jean-Marie Straub and Danièle Huillet fit this bill well, as they made them together, sharing their duties evenly. Their movies also belong to some of the most politically stimulating films ever made. Manuel Ramos-Martinez looks in detail at one of them, *Workers, Peasants* (2000). He argues that the film undermines Marx's assessment of peasants as being politically inferior to workers due to their inability to communicate and forge alliances. *Workers, Peasants* tries to represent these two groups as equal, and by the same token they try to create a new political subject, heterogeneous yet united in their shared struggle. Moreover, by using an elaborate visual and aural style, Straub and Huillet propose a new type of political speech, which bridges the gap between poetry and prose and, in cinema, documentary and fiction film. Ramos-Martinez also draws attention to the fact that the couple of directors invite nonprofessional actors to play in their films, which is another way of reaching a wider audience and learning from those who have a very different experience from them.

The historical part finishes with a chapter by Bruce Williams, who discusses the production and national and international reception of Fernando Solanas and Octavio Getino's *The Hour of the Furnaces* (1968), widely regarded as one of the most politically engaging works ever made and a seminal example of Third Cinema. The film, based on 180 hours of clandestinely filmed interviews and found footage, documents Juan Perón's rise to power, his eventual overthrow and the lasting legacy of peronism in Argentina. One of its important motifs is the direct action of Argentine workers to take over the factories in which they were employed and in this way redress the balance of power in the capitalist world. The change of status of the worker is also reflected in the production of the film, in which the boundary between filmmakers and characters is blurred, as the workers were engaged in making the film. Drawing on the concept of 'functional mediating cultural translation', Williams discusses how the political character of the film was reinterpreted in its subsequent screenings in New York, Montréal, London and Paris. In some places the struggles in Argentina were regarded as similar to that which took place in their own countries or a matrix to be followed. In others, such as contemporary New York, the political 'heat' of the film was largely neglected by the viewers, who merely enjoyed the aesthetic dimension of the film. Williams also pays attention to the influence of Solanas and Getino's work on Jean-Luc Godard during his militant period, especially his production of his *Wind from the East*.

The second part is filled with chapters about contemporary left-wing cinematic activism and its relationship to Marxism. William Brown, in a chapter provocatively entitled 'Contemporary Political Cinema', considers two recent films from around the world, *Elite Squad* (2007), directed by José Padilha, which is a coproduction between Brazil, Netherlands, the United States and Argentina, and *A Screaming Man* (2010), directed by Mahomet-Saleh Haroun, coproduced in France, Belgium and Chad. Brown argues that each of these films in their own way seems to reject a passive attitude towards the contemporary world, and instead encourages viewers to take a more active stance in response to political and economic issues. In doing so, these films also create space for Brown to use Marx's concept of value in order to critique Gilles Deleuze, and especially his work on cinema. Brown identifies how value judgement creeps into Deleuze's work, creating not just a taxonomy, but a hierarchy of image-types that both *Elite Squad* and *A Screaming Man* would seem to refute. By promoting activism, and by condemning passivism, these films also critique Deleuze's idea that time-image cinema, supposedly the superior of his two major image types (the movement-image and the time-image), is a cinema of passive seers.

Haim Bresheeth begins his chapter, entitled 'Cultural Resistance through Film: the Case of Palestinian Cinema', by contrasting the political and cultural identities adopted by Jews: socialist cosmopolitanism, epitomized by the stance of Isaac Deutscher, and Zionism. The author describes Zionism as a particularly regressive position, combining rabid nationalism with capitalism, as presented in the writings of Theodore Herzl. Bresheeth claims that Israel was a brainchild of the latter position; the consequence of the very existence and colonialist policies of Israeli authorities is the occupation of Palestine. This occupation is, inevitably, met with resistance, in which the use of cultural means is particularly important, given the fact that Israel, which is supported by the United States, is a very mighty opponent. Bresheeth sketches the history of Palestinian cinema as a vehicle of resistance, beginning in 1968, the year the Palestine Liberation Organization (PLO) set up their photographic department, which become the Palestine Films Unit two years later, through the period of the First Intifada and the Oslo Accords. He points to the paradoxical character of Palestinian cinema, consisting of the fact that, although it is greatly needed, it does not really receive any support from the state. The last part of his discussion is devoted to recent Palestinian films, such as *5 Broken Cameras* by Emad Burnat and Guy Davidi, as works whose nationality is contested, and which address a European and even global audience, a fact important in light of the European Union's continuous support for Israel. While developments described and analysed in this chapter look back into history and cover recent decades in Palestine and at PLO centres elsewhere, the issues discussed are currently very much at stake, and have become of great importance in Palestinian cultural and political circles, hence the placement of this chapter in the section on current activism.

In the chapter entitled 'The Contemporary Landscape of Video-Activism in Britain', Steve Presence maps the field of video-activism over the last twenty years, paying special attention to the achievements and problems of two of the best-known producers of such material, Undercurrents and SchMOVIES. Although, as Presence maintains, neither of these organizations necessarily make 'Marxist' films, they produce films that resonate with a Marxist audience. Of particular value in Presence's analysis, therefore, is his discussion of the contradictions involved in what is, broadly speaking, 'anti-capitalist filmmaking in a capitalist context'. Pointing to a variety of political, technological, social and cultural factors pertaining to the period known as neoliberalism, he shows how the production of radical video-activism has, for these two organizations at least, involved a compromise between political filmmaking and economic survival, either by incorporating market models into their work or by developing parallel careers in which, as well as being a worker integrated into the capitalist regime, the activist-filmmaker can also operate more or less free from the constraints of the market.

Lars Kristensen, not unlike Steve Presence, discusses a certain type of activism and cinema associated with it, which cannot be described as strictly 'Marxist', but which might appeal to Marxist viewers: the Critical Mass movement. This movement, which started in the early 1990s, consists of groups of bicyclists riding through inner cities in numerous countries. The Critical Mass movement can be assessed in two basic ways: either as a means of combating capitalism by challenging the domination of a private car in the cities and advocating living in a more sustainable and greener way, or as a one-issue activism that diverts attention from the crucial problem of capitalism, which is that of class. Kristensen also discusses the films that represent and advocate bike activism and living according to the 'bike ethos' in terms of their production, textual characteristics and distribution. He draws attention to the fact that cinema is crucial for bike activism and the internet is indispensable for Mass Movement cinema.

Michael Chanan, in 'On the Immaterial Labour of the Video Blogger', draws on the concept of 'immaterial labour' as developed by Michael Hardt, Antonio Negri and Maurizio Lazzarato, the history of cinema and especially the documentary genre, and his own experience as a video blogger, posting blogs on *The New Statesman* from early 2011, to discuss the situation of the contemporary left-wing activist like himself. He mentions that this situation has certain advantages, most importantly allowing for creative freedom. The bulk of activists these days can shoot what they want and make their work available to potentially billions of users on YouTube, with practically zero cost beyond their own labour. Hence, this new situation seemingly creates a utopia, in which everybody can be an artist or an amateur in a wider sense, fishing in the morning and writing political treatises in the afternoon, as pronounced by Marx. This also means that activists are no longer excluded from reaching a wide public. But, as Chanan observes, echoing Steve Presence, this utopia hides a much less attractive reality. Firstly, the blurring of boundaries between video amateurs and professionals (similarly as between professional academics and those who share their knowledge with others for free) brings the risk of lowering the status and the salaries of the former, sentencing them to the fate of 'precarious workers'. Secondly, he points to the solitary character of the video blogger, which on the one hand affords him or her creative freedom, but on the other is a liability because it deprives the video-author of the creative feedback that goes with the teamwork of a crew. Finally, the web, where the products of the new form of political activism are uploaded, is an invention of neoliberal capitalism. By uploading their videos on YouTube, their makers effectively donate for free their work to corporate capital, which makes of it enormous profit.

This part and the book as a whole finishes with Martin Barker's chapter, entitled 'Recovering the Future: Marxism and Film Audiences'. Barker asks when a film is seen as Marxist, and when Marxist films encourage the viewers to behave in ways conducive to Marxist goals. He notes that the bulk of what passes as 'Marxist theory of film' has been restricted to considerations of the textual nature of films and that the prevailing view of film critics and theoreticians, following the formalist experiments in the Soviet cinema of the 1920s and post-May '68 film theory, is that a Marxist film is one which opposes 'mainstream' cinema, is regarded as subservient to the goals of capitalism and 'ideological', and by the same token false. However, he points out that this is not necessarily the way that the 'ordinary viewers' see particular films. Drawing on his own empirical research, he points out that films dismissed by critics as reactionary or at least neutral in relation to Marxist goals due to being spectacular or escapist, such as *Alien* and the Tolkien trilogy, elicit in many viewers a kind of Marxist reaction, most likely to a much greater extent than those heralded by Marxist critics as truly Marxist, which are inaccessible to all but a tiny elite. Barker's purpose, however, is not so much to redeem such popular films for Marxism, as to encourage a more empirical research into the behaviour of audiences and the link (or its lack) between watching a film and acting in its spirit. Barker's conclusions are in fact close to those of Jacques Rancière, as evoked by Jeremy Spencer; we cannot assess the political potential of a given film on the basis of its being 'intellectual' or 'emotional', simple or complicated.

This collection is not only about left-wing film activism, but is also in a large part written by film and political activists: filmmakers, video bloggers, organizers of film festivals, trade union activists and, at least, academics trying to educate their students in the spirit of Marxism. This book is intended to help them and others of similar goals in this task.

Notes

1. In Adorno's writing the difference between a 'real thing' and its pseudo-version plays an important part and he seems to be a sole arbiter of how to discern between the two.
2. Such an opinion was recently expressed by a French director, Nicolas Klotz, who said: 'The events of May '68 opened the door to global capitalism – therein lies their curse' (quoted in Foucault 2008: 30).

References

Adorno, T.W. 1991. 'Resignation', in his *The Culture Industry: Selected Essays on Mass Culture*. London: Routledge, pp. 171–5.
Badiou, A. 2007. *The Century,* trans. A. Toscano. Cambridge: Polity.
———. 2010 [2008]. *The Communist Hypothesis,* trans. D. Macey and S. Corcoran. London: Verso.
———. 2012. *In Praise of Love,* trans. P. Bush. London: Serpent's Tail.

Boltanski, L. and E. Chiapello. 2005 [1999]. *The New Spirit of Capitalism,* trans. G. Elliott. London: Verso.
Bourdieu, P. 1990 [1980]. *The Logic of Practice.* Palo Alto, CA: Stanford University Press.
Burns, T. 2015. 'Marxism and Science Fiction: the Case of *The Matrix*', in E. Mazierska and A. Suppia (eds), *Red Alert: Marxist Approaches to Science Fiction Cinema.* Detroit, MI: Wayne State University Press.
Dahlgren, P. 2004. 'Foreword' in W. van de Donk, B.D. Loader, P.G. Nixon and D. Rucht (eds), *Cyberprotest.* London: Routledge, pp. ix–xiii.
Daly, M. (ed.). 2006. *Karl Marx and Frederick Engels on Literature and Art.* Documents on Marxist Aesthetics 1. Nottingham: CCC Press.
Debray, R. 1979. 'A Modest Contribution to the Rites and Ceremonies of the Tenth Anniversary', *New Left Review* 1(115): 45–65.
Emmelhainz, I. 2009. 'From Third Worldism to Empire: Jean-Luc Godard and the Palestine Question', *Third Text* 23(5): 649–56.
Foucault, M. 1991. *Remarks on Marx.* New York: Semiotext(e).
———. 2008. 'Unbelievable but Real: the Legacy of '68', *Sight & Sound* 18(5): 28–32.
Gombrich, E.H. 2006. *The Story of Art.* New York and London: Phaidon.
Goodman, N. 1968. *Languages of Art: An Approach to a Theory of Symbols.* Indianapolis, IN: The Bobbs-Merrill.
Hall, S. 1988. *The Hard Road to Renewal: Thatcherism and the Crisis of the Left.* London: Verso.
Hamilton-Grant, I. 2001. 'Postmodernism and Politics', in S. Sim (ed.), *The Routledge Companion to Postmodernism.* London: Routledge, pp. 28–40.
Harvey, D. 2006. *The Limits to Capital.* London: Verso.
Iordanova, D. and L. Torchin (eds). 2012. *Film Festivals and Activism.* St Andrews: St Andrews Film Studies.
Jameson, F. 1990. *Late Marxism: Adorno or the Persistence of the Dialectic.* New York: Verso.
Juhasz, A. 2008. 'Documentary on YouTube: the Failure of the Direct Cinema of the Slogan', in T. Austin and W. de Jong (eds), *Rethinking Documentary: New Perspectives, New Practices.* Maidenhead: Open University Press, pp. 299–312.
Kendrik, J. 1999. 'Marxist Overtones in Three Films by James Cameron', *Journal of Popular Film and Television* 27(3): 36–44.
Kleinhans, C. 1998. 'Marxism and Film', in J. Hill and P. Church Gibson (eds), *The Oxford Guide to Film Studies.* Oxford: Oxford University Press, p. 106–13.
Lyotard, J.-F. 1984. *The Postmodern Condition: A Report on Knowledge,* trans. G. Bennington, B. Massumi. London: Routledge.
Marcuse, H. 1964. *One-Dimensional Man: Studies in the Ideology of Advanced Industrial Society.* London: Routledge and Kegan Paul.
Marx, K. and F. Engels. 1947. *The German Ideology, Parts I and III.* New York: International Publishers.
———. 2008 [1848]. *The Communist Manifesto.* London: Pluto.

Meikle, S. 2009. 'Marx, the European Tradition, and the Philosophic Radicals', in A. Chitty and M. McIvor (eds), *Karl Marx and Contemporary Philosophy*. Basingstoke: Palgrave Macmillan, pp. 55–75
Pascal, R. 1947. 'Introduction', in K. Marx and F. Engels, *The German Ideology, Parts I and III*. New York: International Publishers, pp. ix–xviii.
Prawer, S.S. 1976. *Karl Marx and World Literature*. Oxford: Clarendon Press.
Rancière, J. 2004 [2000]. *The Politics of Aesthetics*, trans. G. Rockhill. London: Continuum.
———. 2009 [2008]. *The Emancipated Spectator*, trans. G. Elliott. London: Verso.
Scruton, R. 1995 [2001]. *A Short History of Modern Philosophy*, 2nd edn. London and New York: Routledge.
Torchin, L. 2012. 'Networked for Advocacy: Film Festivals and Activism', in D. Iordanova and L. Torchin (eds), *Film Festivals and Activism*. St Andrews: St Andrews Film Studies, pp. 1–12.
Waugh, T. (ed.). 1984. *'Show Us Life!': Toward a History and Aesthetics of the Committed Documentary*. Metuchen: Scarecrow Press.
Wayne, M. 2001. *Political Film: The Dialectics of Third Cinema*. London: Pluto.
Žižek, S. 2009. *First as Tragedy, Then as Farce*. London: Verso.

Filmography

Alien. 1979. Ridley Scott.
Elite Squad (Tropa de Elite). 2007. José Padilha.
The Hours of Furnaces (La hora de los hornos). 1968. Fernando Solanas and Octavio Getino.
The Last Bolshevik (Le tombeau d'Alexandre). 1993. Chris Marker.
The Matrix. 1999. Andy and Lana Wachowski.
A Screaming Man (Un homme qui crie). 2010. Mahomet-Saleh Haroun.
Workers, Peasants (Operai, contadini). 2000. Jean-Marie Straub and Danièle Huillet.
Wind from the East (Le vent d'est). 1970. Jean-Luc Godard.
5 Broken Cameras. 2011. Emad Burnat.

PART I
Past Activism

CHAPTER 1
Between Socialist Modernization and Cinematic Modernism
The Revolutionary Politics of Aesthetics of Medvedkin's Cinema-Train

Gal Kirn

In his book *Les Écarts du cinéma*, Jacques Rancière poignantly observes that cinema was born with the belief that the cinematic power would be able to create new (hi)story through the language of images (Rancière 2011: 16).[1] Cinema would not only move towards a more adequate representation of reality, but would fulfil an emancipatory promise: it would construct the world and bring us closer to truth. This ambitious expectation embedded the cinematic apparatus with new powers, which one could provisionally name cinematic modernism,[2] and which was famously pronounced in Walter Benjamin's 'The Work of Art in the Age of Its Technological Reproducibility'. For Benjamin film 'presents' and 'interpenetrates' reality with its apparatus; moreover, film was able to explore 'the commonplace millieux ... and exploded this prison-world with the dynamite of the split second, so that now we can set off calmly on journeys of adventure among its far-flung debris' (Benjamin 2002: 117). However, even if one recognizes the inherently democratic potential of the new medium and the cinematic apparatus, which will come into the hands of masses, its historical actualization is not guaranteed. Furthermore, for Benjamin the cinematic apparatus will play an important role in the process of human emancipation only during and after the abolition of capitalist exploitation (ibid.: 113).

Taking this condition seriously – cinema's participation in a revolutionary process – one should take a closer look at the first years after the October Revolution and evaluate the historical actualization of Benjamin's thesis. The revolutionary upheaval of 1917 for art, subsequently, did not consist of only filming the 'storming of the winter palace', but it triggered a complex set of political, socioeconomic and cultural-artistic consequences, which in a plurality of ways made possible a politicized continuation of the avant-garde movement. Revolutionary process and avant-garde movements dissolved bourgeois art autonomy and re-drew, or even dissolved, the borders between art, life and politics (Bowlt 1988). The mass creativity of artists was accompanied by the enthusiastic search and construction of the 'new world', where human emancipation happened by empowerment of the (working) masses.

This historical transformation of art would be most strongly associated with the emerging institution of cinema, which in the early years of the Soviet Union encountered serious financial and infrastructural problems.[3] As is known, Lenin and the Communist Party promoted cinema as the most important art, which propagated revolutionary ideas and educated the masses.[4] In the new socioeconomic circumstances the revolutionary task of cinema did not unfold without tensions, which brings to the fore the following questions that will guide my contribution: how far was it possible for the early Soviet film to perform the task of 'constructing a new world' without falling into complete service to the state? In other words, what was to come of the relationship between state, revolution and (new) cinema? Furthermore, in what way did socialist modernization – processes of industrialization, urbanization and mass investments in the culture – crucially support, but also not completely overwrite the avant-garde movements? My intervention should be read in a critical dialogue with the famous thesis of Boris Groys, who in his seminal work *The Total Art of Stalinism: Avant-Garde, Aesthetic Dictatorship, and Beyond* (2011) argues that avant-garde art logically ended in Stalinism, with socialist realism being its artistic representative.[5] In this article I would highlight how, despite early Soviet art's identification with the October Revolution, one can still find a certain 'excess' of avant-garde art – which Žižek would call 'Real'[6] – that would not so naturally end in Stalinist realism. Groys' argument is unconvincing on two major plains: firstly, *The Total Art of Stalinism* (2011) does not offer any deeper analysis of the role of state, which intervened – bureaucratically – into the cultural field. Furthermore, Groys blends the differentiation between state and politics, between the politics of aesthetics (the avant-garde) and genre (socialist realism). Secondly, Groys' argument downplays the plurality and tensions existent within the avant-garde movement itself.[7] During the 1920s different visions of cinematic communism(s) developed political differentiation and aesthetic novelty, without which the avant-garde would not have existed in the first place. The plurality of orientations pushed avant-garde art beyond the later prescribed genre of socialist realism, which would mean a definite break with the avant-garde.

In the background of a criticism of Groys' simplified view of the relationship between art and state and politics, this contribution initiates two theses on the productive encounter between revolutionary cinema and politics in the early Soviet period. In the first part I shall explore the encounter between communism and cinema ('Communist cinema') by analysing the relationship between a general logic of socialist modernization ('cinefication') and cinematic modernism, where the latter cannot be reduced to modernization as state policy, which completely directs Soviet cinema. In the second part I shall read closely the specific encounter between the cinema and the train in the experiment of Medvedkin's *kinopoezd* ('cinema-train', 1931–33), which introduced a novel political re-appropriation of technologies of motion (train) and vision (cinema). Medvedkin's cine-train might have started as a productivist[8] experiment, but it resulted in what I would call a genuine experience of train-cinematic communism.

On the Encounter of Cinema and Communism

How can one define the encounter between cinema and communism? Let me start with a negative definition: cinematic communism is not merely an application of political, Communist or Marxist formulae to the screen. If we take this direct application, then our research would perform a textual analysis of a certain body of (here Soviet) films that fall under the genre of 'social critique' or political films. At the end of such research one would evaluate how far these films follow (or deviate from) the Soviet state orientation. This type of approach to cinematic communism would reduce the Soviet film to a visual adaptation of state ideology; in other words, the film would be seen as an aesthetic way of pursuing state directives.[9] Contrary to this metapolitical view, another, more fashionable, approach to the role of revolutionary art would argue that the novel practise of Communist cinema testifies to a genuine continuation of the October Revolution. According to this perspective, Communist cinema is defined either as a 'truth-procedure' or as 'utopian space' that stands in for the promise of emancipation. Art, here Communist cinema, continues revolution by other means.[10] This view is largely indebted to the early Romantic approach that gave art powers that go beyond politics. This definition of revolutionary art is predicated upon the necessary failure of politics: the French Revolution can be only fulfilled in German Romanticism and became a central current in the cultural constitution of the nation.

My hypothesis seeks to combine and rectify both the metapolitical (art in service of state) and romanticist (art as realization of utopian promise) positions. To understand the encounter between cinema and communism I will use the concept of 'parallax' view. Drawing from Kant's antinomies, Žižek (2009) used parallax in order to trace and conserve two contradictory and equally valid tendencies within one phenomenon, or one theoretical object, which cannot be resolved or easily reconciled. A typical example is a famous Marxist discussion of whether Marx gave primacy to production or circulation when analysing capital. In my case, a parallax movement could be used to explain the antinomical relationship between revolutionary politics and art. Parallax view means that communist cinema should be understood as an encounter between the emerging socialist state, its policy of socialist modernization[11] and a development of the specific political aesthetics of the new filmmakers. It is then not enough to say that the relationship between revolutionary art and the state is dialectical, but it rather demands a fine-tuning of the dialectical model, which Althusser (2005) coined with the term 'structural causality'. The latter concept puts at the centre of a dialectical movement the detection of concrete historical nodal points,[12] in which we can tackle the effects of the policies of the emerging socialist state upon the creation of a new film movement. Alongside the material analysis of the effects of the cinematic infrastructure, this view of causality refrains from defining (Soviet) cinema as propaganda, which adapted state directives to the screen, but rather seeks to understand the specific autonomous role of revolutionary art in the transformation of the world. Revolutionary art, in this case, cinema, actively participated in the construction of a 'new world' and was not regulated by an unequivocal idea and policy.

Undoubtedly, a progressivist and productivist tendency was present in socialist policies from very early on. Already in 1920, Lenin had famously defined a formula for the advent of communism: 'electrification + soviet power'. Once the soviets were dissolved, electrification became a dominant element that defined the development model of the Soviet plan. Electrification was a precursor of the later Five-Year Plan (Lenin 1977: 280).[13] Stites (1991) rightly detects that the first phase of electrification consisted of massive utopian elements, and in the sense of material progress, it meant a huge leap forward: development of power stations all over the country started to create conditions of production and fuel for industrial capacities. Almost simultaneously Trotsky's famous order 1042 was adopted, which in reality centralized the fragmented railway organization. Trotsky's order was motivated both by the military and practical role of the railways (struggling against famine), and the political struggle within the railways' unions. The reform resulted in another huge boost for the organization and production of transport, which among other things became one of the decisive moments of the Red Army's victory in the Civil War.[14]

The process and the role of electrification and railways in the early Soviet Union has already received a fair amount of scholarly attention (Cliff 1991; Stites 1991). Not many authors have written about the state policy that created conditions for film production and its dissemination. This policy was coined – by the same token as electrification – 'cinefication' and was a major element in socialist modernization.[15] Cinefication was at first carried out by the State Committee for Cinematography and its regional branch offices, while the dissemination was mainly run by a joint-stock company Soukino. Films were transported by boats, cars, coaches and of course by trains. In the early 1920s around one thousand travelling cinemas were in motion, in the second half of the 1920s around two thousand. Thomas Lahusen (2012) observes that:

> in the late 1920s and early 1930s cinefication became a massive, state-run, and centrally-planned enterprise. Soviet statistical sources list 868 urban and 187 rural film stations (cinemas or mobile units) in 1923 for the whole Soviet Union. In 1928, these numbers had grown to 9,700 and 4,100 respectively. In 1933 they reached 27,578, of which 17,584 stations were rural.[16]

Despite a valid criticism of cinefication that pointed to the dangers of centralized control and the dilemma of either political propaganda or profitability, I would agree with Lahusen's assessment that cinefication remains 'an unprecedented example of cultural dissemination, where every citizen was targeted, from the top to the bottom of the social ladder, including more than 150 distinct ethnic groups spread out across the 11 time zones' (Lahusen 2012; see also Kenez 2001: 72–78).

The sheer scope and cultural efficacy of cinefication forces us to add a third element to the famous formula, communism = electrification + soviets + *cinefication*. Yet the expanded formula still remains reductive of the historical complexity of socialist modernization, because it gives primacy to the side of the material progress launched by the 'state'. It should be stated that not only were the processes of intense socialist modernization ambivalent, the constant combination of capitalist and communist elements entailed contradictory and even regressive movements. Even if the most desired goal of the policy of cinefication was education of the masses and their empowerment in the cultural struggle, one should not fail to acknowledge deep political and aesthetical tensions between all the major film authors of that time. Think of the differences between Vertov, Eisenstein, Medvedkin, Kuleshov, Podovkin and many others; their differences are not documented merely in their film works, but also in the endless discussions that promoted very different visions of cinematic communism (Widdis 2005: x).[17] Much more than hiding in a kind of art oasis autonomy, these filmmakers actively moulded new cinematic approaches and with this also participated in the more general project of social transformation. Internal intensification, political differentiation and aesthetic novelty pushed the early avant-garde film beyond the mere adaptation of political directives and the program of cinefication.[18]

The encounter of communism and cinema can thus only be understood in terms of a productive tension between revolutionary political aesthetics that consisted of many avant-garde influences[19] and the general wave of socialist modernization. This tension illuminates a new relationship between Communist art and the emerging state in the early Soviet period. As mentioned earlier, the new socialist state supported and largely invested in the conditions of new cinema/art,[20] but also the artists themselves were politically organized on many levels: they participated in the new state apparatuses and creation of new academic departments, and in addition were also organized in trade unions and journals (Bowlt 1988: xxxiii–xxxix). It was the political organization of artists, their own political struggle, which actually contributed to a construction of specific socialist art autonomy. Against vulgar determinism that argues that economic policy determines all other social instances, the principle of overdetermined causality advocates a more complex view of the mutual determination of instances. Moreover, in a specific conjuncture, for example in post-revolutionary Russia, the primacy of social determination is displaced to politics or even culture.

From this it follows that the policy of cinefication did not only follow economistic logic – either of the NEP or later planned economy – but that the determination of the cultural by the economic would mean that after the material cinematic infrastructure was established, the propagandistic construction of socialism (socialist realism) naturally followed. According to this economistic logic, all cinematic products would fulfil the task of mirroring state directives. Contrary to this, I argue that cinefication opened a path for the flourishing of contradictory artistic tendencies, which meant that art was not simply subjugated to the service of state politics, but rather new art internally subverted the existing coordinates of the socialist system. Just as in the established relationship between the sayable and the visible, the field of intervention is widened to the extreme by and for new artistic movements. Moreover, the avant-garde/Communist art not only underlined the necessity for the continuation of revolution by poetic means, it also acquired a specific role in structural terms; it worked as an overdetermining element in the revolutionary process that participated in a new 'distribution of sensible'. Rancière's (2006) concept, the 'distribution of sensible', is central to his theory of the politics of aesthetics, which implies that any new (and democratic) politics consists of an aesthetical moment, which breaks with the established genre of the visible; vice versa, the aesthetical forms are often accompanied by properly political acts that include either certain groups, topics and gestures that were previously not included in the art genre. However, despite the importance of avant-garde movements and their artworks in the early Soviet period, one should not underestimate the crucial role of the state apparatus and its launch of the cinefication campaign. It is precisely on this nodal point between a newly emerging state and the mass of artistic experimentation that one should register the overdetermined character of the encounter between art and politics in (post)revolutionary times.

The encounter between cinema and communism could be evaluated in Rancièrian terms such as the 'politics of aesthetics' of early Soviet films. The political aesthetics of the early Soviet films dealt with the excess that could not be tamed by the established definition of cinefication. Recently, Pavle Levi (2012), in his book *Cinema By Other Means,* defined the process of cinefication in avant-garde film not only as the development of the material infrastructure for film, but much more in terms of a deeper procedure, which cinetifies the whole of reality:

> cinefication *of reality – its growing contamination by both the technological features and the perceptual-aesthetic functions of the film medium (as diagnosed by Benjamin) – is to be understood simultaneously as the ultimate consequence of and a condition for the successful proliferation of the conceptual-materialist art of 'cinema by other means'. (Levi 2012: 83)*[21]

Levi (2012: 144) traces this 'cinematic desire'[22] in avant-garde manifestations of 'cinematic cuts', which result in the 'impression that there is always more than meets the eye, there is an excess beyond the frame of the image: *an impression that closure is never total*'. Levi goes through a close analysis of different avant-garde works and their aesthetical excess(es) from 1920 to the late 1970s, and locates the primary source of cinefication in noncinematic media. This means that what the viewer sees as the most evident progression within the filmic process (montage of shots) was actually developed by avant-garde filmmakers through many other media and arts: from theatre and photography to abstract painting and architecture.[23] Along these lines I argue that Soviet film works transgressed the policy of state-organized cinefication, with both political and other noncinematic means. Let me take the example of the works of Eisenstein, who did not want to only represent the October Revolution or class struggle in Tsarist Russia in his *October* (1928) and *Battleship Potemkin* (1925), where the political message would be immediately accessible to the masses; rather, his aesthetical procedures were meant to incite the intellectual capacities to explore and question social injustices and emancipatory struggle. The dialectical movement of history was inscribed in the cinematic medium through what one could name the montage apparatus, which so dramatically affected the new Communist and cinetified reality. These procedures were meant to advance new cinematic form via aesthetical-formal means (montage, new documentary forms) and develop the 'Communist decoding' of reality[24] that opposed a consumer-driven reception that strengthened the entertaining function surfacing in Hollywood cinema, and in the later socialist realist film factory of the 1930s. This quest for a different decoding of the new world is not a pure and authentic construction of reality, but on the contrary, it consists of the laborious work of editor-author, who applies a mathematical-scientific method to the exploration of the visual field. Also, Eisenstein and Vertov struggled around their approaches that would influence the perception of the cinematic audience – either the fist or eye –while the case of Alexander Medvedkin brought the camera and cinema to the people.[25]

Boris Groys' argument that avant-garde groups were 'infected' with a strong political mission is an historical fact. It could be even said that at times the avant-garde art was overidentified with the October Revolution: it strictly followed and continued social transformation with its own means. Thus, we conclude that film works tackled with the excesses of revolution and the formalization of the Real within their own cinematic field, while also recognizing the common feature of certain tendencies (e.g. productivism) that moved in the direction of dissolution of art. In other words, certain avant-garde tendencies did work in the direction mentioned by Groys, towards the dissolution of the border between art, politics and life.[26] The explosive cocktail of ambivalent avant-garde tendencies unfolded intensively during the 1920s and came to gradual restraint and demise after 1932.[27]

Groys is correct to argue about the more ambivalent role that socialist realism played in this process: many socialist realist films were in certain ways postformalist, or postmodernist *avant la lettre*, taking some procedures from the avant-garde legacy. However, it would be wrong to overlook the role the state played in introducing socialist realism. The demise of the avant-garde should be historically correlated to times after 1932, which in reality meant more intense ideological control, which was directly instructed by the state apparatuses. Thus, socialist realism functioned as an important ideological weapon that targeted all forms of aesthetical and political orientations, which at the end of the day subjugated art to the service of the state. This resulted in the repression of individual artists through executions and restraints, while in terms of aesthetical forms, it meant a return to the bourgeois conceptions of art. The biggest goal of art should be to entertain the masses. This artistic orientation was foreign to any avant-garde experimentation in the 1920s, and in many respects even betrays the initial doctrine of socialist realism that advocated the depiction of 'reality in its revolutionary development' (Bowlt 1988: 293).[28] Its realization promoted socialist romanticism, which idealized the new Soviet society and portrayed a heroic new man of the future. Romantic musicals and comedies proliferated during the 1930s,[29] which contrary to the avant-garde legacy served as an ideological consolidation of the masses and the strengthening of new state. We should, however, be attentive not to simply proclaim socialist realism as the logical development of the avant-garde. Furthermore, Groysian lenses block any productive return to reassess and perhaps even reactualize this legacy and instead feed into the 'anti-totalitarian ideology' condemning anything avant-garde as necessarily containing a totalitarian and irrational core and thus inevitably ending in the totalitarian regime of Stalin (Kirn Forthcoming). In the following section I will take into close consideration a cinematic experiment that took place in times of Stalinist ideological restraint: Medvedkin's project kinopoezd.

On the Encounter between Communist Cinema and the Train: Medvedkin's Kinopoezd

Within this general framing of encounter between cinema and communism, I would like to tackle another encounter in (film) history, the encounter between Communist cinema and the train. The cinema and the train share a very peculiar, but often overlooked history. Both the train and cinema were major sources of visual production and predominant symbols; furthermore, they both became apparatuses and institutions of industrial revolution and modernization (Schivelbusch 1986). For Christa Blümlinger, who has analysed the connection between the cinema and train in her research, this relationship runs very deep and is not merely metaphorical:

> *The railway stands for the loss of the experience of travel as a spatial continuum, insofar as a train passes over or travels through an interstitial space. Thus the train, like cinema itself, functions both as a machine to organize gaze and as a generator of linearity and movement. There is therefore a technical affinity between cinema and the railway, or rather between the machines that comprise them: the locomotive, the wagon and the projector.* (Blümlinger 2006: 246)

This relationship and appropriation of cinema-train receives a political twist in the early Soviet period. The encounter between the cinema and train begins in the times of Civil War. As Linhart states, trains played a crucial role in this period:

> trains supply food and fuel, trains for transport of troops and for the commanding (a famous blind train of Trotsky and the general staff that was constantly traveling between different fronts of the civil war). But also propaganda trains with cinema, printing, wagons that were painted with revolutionary frescoes. Throughout this period railways were an important flow of blood innervation; the State in movement. *(Linhart 2010: 122)*

During and after the end of Civil War, many important filmmakers and theatre groups were involved in the so-called experience of agit-trains or propaganda trains that were used to transport films, prints, posters and theatre groups (Tode 2008). Official documents show that the Communist Party and Lenin especially valued film and also granted special rights to agit-trains: all the developments were to be reported to Lenin directly (Christie and Taylor 2002: 56–57). Also, as already mentioned, the cinefication process was executed with the help of travelling cinemas, which were predominantly organized on trains.

Here I will focus, however, on the experiment of Alexandr Medvedkin that took place a decade later. In the early 1930s Medvedkin started writing one of the most exciting chapters of the history of cinema, which for long time remained largely overlooked:[30] the adventures of kinopoezd. Kinopoezd is often translated as 'film-train' (Widdis 2005), but I propose to use the term 'cinema-train', which runs, as we will see in the next sections, conceptually closer to Medvedkin's experiment. In Chris Marker's documentary *Last Bolshevik* (1993), Marker explicitly draws a demarcation between film and cinema. He understands the body of Medvedkin's work can be understood along the lines of the old Chinese proverb: give a person a fish and he will live for a day (film), teach a person how to fish and he will live forever (cinema). Especially, in the course of the cinema-train, as both parts of the syntagm gained an added value: the train was not only basic infrastructure for the distribution of films (train as technology of motion), but more importantly, the train participated in the organization of labour, the vehicle for distribution became the production unit. My thesis is that this implied a politicization of the production and distribution process, making the film process ever more intense, open and mobile.

Figure 1.1. Agit-train 'Lenin'. Image from Red Files Website.

The cinema-train became the nodal point around which the technology of motion and vision connected in a new way, moving away from a more aesthetical and technological account of the early silent cinema and train.

Kinopoezd

Medvedkin was very familiar with agit-trains; he also started to make his first short agitational films during the Civil War, but only in the late 1920s was he to become more involved in the film profession (Widdis 2005; Taylor and Christie 1994: 165–67). The actual idea for kinopoezd came during a walk with his good friend Mikhail Guindine, when they discussed how to transform a train wagon into a mobile film laboratory. The central idea of kinopoezd would be to move from distribution to production on the way. Cinema-train would be able to travel between factories and collectivized farms across the Soviet Union, which would simultaneously allow the crew to shoot and edit the films about the working collectives. This idea did not immediately receive support by the authorities: Soiuzkino rejected the proposal, but Medvedkin insisted and finally the Central Committee of the Communist Party conceded to the plan – approval came from the Minister of Heavy Industry. This political instance made the project directly responsible to the propaganda section of the party (Widdis 2005: 23). As can be learnt from Medvedkin's testimony and Chris Marker's documentaries, one should take into account that Medvedkin remained a sincere and dedicated Communist until his death. He openly affirmed the official policies of the first Five-Year Plan and one could argue that the initial intention for the cinema-train was indebted to productivist reasoning (Layda 1960). As Medvedkin stated, kinopoezd aimed to 'liquidate the delays in the production' and report on troubleshooting with the implementation of the plan.[31] If one evaluates kinopoezd only by these initial intentions, then one could ask if the whole experience is not simply a state experiment, or a spontaneous ideology implemented by cinematic means? But assessing the whole experiment by its initial intentions would remain idealist; for a Marxist analysis worthy of its name it is necessary to look into the effects of the social practise of kinopoezd.

Organizational Principles: Productivism and the Political Activism of Self-Management

Chris Marker's documentary *Le Train en marche* (*The Train Rolls On*, 1971) presents the modus operandi of Medvedkin's experiment: kinopoezd's team gathered thirty-two people, in Medvedkin's words 'all revolutionary enthusiasts', who travelled, worked and slept together on the train. Each member of the crew had at disposal approximately one square meter. They had four wagons; one was dedicated to accommodation, part of the second wagon was turned into a film laboratory with a complex water system on the top, while the last part of this wagon was used as an editing room where ten people could work simultaneously. The next wagon consisted of an animation stand, where they inserted the intertitles, made animations and edited newspapers and pamphlets, which was followed by a small projection space, which ended the production cycle. The final wagon had also a car and bicycles, so the crew could be mobile.[32]

The cinema-train crew was extremely productive in terms of output: in the time span of the first travel that lasted 292 days, they produced seventy-two films, each of them around fifteen minutes long; this roughly makes two films a week and is most adequately condensed in the central slogan of kinopoezd: 'We film today and screen tomorrow'. Cinema-train could stop anywhere, film anyone and show films to everyone. Despite this freedom to film, they chose their spaces carefully and were mostly travelling between the villages that underwent collectivization in early 1930s and the bigger factory complexes which were built in the first Five-Year Plan (1928–32).

Once they arrived at a location to shoot, they sent out a team that would research social circumstances and talk to the workers and peasants. As Medvedkin claimed this would be the essential part of their work, which he named a direct intervention and direct criticism of a concrete situation. In this respect, the work of the crew was directly activist, attempting to detect the central problems in production. Kinopoezd would expose the problems in the process of filming: absenteeism, laziness, lack of working discipline, bad co-ordination between collectives, bureaucratization of local party committees, poor working conditions... everything that contributed to bad results of the working collective and the life of workers. For kinopoezd the division between political and artistic work did not exist, their mission was inscribed in the quest of the improvement and advancement of socialism. Most of the remaining films of the cinema-train[33] were socialist realist reports, which could be seen as transmitting the form of *kinopravda* in the newly industrialized and collectivized landscapes of 1930s. All the mentioned features of kinopoezd, such as high output, treatment of topic and their initial mission, completely fit the productivist paradigm.

However, it is important to note that the central organizational principle of the crew did not follow any plan or special guidelines from the propaganda section of the party, but on the contrary, the cinema-train always began with Lenin's well-known call to 'concrete analysis of the concrete situation'. Instead of applying 'orthodox' formula (e.g. industrialization) to every context, any serious Communist project (analysis, policy, cinema...) should depart from the singularity of context. More than a strict party discipline imposed by commissars, political activism was based on the genuine involvement in the community. As Medvedkin recounts, there were many occasions when the crew even helped to renegotiate and reconstruct the plan bottom-up within the working collectives. In more contemporary jargon one could name these instances as forms of democratic planning.

The next important feature that makes Medvedkin's experiment divergent from the top-bottom productivist paradigm was actually the guiding organizational principle that the crew practised: rotation of all tasks. It is noteworthy that within the crew it was only Medvedkin and Nikolay Karamzinsky who had experiences with film, while other members were complete amateurs. This meant that the whole working process was designed as a learning process; moreover, every member participated in different stages of the film production and distribution. In kinopoezd anyone could become a film director and editor. In this vein, the principle of rotation undermined the division of labour in the established film industry. Instead of professionalism, they would promote amateurism. Instead of following a hierarchical principle, where the producer and director command the whole film process, the cinema-train was deeply marked by the idea of collectivist utopia, which stems from Marx's famous passages from *German Ideology* that conceive Communist society as the place where every human being will realize the full extent of their capacities.[34] The fundamental thesis of kinopoezd thus was designed to give its members self-managing authority freed from a director's despotism.[35] The principle of rotation attempted to abolish the division of labour, but only at the expense of the constant activity of the members. This task could be achieved only by very intensive collective and individual efforts. Medvedkin recounts that often their working day was stretched up to eighteen hours and they would be working in shifts.[36] The division of labour was surpassed, but thanks to enormous expense of superhuman efforts, which in a certain respect resembled the promoted figure of shock worker. Once we apply this ideal to the whole society, we get a productivist society.

Additionally, crew-members were not only involved in a strict film production, they also edited a newspaper and helped in organizing social life (e.g. harvesting, learning some working skills). This fluid transition between political art and life was further undermined by an organized attempt to integrate workers and peasants into the film production and distribution. They were helping the crew with the gathering of information; they edited newspapers, inserted intertitles and at times moderated discussions.

On the Distribution and Social Effects of Cinema-Train

Kinopoezd was not only productive in terms of the quantity of films, but also in terms of their distribution and exhibition. They organized a huge amount of screenings and distributed and archived few copies.[37] In the first three months of 1931 they organized 105 screenings with more than thirty-five thousand spectators, and these numbers only rose in the following years (Widdis 2005: 24). There are no existing records of how much the copies were used by local communities, though Medvedkin recounts that some communities asked them for a few of their copies, which were used both for educational and entertainment purposes.

What became quite clear from the early stage in the project was an experience that the cinema crew cannot simply impose directives from above and educate the masses; quite the contrary, the crew, due to its research and rotation, was involved in the learning process. The crew and spectators were themselves educated. At first one should mention that critical documentaries of the cinema-train entailed a critical pedagogy; this point reflects best Medvedkin's influence on the group of film enthusiasts.[38] Medvedkin already in the 1920s had started to develop a pedagogy that was directed against the established propagandistic agitational films. For him, effective pedagogics could be achieved through the narrative that was permeated by humour and satire. There is no doubt that kinopoezd used very direct agitational methods of naming the ills in the new working collectives, at times even naming the bad workers. However, the primacy was given to the method of satire, which would work with displacements, mimicry and awkward repetitions. The whole journey was accompanied by a very surrealist character, which they called the 'camel of shame'. A cartoon-like character, the camel would be inserted in the real film and would act as a substitute for the worker. For example, it would imitate bad practise in the workplace: being drunk, clumsy, absent or lazy. According to Medvedkin, the camel and its gestures always incited laughter among spectators and would in many ways push beyond the limits of the direct 'policing' of workers. In the context of the already highly intensified ideological situation of collectivization and industrialization of 1930s, satire and the figure of the camel were creative rhetorical and visual devices that in a comradely fashion decoded and criticized the economic processes and reactions, both from the system and the agents themselves.[39]

The satirical process was related to another method of kinopoezd, which attempted to reconstruct the division between the film stage and audience. It is noteworthy that Medvedkin was not only engaged in the amateur theatre, but also assisted Nikolay Okhlopov, who in the 1920s famously targeted the traditional divide within the theatre situation (Layda 1960).[40] As mentioned above, workers and peasants were integrated in the film production; further-

Figure 1.2. Camel of Shame, animated character from cinema-train films. Screen capture from Chris Marker's *Last Bolshevik* (1993; DVD, Icarus Films 2008).

more, they did not remain simple spectators, consumers who would watch (and listen) how the Five-Year Plan should be executed, and according to which guidelines they should act. The cinematic experience was immediate: workers became engaged as actors and were, even after the screening, the main agents of the process. Kinopoezd films could be seen as the first kind of *avant-la-lettre* political 'reality show': spectators were able to see themselves on the screen the day after they were filmed. For many of them, this might have well been first time they saw film, but what is even more powerful is to imagine that their very first moving images showed the workers themselves. The filming procedure of the cinema-train was reversed: the spectator entered the film before s/he watched it, leading to the undermining of the division between professional actors and spectators on the one hand and between distribution and production on the other.

The interactive modality of the new mobile medium (cinema-train) was further strengthened by the exhibition of films. One has to have in mind that the spaces for exhibition were improvised; bars, local committees, parts of factories, train wagons, walls of the farm/barn, everything was re-used for cinematic purposes. Also, the screenings themselves were attended by a hundred, even a few hundred people. The projections were only the start of the much longer public event, because they were used as a kick-off for discussion. One has to imagine that the normal length of this film was around ten to fifteen minutes; the film on the specific community would be at times accompanied/juxtaposed with a film from another working collective. Through Medvedkin's testimony and some memories on these experiences, it is well known that the discussions that followed screenings were long and often heated. Medvedkin recounts how on many of these occasions workers started to reconstruct the plan in their factory and find solutions to the exposed problems.[41] Workers became political and this implied that workers stood beyond the economic field of the production process. Kinopoezd enhanced and triggered the political language and in the moment after the screening the working collective that took initiative became political. This resulted in the further enabling of workers' self-organization, making conflicts visible and sayable, which contributed to the construction of a new Communist community, where workers did not only work, but also spoke and participated.

Concrete Example: *How Do You Live, Comrade Miner?*

In the concluding section I would like to make a few comments on the most famous of conserved cinema-train films, *How Do You Live, Comrade Miner?* (1932), directed by Nikolay Karamzinsky. The film begins as a typical socialist realist display of the mine October. The camera follows the path of one miner and tends to lead us through the production process. However, soon the film embarks on a very different story: after his shift is done, comrade miner walks home to the mass residential complex that harbours 1,500 miners and their families. The film displays the worker's living conditions, what happens after work, in the so-called sphere of reproduction. The relationship between intertitles and movement of camera was based on a naturalist connection: what we read first is then confirmed by a camera shot or a close-up. Our worker is followed to his residential complex, which is marked by misery: roads are muddy, toilets scarce and open, platforms in front of the housings are used for cooking (the intertitle breaks with the naturalistic relation with the camera in the moment when it adds that money allocated for roads is not spent for that purpose), and greenery/trees are not growing. Afterwards the camera-eye is invited into the house and enters into the flat of the worker. Different families share the flat with single men, who all live, cook and sleep together. Privacy is absent and there are also not enough mattresses or covers that were, as the intertitle warns, supposed to be provided by the house management. The intertitle comments that one can find no real culture for the workers here, and concludes that comrade miner is destined to stay here since he receives such a low salary. Communal housing is in fact a barrack, which does not provide the conditions for decent social life.[42] The departing images of the industrialist development and machinization are juxtaposed with the images of misery in the collective mode of living.

Everything so far leads us to the assertion that this is a typical social realist documentary with some critical and pedagogical moments. However, the film ends in a rather surprising way, in political and aesthetical terms. After the display of the communal residence, the camera brings us to the local party meeting, where members discuss the problems of the community and keep drinking. The camera zooms in and out, and this time the naturalist relation between images and intertitles is broken with a very strong aesthetical procedure. The camera is now on a mission of (critically) evaluating two consequences of these party meetings. Firstly, instead of bureaucrats we now see their pants that are hanging in the air; the camera zooms in and focuses on many holes in their pants.[43] This displacement of subject into objects suggests that in multiplying party meetings there is also a corresponding multiplication of holes in pants – it renders the situation humorous. In the following sequence we see the comic line continued in a surrealist evaluation of the second consequence of the meeting. We see a desk with papers, and then the camera follows, in a Vertovian way,[44] one piece of paper, which on its own flies into a map and then, as if taken by the wind, the map dances to the cupboard, which is full of other maps. This visual take tackles the problem of the mechanical and repetitive aspect of the official political process, where bureaucratic meetings are put on the same level as paper accumulation.

But the critical eye does not rest its case here: what follows is politically even more surprising, we meet a socialist realist *deus ex machina*: a portrait of Stalin. The portrait is followed by his quote that addresses and praises the new heroes, shock workers and to who the party needs to fully commit. Obviously, this insert and quote should be read in a satirical way; it is not only because the whole film does not tackle the question of the shock worker, or more specifically work (rather reproduction than production; rather critique of bureaucracy and Stalinization than praise of Stalin). Also, the film's political position is empowered through a reference to Stalin, which is done in an ambivalent way. By acknowledging Stalin as the 'master signifier' in those historical circumstances, the film does not wish to launch any concrete programmatic points for the Five-Year Plan, but places its intervention in the midst of Stalinist authority; it exposes and challenges bureaucratic machinery and the negative sides of socialist modernization from within. It means that kinopoezd does not have recourse to art as an oasis, or a dissident external position, but struggles in the politico-aesthetical form from within: using the social realist scenography and iconography. Kinopoezd deploys techniques that are at once subtle and satirical in order to criticize the blind spots of socialist development and to defend itself against the critique of the state.

Stalin's quote is followed by a brief display of a worker in the mine, which then brings us to the last sequence of the film. Karamzinsky juxtaposes the 'alienated' bureaucracy that does not commit to the political work with our worker, who sleeps in the scarce living conditions. Should this comrade really live in this way? The film ends on a highly critical note and is directed towards the socialist power itself, in particular to the negative sides of socialist industrialization. We see no critique of absenteeism, lack of discipline or workers' motivation. Rather, the film is the instance of paradigmatic shift of kinopoezd, which stepped miles away from service to the state. *How Do You Live, Comrade Miner?* (1932) steps to the service to the people, and could be read as a sort of continuation of revolution, both in terms of political stance (critique of bureaucracy and expansion of production to reproduction) and aesthetical stance that embodies also anti-naturalist, surrealist, even Vertovian elements. The film can be seen as one of the most creative documentary works of the early 1930s in the Soviet Union.

Conclusion: Arrested Development of Kinopoezd?

This chapter tackled the question of the encounter between communism, cinema and the train in the early Soviet period. Reinstating the importance of the material infrastructure in the frame of the cinefication policy for the emerging socialist state, I argued that besides this socialist modernization also a genuine movement of cinematic modernism emerged, or what I called cinematic communism. The more abstract analysis was concretized through an analysis of the historical example of train cinematic experience: Medvedkin's kinopoezd. The experiences of kinopoezd remain inspiring for political activism and cinema today. Kinopoezd was an independent, self-managed unit of production, distribution and consumption, a mobile film factory that travelled across the expanse of the Soviet Union. Not only educating people and bringing them films, rather cinema-train was there to produce films with and among people, to get critically involved in the process of the 'building of socialism'. The method of work shifted the established division of the film labour process and also tended to abolish the border between professionals and amateurs, and actors and spectators. In many ways it expanded and rectified experience of agit-trains from the early 1920s, where the primacy was given to distribution and cultural dissemination of 'ready-made films'. Production of a series of critical documentary films was accompanied by a development of satirical pedagogy, which was designed to self-educate the working collective. These critical interventions stirred many heated discussions, which influenced a novel construction of working collective. In this respect, kinopoezd is of the most exciting revolutionary forms in history of cinema, indebted to Marx and the October Revolution.

Marx spoke about 'revolutions as the locomotives of history' (Marx 1962: 217), while later Benjamin hurried to correct him by saying that 'revolutions could be seen as humanity pulling the brake on this train' (2003: 402). Medvedkin's cinema-train, however, displayed two different tendencies: that of accelerating and arresting the revolutionary movement. Kinopoezd was not only a productivist experiment that brought revolution from above, the locomotive that propagates the inevitable and linear material progress;[45] rather, cinema-train was not afraid to pull the brake from below and stop the movement, while at the same time also accelerating it, discussing and showing the inconsistencies of socialist modernization. This was not done from a comfortable dissident position from without, but internally from a dedicated belief of the Communist activism of the whole crew. As Linhart at some point claims that we should see the early Soviet train as a proper 'state in movement', I can conclude that Medvedkin's encounter of cinema and train was a cinematic state in movement towards communism.

Notes

I thank the editors of this volume for their valuable comments on the chapter and Alexander von Humboldt Foundation for the postdoctoral fellowship to research on this topic.

1. It is noteworthy that one of the early cinematographers, Boleslaw Matuszewski, who worked with the brothers Lumière, wrote that film will not only offer a source of historical research, but will become the most suitable medium for historical narration (1898). There is no coincidence that the brothers Lumière took the name that is so clearly bound to the metaphors of modernization. One century later, Jean-Luc Godard finished his master work *Histoire(s) du Cinema* (1998), where he attempted to answer the call of Matuszewski, this time in terms of re-viewing the history of the whole twentieth century by skilful editing of the famous moving images (see Mazierska 2011: 10–16).
2. Adams Sitney aptly remarks that modernism brings together an ambivalent feature of both radical discontinuity and at the same time continues to re-inscribe it into earlier traditional art forms (Sitney 1992). For a detailed discussion on the question of Modernism in cinema see Kovacs (2008).
3. For a good analysis of institutional changes and how the income from distribution of foreign films was transferred into domestic film production see Kepley (1994: 60–80).
4. Lunacharsky's famous report of what Lenin told him in 1922: 'you must remember that of all the arts for us the most important is cinema' (Lenin in Christie and Taylor 2002: 57). Also, Trotsky claimed that film will awaken 'human personality in the masses' (Trotsky in Cliff 1991: 98).
5. 'Under Stalin the dream of the avant-garde was in fact fulfilled and the life of society was organised in monolithic artistic forms, though of course not those that the avant-garde itself had favoured' (Groys 2011: 9; see also 44 and 64–65). It would be also wrong to claim that all socialist realism was Stalinist, or even state art. There were some important examples of social(ist) realism that demand a more concise and less disdainful analysis. It is also noteworthy that what dominated 1930s film production was something that cannot be easily defined as 'socialist realism', but could be much more depicted as romantic idealization and socialist kitsch. I will return to this question later.
6. 'Real' is a traumatic kernel, one of the fundamental dimensions of unconscious, which Žižek (2011) and Badiou (2007), most notably, deployed in rethinking revolutionary politics and art of the twentieth century. To simplify Wajcman's psychoanalytic argument (1998), the Real in art exists in its elementary gesture to show towards something that the gaze/viewer does not want to see, or is not able to see in the existing aesthetic constellation of the dominant genre. This Real is more real than reality and, in a specific way, it makes visible a blind spot in aesthetic production and reception. This gesture can be either extremely political, or also, as

Rancière would claim, it can be depoliticized and purely in an aesthetically novel form (Rancière 2006).
7. Ross Wolf (2013) made a good criticism of Groys' arguments by situating them within the general postmodern malaise that comfortably denunciates 'totalitarian modernism'. I work on the problems of Boris Groys' return to avant-garde in details elsewhere, see Kirn (forthcoming).
8. Productivism was one of the avant-garde tendencies that operated mostly with the transgressing of the border between art, technology and economy; in some instances, it also announced the dissolution of art in favour of industrialization (Bowlt 1988). See also Steyerl (2009), who argues that Medvedkin is a 'productivist' documentary maker.
9. Emanuel Barot (2009: 27–33) contributed an important critique of this metapolitical approach in his book *Camera Politica*, where he rightly diagnosed the regressiveness of the position (both formally and politically), which remains merely stuck with the application of a formula or political message onto the screen.
10. This type of argument was developed by Alain Badiou (2005) when reading Mallarme's poems as certain continuation of Parisian Commune after its historical defeat as an 'action restrainte'. In a similar vein, Adorno (2007) advocated the defence of artistic form against a direct application of politics onto art.
11. Socialist modernization consists of intense and interconnected processes of urbanization, industrialization and the emerging industrial working class, but also the repression of workers' opposition, economic compromise in the NEP (New Economic Policy), as well as the collectivization and repression of peasantry. Also, within cinema, there is a conflictual relationship between more popular art and the avant-garde.
12. A historical example of the nodal point was for Althusser contained in his reading of Lenin, locating the rupture of the October Revolution. For Althusser, it was important to stress the political and ideological dimension of the rupture against the false readings of the Second International that predicted the revolution would take place in the more developed Western countries first (Althusser 2005: 87–129). Russia cannot be regarded only as the 'weakest link', but should be seen as a new nodal point (politics, ideology, anti-imperialist struggle), which opened a path towards a different reading of revolution, but also a different political strategy within the international workers' movement. Althusser criticized the classical model of simple causality where the economic base determines the superstructure, and developed a model of structural causality that allowed him to think 'double determination', or rather how the alleged centre of society (economy) is decentred or how structural efficacy is to be only detected in its effects. This dialectical model can help us understand the complex interrelationship between economic policy, revolutionary politics and art/cinema.
13. The formula comes from his famous 'Note on Electrification' from 7 February 1920, when the All-Russian Central Executive Committee of the Soviets announced the

14. formation of a State Electrification Commission (GOELRO). For the discussion on the utopian kernels of state modernization see Stites (1991: 41–53).
14. Trotsky discusses the relevance of the order 1042 in the chapter seven of the book *New Course* (1965). This order dealt with the railway plans and future socialist economy (Swain 2006: 125–26; Linhart 2010). In an analogy to the military and economic importance of train one should mention Paul Virilio's (2009) assertion that the cinema is firstly military and only secondly artistic. I owe this remark to Lars Kristensen.
15. Anything that was connected to logistics (circulation) was pivotal for the new revolutionary state and the Bolsheviks (Linhart 2010). For the historical account of cinefication see Taylor (1979) and Kepley (1994).
16. Lahusen, together with a group of researchers, is currently working on the film documentary *Celluloid Road*, which will present the cinefication of Kyrgyzstan.
17. There are certain authors, Medvedkin included, who have not been properly addressed in the film history cannon, either due to their less prestigious status or due to the more difficult accessibility of their works. This contribution attempts to further investigate Medvedkin's work. The question on the relationship between communism and cinema was of particular importance in early Soviet times, but also in some later historical sequences, such as the French context of the late 1960s (Group Vertov and Group Medvedkin), Yugoslav Black Wave cinema (see Kirn 2012), streams in Third World cinema (Wayne 2001).
18. Many of the early avant-garde and political films were criticized for being neither comprehensive nor pedagogical enough, or for being too stylistic/formalistic. This critique actually confirms the relative autonomy of a body of film works that I am interested in analysing here. For important critique of art autonomy and specifically of (Yugoslav) partisan-revolutionary art see Komelj (2009).
19. For a valuable account of collective and aesthetical communist practises see Stites (1991).
20. Taylor 1979; Kepley 1994; Sochor 1988.
21. For details on the new conception of cinefication read the whole section, see Levi (2012: 77–84).
22. 'Cinematic desire ... can be successfully reproduced even under the conditions other than those of watching an actual film' (Levi 2012: 138). In other words, it was through many non-cinematic media that avant-garde film-makers generated filmic seriality and movement.
23. Levi states the influences from Leonardo da Vinci (2012: 129) to Meyerhold's theater for early Soviet filmmakers, as well as a series of exciting intermedial experiments taking place in very different historical conditions (2012: 25–46).
24. The communist decoding of reality was, as both Levi (2012: 79) and Rancière (2011: 35–42) correctly pinpoint, of extreme importance for the work of Dziga Vertov.
25. Wollen (1972: 41) describes well how Eisenstein's cinema-fist replied to Vertov's cinema-eye.

26. These different tendencies ranged from the question of abolishing/transforming the border between art and life/politics, at times in service of industrialization (industrial design, productivism), at other times in service of pure art (formalism, futurism) or pure politics (proletcult). See Bowlt (1988).
27. At a broader level, the belief in cinematic modernism was further suspended a decade later with the tragic events of WWII (Auschwitz, Hiroshima). Deleuze (2000: 6) tackles this topic of crisis through the attempt of Italian neorealismo to restore the belief in humanity.
28. Rather than simply imitating or even romanticizing reality, socialist realism would both critically evaluate the social conditions and affirm or negate the developing tendencies. Interestingly, Slavoj Žižek advocates a more affirmative view on the romanticized version of socialist realism. The latter:

    should depict 'typical' heroes in 'typical' situations. Writers who for example, presented a predominantly bleak picture of the Soviet reality were not accused simply of lying – the accusation was that they provided a distorted reflection of social reality by focusing on phenomena which were not 'typical' which were sad remainders of the past, instead of focusing on phenomena which were 'typical' in the precise sense of expressing the deeper underlying historical tendency of the progress towards Communism. A novel which presented a new Socialist type of man who dedicated his life to the happiness of all the people, of course, depicted a minority phenomenon (the majority of the people were not yet like that), but none the less a phenomenon which enabled us to identify the truly progressive forces active in the social situation. (Žižek 2000: 175)

    Žižek's evaluation of the figure of shock workers ignores the etatist and ideological function.
29. Paradigmatic films from Grigori Aleksandrov's *Jolly Fellows* (1934) and *Volga Volga* (1938).
30. Very little research has been done on Medvedkin in film history. Jay Layda (1960) was one of the first to mention Medvedkin's experiments of cine-train, but it has been largely thanks to Chris Marker, who in the late 1960s discovered Alexandr Medvedkin. After Medvedkin's death, Marker made an extraordinary homage to him with *Last Bolshevik* (1993). There has not been much written on Medvedkin, the first serious mention – at least in the West – as already noted came from the pen of Leyda (1960), while the first monography on Medvedkin came only in 2005 from Emma Widdis. Furthermore, in the book edited by Taylor and Christie (1994: 165–75), one finds an interview with Medvedkin, which among other things explains well Medvedkin's take on the relationship between politics and art.
31. Medvedkin stated that the 'train would be a kind of special fire brigade to put out problem fires … with that most effective of extinguishers: film' (Medvedkin in Widdis 2005: 23).
32. For details see Chris Marker *Le Train en marche* (1971).

33. A few conserved examples are available on the new DVD of Alexander Medvekin's *Happiness* (1935). A few years ago an Italian public broadcaster screened a series of eleven films from cinema-train (accessible on the internet: https://www.youtube.com/watch?v=0usOIw3Kuys&list=FLPODexyrsVoQ9aUs6tizXww). News reels and short insights in the life of workers or modalities of production processes were a few different film forms that they used during the journeys.
34. See Marx and Engels (MECW 5(47)): 'each can become accomplished in any branch he wishes, society regulates the general production and thus makes it possible for me to do one thing today and another tomorrow, to hunt in the morning, fish in the afternoon, rear cattle in the evening, criticize after dinner, just as I have a mind, without ever becoming hunter, fisherman, shepherd or critic'.
35. In this respect, cinema-train employed a similar criticism and principle that was practised by Persimfans, the first orchestra that preformed without a conductor and where all members managed the orchestra (Stites 1991: 135–40).
36. This modus operandi could be described as the train that never stops, which is a central metaphor of the influential science fiction novel from China Mieville's *Iron Council* (2004).
37. Usually they made around five copies of each film. A few were sent to the propaganda section of the Communist Party in the concerned region, some were left with the working collectives and others remained on the train.
38. This enthusiasm and way of doing films was in its own way repeated and explored in France in the late 1960s, when Medvedkin's group was created. As already mentioned, Medvedkin's work in many ways influenced Chris Marker's path (see also Jon Kear's chapter in this volume).
39. Walsh (1981: 22–37) pointed to the Freudian lesson of the economic character of the joke. Obviously, the role of satire in these circumstances operated on a thin line, which would in the second part of the 1930s be severely sanctioned and prohibited by the Stalinist apparatus. I leave the discussion on the more general role of satire in Medvedkin's work and in the 1930s for another occasion.
40. In this respect we should mention the whole series of the experiments that targeted different divides and called for a sort of mobility (Stites 1991: 190–223). One of the most influential figures was undoubtedly Velimir Khlebnikov, who theorized mobile cities and in what way to start a different way of communal living.
41. See Chris Marker's *Le Train en marche* (France, 1971).
42. This portrayal is critical also towards otherwise utopian attempts of communal workhouses (see Stites 1991: 200–04). If collective communal housing is in reality merely a strategy of survival, then it has failed to achieve its mission: to improve social life for new workers.
43. One is reminded of Mayakovsky's (1940: 74) famous poem 'Lost in Conference', which speaks of the demise of revolutionary fervent and the bureaucratization of society through countless meetings and conferences. Half of a person is at one conference and the other half at another (see http://www.unz.org/Pub/AmQSo

vietUnion-1940jul-00074). Mayakovsky ends the poem with the utopian slogan, just after he wakes up: 'One more conference/one last conference/one/to liquidate all conferences!'.
44. A Vertovian move that reminds us of the famous dance of the camera (*Man with a Movie Camera*, 1929).
45. In this respect, and even more in his masterpiece *Happiness* (1935), Medvedkin's work, in particular on peasantry, went well beyond either Dovzhenko's *Earth* (1930) and his naturalistic/organistic representation of the soul of peasant, and also the metaphor of the tractor as the technological advancement in Eisenstein's *General Line* (1929) or Vertov's *Enthusiasm* (1931).

References

Adorno, T. 2007. 'Commitment', in *Aesthetics and Politics*. London: Verso, pp. 177–95.
Althusser, L. 2005. *For Marx*. London: Verso.
Badiou, A. 2005. *Metapolitics*. London: Verso.
———. 2007. *Century*. Cambridge: Polity Press.
Barot, E. 2009. *Camera Politica*. Paris: Vrin.
Benjamin, W. 2002. *Selected Writings, 1935–1938*. Cambridge, MA: Harvard University Press.
———. 2003. *Selected Writings, 1938–1940*. Cambridge, MA: Harvard University Press.
Blümlinger, C. 2006. 'Lumiere, the Train and the Avant-Garde', in Strauven Wanda (ed.) *Cinema of Attraction Reloaded*. Amsterdam: Amsterdam University Press, pp. 245–65.
Bowlt, J. 1988. *Russian Art of the Avant-garde: Theory and Criticism 1902–1934*. London: Thames and Hudson.
Cliff, T. 1991. *Trotsky 1923–1927: Fighting the Rising Stalinist Bureaucracy*. London: Bookmarks.
Deleuze, G. 2000. *Cinema II*. Minneapolis: University of Minnesota Press.
Engels, F. and K. Marx. 1962. *Selected Works, Part I*. Moscow: Moscow Publishers.
Groys, B. 2011. *The Total Art of Stalinism: Avant-Garde, Aesthetic Dictatorship, and Beyond*. London: Verso.
Kenez, P. 2001. *Cinema and Soviet Society: From the Revolution to the Death of Stalin*. London: Tauris.
Kepley Jr, V. 1994. 'The Origins of Soviet Cinema: a Study in Industry Development' in I. Christie and R. Taylor (eds), *Inside the Film Factory*. London: Routledge, pp. 60–80.
Kirn, G. 2012. 'New Yugoslav Cinema: a Humanist Cinema? Not Really', in G. Kirn, D. Sekulić and Z. Testen (eds), *Surfing the Black: Black Wave Cinema and its Transgressive Moments*. Maastricht: JvE Academy, pp. 10–46.

Kirn, G. forthcoming. ' Critical Notes on Boris Groys' Blockage of Avant-garde, or on the defense of Socialist Realism', in B. Dimitrijević and A. Sekulić, *En Garde, Avant-Garde: 20/21 Covjek posle rata*. Belgrade: CKZD.

Komelj, M. 2009. *Kako Misliti Partizansko Umetnost?* [How to Think Partisan Art?]. Ljubljana: Založba *cf.

Kovacs, A. 2008. *Screening Modernism: European Art Cinema, 1950–1980*. Chicago: University of Chicago Press.

Lahusen, T. 'Cinefication: a History of Soviet Film Dissemination'. Retrieved 18 September 2013 from http://www.chemodanfilms.com/cinefication-a-history-of-soviet-film-dissemination/.

Layda, Y. 1960. *Kino: a History of the Russian and Soviet Film*. Princeton, NJ: Princeton University Press.

Lenin, V. 1977. *Collected Works* 42. Moscow: Progress Publishers.

———. 2002. 'Directive on Cinema Affairs' in I. Christie and R. Taylor (eds), *The Film Factory*. London: Routledge, p. 56.

Levi, P. 2012. *Cinema by Other Means*. New York: Oxford University Press.

Linhart, R. 2010. *Lenine, les Paysans et Taylor*. Paris: Seuil.

Marx, K. and F. Engels. 1975–2005. *Marx and Engels Collected Works* (MECW). New York: International Publishers.

Matuszewski, B. 1898-2006. 'Une nouvelle source de l'histoire du cinéma', in M. Mazaraki (ed.), *Écrits cinématographiques*. Paris: Association française de recherche sur l'histoire du cinéma/Cinémathèque française.

Mazierska, E. 2011. *European Cinema and Intertextuality: History, Memory and Politics*. Hampshire: Palgrave Macmillan.

Mayakovsky, V. 1940. 'Lost in Conference', *American Quarterly on the Soviet Union* 3(1): 74. Retrieved 18 September 2013 from http://www.unz.org/Pub/AmQSovietUnion-1940jul-00074.

Medvedkin, A. 1994. 'Interview', in I. Christie and R. Taylor (eds), *Inside the Film Factory*. London: Routledge, pp. 165–75.

Mieville, C. 2004. *Iron Council*. New York: Del Rey Books.

Rancière, J. 2006. *Politics of Aesthetics: the Distribution of the Sensible*. New York: Continuum.

———. 2011. *Les Écarts du Cinéma*. Paris: Editions Fabrique.

Schivelbusch, W. 1986. *Railway Journey: the Industrialization of Time and Space in the 19th Century*. Leamington Spa: Berg Publishers.

Sitney, A. 1992. *Modernist Montage: The Obscurity of Vision in Cinema and Literature*. New York: Columbia University Press.

Steyerl, H. 'Truth Unmade: Productivism and Factography', *Transversal / EIPCP Multilingual Webjournal*. Retrieved 18 September 2013 from http://eipcp.net/transversal/0910/steyerl/en.

Stites, R. 1991. *Revolutionary Dreams: Utopian Vision and Experimental Life in the Russian Revolution*. New York: Oxford University Press.

Sochor, Z. 1988. *Revolution and Culture: the Bogdanov-Lenin Controversy*. Ithaca, NY: Cornell University Press.
Swain, G. 2006. *Trotzky*. Edinburgh: Pearson Publishers.
Taylor, R. 1979. *The Politics of the Soviet Cinema 1917-1929*. Cambridge: Cambridge University Press.
Tode, T. 2008. 'Agit-trains, Agit-steamers, Cinema Tracks Dziga Vertov and Travelling Cinema in the Early 1920s in the Soviet Union', in M. Loiperdinger (ed.), *Travelling Cinema in Europe: Sources and Perspectives,* Frankfurt: Stroemfeld/Roter Stern, pp. 143-57.
Trotsky, L. 1965. *New Course*. London: Cresset Press.
Virilio, P. 2009. *War and Cinema: Logistics of Perception*. London: Verso.
Wajcman, G. 1998. *L'Objet du Siècle*. Paris: Editions Gallimard.
Walsh, M. 1981. *The Brechtian Aspect of Radical Cinema*. London: British Film Institute.
Wayne, M. 2001. *Political Film: the Dialectics of Third Cinema*. London: Pluto Press.
Widdis, E. 2005. *Alexander Medvedkin*. London: Tauris.
Wolf, R. 2013. 'Stalinism in Art and Architecture or the First Postmodern Style', *Situations: Project for the Radical Imagination* 5(1): 101-11.
Wollen, P. 1972. *Signs and Meaning in the Cinema*. Bloomington: Indiana University Press.
Žižek, S. 2000. *Did Somebody Say Totalitarianism?: Five Interventions in the (Mis)use of a Notation*. London: Verso.
———. 2009. *Parallax View*. Cambridge, MA: MIT Press.
———. 2011. *Living in the End Times*. London: Verso.

Filmography

How Do You Live, Comrade Miner? (*Kak zhivesh', tovarishch gornyak?*) 1932. Nikolay Karamzinsky.
The Last Bolshevik (*Le tombeau d'Alexandre*). 1993. Chris Marker.
The Train Rolls On (*Le Train en marche*). 1971. Chris Marker.

CHAPTER 2

Politics and Aesthetics within Godard's Cinema

Jeremy Spencer

In this chapter, I highlight different ways political aesthetics and art are defined as the context of the radical or militant cinema of the filmmaker Jean-Luc Godard. I survey the arguments generated by the practices and representations of twentieth-century radical film and art, indicating different ways in which they can be politicized; which are pertinent to, which make reference to or involve Godard's intellectual and aesthetically conscious cinema. These arguments are elaborated on in journals concerned with the theoretical foundations for the study of film, which emphasize the articulation of cinema, ideology and politics. I conclude with the challenge to the presumptions and efficacy of the political culture established by the avant-garde in art and film in contemporary writings of Jacques Rancière.

In a 1950 article on Soviet film for *Gazette du Cinéma,* 'Towards a Political Cinema', Jean-Luc Godard associates the possibility of a 'cinema of revolution' with repetition, self-consciousness and 'the dynamic' (Godard 1986: 16). Drawing upon Marx's *The Eighteenth Brumaire of Louis Bonaparte* (1852) and art critic Harold Rosenberg's 'The Resurrected Romans' (1948), Godard contrasts the representation of gestures in film that are unconsciously repetitive or mimetic, that have been played before and are meaningful only through their allusion to history and culture to those which are spontaneous and passionate. Godard understands this distinction and political film in light of Marx's depiction of the proletarian revolution as self-conscious and critical in its relationship with history, understood as a drama of creative self-recognition that occurs through struggle. Marx contrasted the proletarian revolution to the bourgeois revolutions in terms of their different relationships to the past. In periods of revolutionary crisis the bourgeoisie borrowed the imagery and language of dead generations to accomplish its task of social transformation. To establish modern bourgeois society the heroes of the French revolution parodied revolutionary traditions, appropriating their names, battle cries and costumes. This conjuring up or the awakening of the dead distinguishes the bourgeois revolution from 'the social revolution of the nineteenth century' (Marx 2010: 146–49). This revolution does not repeat past history or aestheticize politics to conceal its content; it is self-critical and reflective and, unlike the revolutionary bourgeoisie, the proletariat completely abandons the past, as it has no 'recourse to myth' (Orton 1991: 9).

Godard's 1950 article relates political film with questions of signification and the analysis of the linguistic sign, suggesting the science of signs and what constitutes them, as conceived by the linguist Ferdinand de Saussure; Godard's semiotic analysis of the shot challenges cinematic illusionism that requires the subjection of the image to the referent. A sign finds its meaning through its position and relation as an element within a system; its meaning is differential rather an innate. Sergei Eisenstein had created independent and specifically filmic spaces and times by reading or interpreting the referent; Bergman's *Persona* (1966), Buñuel's *Belle de Jour* (1967) and Godard's *La Chinoise* (1967) – 'the writing of a spectacle that imposes its own time and space' (Narboni 2001: 301) – also exemplify a practice of cinema that is self-reflexive, for Godard, a cinema of 'formal aggression', which is concerned with the independence of the film image from the referent. In Godard's post-'68 film in particular we see a tendency to work with the modernist disjunction of signifier and signified. Twentieth-century modernism developed towards abstraction to become 'an art of pure signifiers detached from meaning as much as from reference' (Wollen 1976: 79). Robert Rauschenberg and Jasper Johns' work of the later 1950s investigated the arbitrariness of the sign to the point of its actual dissolution. The avant-garde's defining theoretical and practical work upon the sign informs the debates of political film aesthetics. Brechtian dramaturgy proposes a semiological problem because it posits that the responsibility of 'dramatic art is not so much to express reality as to signify it'; political art acknowledges 'a certain formalism', admitting 'a certain arbitrary nature of the sign' (Barthes 1972: 74). For the film journal *Screen* of the 1970s, the construction of semiology, particularly in relation to historical materialism and the necessary appropriation of Freudian psychoanalysis for a theory of the construction of the subject, made it possible to question conventional modes of thinking about film and metaphysical notions of origin, centre, and expression, and understand signification or sense as a specific practice or process of production. Semiology becomes more than the analysis of the sign; it engenders its actual dislocation to challenge the symbolic.

The avant-garde fascination with the arbitrariness of the sign became an important critical reference for Godard's practical analysis of the processes of cinematic representation, named by Sylvia Harvey (1982) as 'political modernism': the attempt to unite semiotic and ideological analysis for the sake of a radical aesthetic practice that would have radical social effects. Godard's films are engaged with contemporary politics but it is their disassembly or dislocation of the diegesis of bourgeois cinema that makes them politically effective. While keeping in mind the difference between the linguistic sign and analogical representations, Godard's film seems capable of dislocating the sign, it typically separates images from the sound track; the narration of a voiceover will be unrelated to the accompanying image the spectator sees: words – in the form of slogans, titles, posters and captions – criticize, interpret and transform images. *British Sounds* (Godard 1969), a documentary of six sequences analysing contemporary British capitalism, promotes the construction of a 'science of the image' that could exist through the appropriation of Marxist theory. The documentary begins by 'rewriting' a line from the *Manifesto of the Communist Party* (1848): 'In a word, the bourgeoisie creates a world in its image. Comrades! We must destroy that image! … Sometimes the class struggle is also the struggle of one image against another image, of one sound against another sound … in a film, this struggle is between images and sounds'. Its first sequence is a long, continuous tracking shot of unidentified workers on a sports car production line, only interrupted by two handwritten placards alluding to the October Revolution and work; the sounds that accompany or are superimposed over the image that we experience independently or separately are shrill, screeching and mechanical; a voiceover reads out altered passages from Marx and Engels' writings (*The Manifesto of the Communist Party*; *Capital*). This sequence denies cinema's privilege, the complete unity of sound and image assumed in Hollywood film to present a true presentation of reality; Godard politicizes sound and image (reactionary/revolutionary), seeing their opposition, their relation as one of continuous struggle.

Making Films Politically

The 'political group' Dziga Vertov made the English-language film *British Sounds* (1969), produced by Irving Teitelbaum for Kestrel Films and commissioned by Stella Richmond at London Weekend Television, which refused to transmit it. Godard formed the group in 1969 with the intention to make films politically. The group produced eight films between 1969 and 1971, with Godard collaborating with the journalist and militant Jean-Pierre Gorin and Jean-Henri Roger.[1] Godard considered himself 'no longer a filmmaker' or a 'painter in letters' but instead 'just a worker in the movies', a self-identity that emerged in the events of May '68. Gorin made film only provisionally because of its importance to contemporary class struggle. Of his earlier political films Godard remarked: 'They are just Hollywood films because I was a bourgeois artist. They are my dead corpses' (Carroll 1972: 61).

In naming this experiment in collective and engaged filmmaking the 'Dziga Vertov Group', Godard claimed the relevance of Soviet cinema to 1960s France. He chose the name of the Soviet filmmaker 'to indicate a programme, to raise a flag' (Carroll 1972: 50); Vertov symbolized for Godard 'the synthesis of formal and political revolution' (Stark 2012: 39). In explaining what it meant to make films politically, Godard referred to Vertov's instructions for editing from a 1927 text, 'Provisional Instructions to Cinema Eye Groups'. Vertov attributed a different significance to editing than that of 'artistic cinema', defining it as intrinsic to filming and an 'organization of the visible world'; the voiceover in *Pravda* (1969), a documentary filmed in Czechoslovakia in March 1969 in collaboration with Jean-Henri Roger, refers to editing as the organizing of sounds and images differently and politically with the aim of producing a 'militant film' that presents a 'concrete analysis of a concrete situation' with the intention of transforming it (Godard cited in Harvey 1978: 30).

In a 1967 interview published in *Cahiers du Cinéma* discussing Chris Marker's work with strikers at the Rhodiaceta textile factory in Besançon, described as a 'travelogue' in *Pravda*, Godard expressed the difficultly of making films politically: 'the men who know film can't speak the language of strikes and the men who know strikes are better at talking [Gérard] Oury than Resnais ... Union militants have realized that men aren't equal if they don't earn the same pay; they've got to realize now that we aren't equal if we don't speak the same language' (Bontemps et al. 1968–69: 22). Hollywood fiction film effaces the marks of its construction and does not usually address the spectator directly; in contrast, Godard and Dziga Vertov used a different language, as outlined by Peter Wollen (1972), of 'narrative intransitivity, estrangement, foregrounding, multiple diegesis, aperture, unpleasure, reality'. This language or set of strategies – Godard's 'politicised, socially aware formalism' (Harvey et al. 1985: 43) – associated with Brechtian theatre and, for Wollen, the aesthetics of the radical avant-garde, are central to making films politically compared to just making political films. For Godard, films that contained 'political signifieds', such as Gillo Pontecorvo's *Battle of Algiers* (1966) and Costa-Gavras' *Z* (1969), were at best 'liberal' because they recorded but were not part of national liberation or class struggles. These films 'confuse reality with reflections', they confuse the film image, which is a reflection of reality, with reality: 'Bourgeois filmmakers focus on the reflections of reality', Godard argues, whereas, the Dziga Vertov Group were concerned with the nature or the reality of that reflection. Their exploration of film language, with the 'reality of [the] reflection', led to their ghettoization; Godard comments that their commissioned films were rejected by television companies, such as London Weekend Television, because they were 'fiercely attacking' them. Godard regarded film as the most 'economically and culturally enslaved' of all the arts; he discovered imperialism via aesthetics, in trying to make films in a different way, an aesthetic struggle. There appeared to be a right way to make films, a structure imposed on production that eliminates all others; film in socialist countries imitated the conventions of U.S. cinema: 'Fifty years after the October Revolution, the American industry rules cinema the world over' (Godard 1972: 243). Godard describes this as cultural or 'aesthetic imperialism', insisting that films could not keep being made in the same way.

Theorizing Militant Film

In a 1969 interview with *Cinéthique,* Marcelin Pleynet, editor of the theoretical journal *Tel Quel,* argued that the question was not what was a political film in bourgeois society – 'a cinema whose political effectiveness is real' – but which films were made through theoretical work. By naturally and directly reflecting the real, avowedly 'politicised films' were 'invested' by bourgeois ideology, a powerful, well-constructed and coherent system of representations. Costa-Gavras' *The Confession* (1970) delivered an authentic political message but it did not attempt to transform conventional cinematic aesthetics or ideologies. A politically effective or valuable film carried out a scriptural operation or work – it possessed a self-conscious understanding of how meanings are produced. *The Confession* does not work upon or with its images as signs, which guarantees that it is accessible to a wider audience and its political message is blatant, but it fails the most important test of political aesthetics: the questioning of its own conditions of existence and its means of representation. It reproduces the aesthetic conventions of bourgeois cinema and its own politics are deformed because it has adopted conventional aesthetics, means of production and dissemination. Revolutionary or militant film, however, engaged representation at the level of the signifier, an argument expressed in Benjamin's essay 'The Author as Producer' (1934). Benjamin argued that it was not sufficient for an artwork to show the 'right tendency' or contain a political signified. He raised the question of 'technique' and of which forms possessed 'revolutionary use-value' through not merely supplying but changing an existing cultural apparatus from within.

In the *Cinéthique* interview, Godard's cinema of the 1960s is judged 'limited to agitational dissent'; it was recognized to be valuable in its understanding of cinema as 'ideological production', but it was not revolutionary because it did not directly participate in 'real class struggle' or consider cinema theoretically as a signifying practice. His more interesting films expressed a personal ideology that was anarchist, and this was how they contested or upset bourgeois ideology. 'Signifying practice' raises the question of the position of the spectator created for the film. 'Signifying' indicates and recognizes film as a system or articulation of meaning or the production of signs, while 'practice' emphasizes the labour of producing meanings and the process of its articulation. The ordering or arrangement of signifiers does not passively carry, reflect or express meanings but produce and transform them. A practice of film that is specifically cinematic is materialist and formalist to engender political effects, even if it lacks an explicit or avowed political message. It is unnecessary for it to include any explicitly political signified to be political. Indeed, explicitly or avowedly politically committed cinema failed to challenge ideology if it uncritically adopted the conventional language and imagery, the same expressive forms of bourgeois cinema. So, although Godard's *La Chinoise* was splashed with politics it was politically unthreatening and easily digestible, 'entirely invested in bourgeois ideology' (Pleynet in Harvey 1978: 156), because it did not deconstruct the optical apparatus or force the spectator to question the nature of cinema, which was left entirely free to produce the intrinsically specular images of ideology.

For Pleynet, an important but neglected task for filmmakers was investigating the camera as an ideological apparatus that disseminates bourgeois ideology in its structuring of reality. Filmmakers that did not lead the spectator to question the institution of cinema had not recognized that they film through 'a particular apparatus, built for particular purposes, possessing, so to speak, a particular mental ideological structure' (ibid.: 156). A political signified is mediated by, it is put through, an apparatus imbued with its own ideology. It is not just the image or slogan – those written on the walls of the students' summer apartment in *La Chinoise* – that speaks, but the apparatus that doubles them according to its own ideology. Godard had not fully recognized that the film camera was not an impartial but an ideological instrument – with an unrecognized 'ideological bias built into it mechanism' (Leblanc 1977: 15) – which reproduces 'the code of specular vision as it was defined by Renaissance humanism … the ideology of the code of perspective, its norms and its censorships' (Pleynet in Harvey 1978: 156).

Baudry (1974–75: 40) also questions the critical emphasis upon the ideological effects of films as finished products and the 'field of what is signified' rather than 'the technical basis on which these effects depend'; because of its scientific and technical nature, the optical apparatus has seemed inviolable, he argues. What Pleynet labels as 'the whims of avant-gardist empiricism', the kinds of formal effects that Godard employed – 'deconstruction of the story, of shots, of modes of camera movement, deliberately arbitrary montage' – are symptomatic of the failure to think of cinematic practice theoretically, to consider the ideological function of the cinematographic apparatus (Pleynet in Harvey 1978: 157). Technologies of representation possess ideological effects that are concealed in the film's consumption, in its viewing. With the exception of the montage experiments of 1920s Soviet film, he argued, cinema had not critically examined its relation to the ideologies embedded in its own technologies or apparatuses.

The camera guarantees the subject as centre and origin of meaning whereby the representation becomes the spectator's. His/her identification with the camera is deeper than his/her identification with the film's protagonist; the camera obliges the spectator to see exactly what it sees. Baudry, writing in *Cinéthique* in 1970, considers the specific ideological effects of the technological basis of cinema and what ideological effects result from either its concealment or its inscription or manifestation. The camera constructs images analogous to those of the perspectival views of the Italian Renaissance, in which paintings are transformed into windows on views, negating their material surfaces. It guarantees the realism of the image or the impression of reality produced by bourgeois cinema; we forget that it is a specific ideological and cultural structure. Renaissance painting, which is a model for and is realized by the camera, elaborates a 'centred space' for the subject and presents 'a motionless and continuous whole'; in the same way, the camera's monocular vision organizes objects within the visual field in relation to the position the subject occupies; it 'lays out the space of an ideal vision' (Baudry 1974–75: 41). Its 'total vision', Baudry (ibid.: 42) writes, 'corresponds to the idealist conception of the fullness and homogeneity of "being"' and so contributes to the ideological function of art, namely, 'the tangible representation of metaphysics'.

The subject emerged as the crucial concept in the development of a Marxist theory of ideology: Louis Althusser calls the positioning or the inclusion of individuals as subjects within ideological formations or apparatuses (family, school, church, culture), 'interpellation'. Following his essay 'Ideology and the Ideological State Apparatuses' (1969), the function of ideology is to constitute concrete individuals as subjects – ideology establishes or positions individuals as subjects – as such, the subject is a constitutive of ideology and its theorization. The function of the cinematic or optical apparatus was to constitute the subject as centred and powerful, which is conditional upon his/her ignorance; it petrifies the spectator in a position of pseudodominance; this apparatus seems to extend the reach of our sensory organs so that we can more easily dominate our environment. The problem of specifically political aesthetics and the purpose of political film is the possibility of transforming the subject's position and relation to ideology, at least while the film lasts: 'the spectator is to be broken from the continuity of an identification-position which holds him as the blind-spot of ideology, its vision and its image' (Heath 1975: 39). In contrast, bourgeois cinema permits the audience 'to live an imaginary life within a non-existent reality' as consolation or escapism in face of 'the different kinds of alienation engendered by capitalism' (Leblanc 1977: 15). Cinema should confront the conditions of existence with the intention of transforming them rather than offering the spectator an imaginary escape. But if entertainment cinema constructs spectators for its products then its success rests on addressing their actual needs, especially the need for escapism from a dissatisfied life. 'Entertainment cinema provides surrogate or pseudo-satisfactions' to make alienated life more bearable (Leblanc 2005: 280). Films can appear to be without origin, 'born by magic on the screen' (Leblanc 1977: 17) or fathered by the director who creates them in his own image. They conceal their production and efface the work that produces their sounds and images. An adequately political film practice would reveal the economic origins and motivations of film production – a film is a commercial product like any other that has to make money – and thwart film's entertainment function.

The object for *Cahiers du Cinéma* was film in relation to the ideology it conveyed and the intertextual space in which films were held; film and art were 'branches of ideology' (Comolli and Narboni 1977: 4). But films related to ideology differently; the question was which of the films that are produced and distributed within the economic system and ideologies of capitalism transmit the dominant ideology with crystal clarity, are vehicles for it, and which films intercept, block and establish an ideology as a visible object. The dominant ideologies in society belong to and articulate the experience of the bourgeoisie and the defining material relationships of bourgeois society. In a similar way, Pierre Macherey (1989: 132) argued that the literary text could construct 'a determinate image of the ideological, revealing it as an object rather than living it from within as though it were an inner conscience'; literature could explore, test and crystallize ideology. In that ideologies permeate and are indistinguishable from lived experience, they are not easily or usually *perceived*. The system of representations constitutive of ideology is not immediately visible to the men and women who live it. The transformation of ideology through the practice of art is 'to change the position of the subject within ideology' (MacCabe 1974: 24).

A central ideology of the cinema is that the cinematic apparatus and available technologies can accurately reproduce a tangible reality. The ideological character of cinematic illusion is the denial of the existence of the screen and therefore the spectator's confusion of 'reflections and shadows' for reality 'as it really is' (Fargier 1977: 28). Cinema is a system of representation predicated upon the technological reproduction of illusion that conceals its own signifying production. The majority of films unconsciously reproduce an imaginary relationship to reality – 'the world as it is experienced when filtered through the ideology' (Comolli and Narboni 1977: 4). A 'principle task' of ideological struggle was 'the theoretical and practical deconstruction of the specific hold of Representation on the cinema' (*Cahiers du Cinéma* 2001: 288–89). Films that constituted 'the essential in the cinema' and were the 'chief subject' of *Cahiers du Cinéma* unravelled or deconstructed traditional cinematic conventions for depicting reality.

Lef and Political Film Aesthetics

What constituted a political, or in the early Soviet Union, a revolutionary art and culture was debated by writers and critics on the left. In writings of the early 1920s, Lenin had asserted the necessity of a cultural revolution in establishing a socialist country.[2] The past was overthrown but it had not been overcome; a durable culture had not yet established itself. A higher level or standard of culture was required, at least to the standards of Western Europe, in building socialism; Lenin argued for the development or refashioning of the best of existing bourgeois culture rather than its repudiation or abandonment through the invention of an antithetical proletarian culture. Artists, writers and filmmakers associated with *Lef* searched for innovations in a form appropriate to these tasks. Osip Brik launched the avant-garde review *Lef* (1923–25) with the poet Vladimir Mayakovsky in 1923. *Lef* was essentially a literary journal; it closed in 1925 and was revived as *New Lef* in 1927, following which twenty-four monthly issues were published by the 'Left Front of the Arts' between January 1927 and December 1928. For *New Lef*, the most important cultural task was the critique of existing and pre-revolutionary culture and to finally and concretely establish the 'real social purpose' and 'function' of the 'things produced by workers in art' and the effects of those things – art, literature and film production ('We are Searching' 1977: 298). *New Lef* promoted film and photography and was critical of some but not all traditional forms of art practice; new practices and technologies would displace and overtake the old and outworn, the photograph and the placard were opposed to the easel – 'easelism' narrowed the artist's 'creative path' for Brik – and reportage, a practical writing of eyewitness and primary documents for newspapers and periodicals or *factography*, was opposed to *belles-lettres*. The photographic depiction of Soviet reality in newspapers was more essential than its appearance in an exhibition of easel paintings. Photographs, because they were precise, factual documents, displaced artistic images refracted through the sensibility or the imagination of the artist. The necessity to grasp or fix facts and practices with a 'definite agit function' was now the basic function of art practice and determined its obsolescence or otherwise in the new society. The cinema was considered an important device for realizing the political or social function of art – 'the fixing of fact and agit' ('We are Searching' 1977: 298–99). Eisenstein's film was agitational, whereas the function of Dziga Vertov's film was informational. The poet and critic Sergei Tretyakov (2006: 38) describes Vertov's sophisticated journalistic montages as the 'enemy' of the acted film involved in the 'dense matter of real life', rather than the invented and illusory worlds of an acted cinema of 'diversion and social anaesthesia'. Leftist cinema fulfilled an informational and an agitational function in opposition to an art that was merely entertaining, spiriting the spectator into an illusory and aesthetic world. A left cinema, either through emotionally stimulating the spectator or by factually chronicling or delivering the actual experience of Soviet life, provoking an expert or intellectual interest in its development, serves the revolution.

Debates in *New Lef* centred on the difference between played and unplayed, which depended on the extent the raw material of film was deformed, its 'arbitrary distortion and displacement', or interpreted; deformation was minimal in Vertov's films that get close as possible to, and were orientated towards, the raw material. However, film that was emotionally stimulating required different methods, the method of making films through the 'montage of attractions' of Eisenstein, defined as a unit or primary element designed to shock or stimulate the spectator emotionally or psychologically. Art theorist and a founder of *Lef,* Boris Arvatov summed up positions on what constituted a specifically left cinema in his 1928 article 'Film Platform'. Arvatov (1977: 311) wrote: '*Lef* theory considers cinema of the right to be characterized by "play", narrative structure (*fabula*) and deformation of the object, while a film of the left is "unplayed", non-narrative and does not deform the object'. If the 'cinema of the right' was concerned with play, narrative and the 'deformation of the object', left cinema was the opposite: this cinema was unplayed, non-narrative and did not 'deform the object'. Vertov's films consisted of the montage of unplayed film material shot on location; a play or played film is motivated and structured by a narrative; this is an explicit 'inner thematic link' to the film material. Vertov was highly critical of what he considered as the outmoded – 'decrepit and degenerate' – acted or actor-based film, exemplified by Eisenstein's *Strike* (1924), and of directors who produced 'art cinema': he thought that Eisenstein's films of the 1920s were 'acted films in documentary trousers'. In the discussion of unplayed versus played films in *New Lef*, Tretyakov defended the unplayed documentaries by Esfir Shub and the played films by Eisenstein and Vsevolod Pudovkin. But the consensus was that the art practices that *Lef* should defend were the agit-film and documentary; although, Arvatov warned that the exclusion of play, fiction or acting did not guarantee a documentary film's belonging to the left. He was generally critical of the terms and conclusions of the debate: narrative is an important factor of aesthetic expression and he was wary of forfeiting it; moreover, the view that the camera should simply reproduce real life he believes ends in a kind of aestheticism of well-composed interesting images. Arvatov argued against the view that even agit-films, his example is Eisenstein's *Battleship Potemkin* (1925), were intrinsically left; the politics of film are extrinsic to it, located in the ways a film is produced and consumed, or that the politics of *Battleship Potemkin* are intrinsic to it but the film became 'ordinary aesthetic cinema' when enjoyed by a European bourgeois audience.

Questions of cinema's politicization that occupied the Soviet avant-garde were of contemporary relevance to French film theory and criticism. *Cahiers du Cinéma* was committed to an ideological struggle for a materialist conception of cinema and the elaboration of a Marxist-Leninist theory of film: a 1971 editorial refers to the 'intervention of Marxism-Leninism in this magazine' (*Cahiers du Cinéma* 2001: 335). It identified the importance of the theoretical writings of Soviet film-makers, publishing texts by directors involved in the development of montage, such as Kuleshov, Vertov and Eisenstein, who thought through a materialist practice of cinema theoretically. In publishing and making accessible texts that seemed indicative of an emergent proletarian culture (although often quoted, they were then unavailable in France), *Cahiers du Cinéma* (2001: 113) saw them as '*still* part of our present' and a 'cutting edge': the magazine was not interested in merely reconstructing an era that cinema reflected. French film theory shared with the earlier Soviet avant-garde a concern with cinema as a signifying practice. In opposition to ideologies of artistic creation and expressiveness embodied by the *auteur, Cahiers du Cinéma* and the film journal *Cinéthique* developed theories of signifying practices and of ideology indebted to Althusserian Marxism. The magazines were self-consciously engaged in cultural politics and 'ideological struggle at the level of the superstructures'. The stakes of this political and ideological struggle were the reign of bourgeois ideology in the domain of cinema. *Cinéthique*, first published in January 1969, theorized a 'class cinema' and elaborated an analysis that recognized that films only existed in and through a 'class apparatus': the practice of film was ideological. So, avant-garde films are the products of ideology and also commodities; their critique as pleasurably consumable products manufactured according to dominant ideologies and for a cultivated bourgeois spectator. Films were assumed to possess a definite role in the class struggle, although how and under what conditions cinema could specifically serve the interests of revolution or the 'proletarian cause', and what form cinema should actually take in capitalist and in revolutionary societies, remained largely unresolved.

Brechtian Cinema

The possibility of a Brechtian cinema is explicitly assumed in Godard's cinema, especially the films made under the name of the Dziga Vertov Group. Political aesthetics for Brecht is a struggle in ideology on the grounds of the subject's interpellation through strategies of distanciation, the mode political art takes, which will pose another, different subjectivity. Ideological representations are represented or shown but they are distanced; the representation is displaced politically: Brechtian theatre transforms the spectator's attitude towards the performance so that familiar or self-evident events and characters become remarkable or astonishing, he/she is unable to empathize or lose him/herself completely in the theatrical spectacle. The result is a spectator who is no longer intoxicated or hypnotized by the performance and therefore an essential part of it; instead he/she becomes a critic of a situation, from which he/she can learn. There is still a sense of inclusion here, but it is active, the spectator does not just receive a representation but can engage critically in an activity of reading, which is realized through montage. Brecht tells a story of the censor's objections to his film *Kuhle Wampe*, screened in Berlin in June 1932, and made in collaboration (itself recognized as aesthetically and politically significant) with director Slatan Dudow. The 'acute censor' objected on the 'artistic grounds' that an audience is unable to identify or become emotionally involved with the unemployed worker who commits suicide. He recognized that the worker is depicted as a type rather than as an individual human being;

as such, Brecht and Dudlow has failed artistically. However, Brecht's point is not that spectators will take theatrical illusion as reality – he is critical of the illusion *of* reality, of a realism that denies the spectator knowledge of its production. Brechtian theatre self-consciously draws attention to the artifice of art and expresses the relation between the staged action and the conditions of its staging, breaking, therefore, with the illusion of watching unobserved a natural, unrehearsed event. Neither Brecht nor Godard's film abandons reference to become entirely self-referential, but reminders of the cinematic process, the visibility of (camera) equipment, the self-conscious foregrounding of how images are technologically produced, actors acknowledging they are playing a role and reflecting upon it, are all 'Godardian'.

Brecht emphasized that the simple reproduction of reality told us nothing about it and therefore necessitated 'literalizing' the theatre through the projection of the titles of scenes onto screens. The intention was to change the function of theatre from an evening's pleasurable entertainment, through its contact with 'intellectual activities' and written media. MacCabe criticized the 'Brechtian experiment' of Godard's *Tout va bien* (1972), which starred Yves Montand and Jane Fonda; the film played ironically with existing cinematic codes but its abandonment of writing or literalization risked its lapsing into a plenitude of the full and believable image that denies the place of the viewer in focusing its multiplicity. For Brecht (1964: 43), the 'punctuating of "representation" with "formulation"' transforms rather than continues to merely supply the apparatus; it would transform a spectator's passive attitude and fixed position, and determine a different kind of acting. The actor becomes detached from the events he/she portrays and *shows* characters rather than completely becoming them; the actor will quote his/her part, simulating the characters' gestures, actions and words, and showing an audience what s/he thinks of the character. This critique of reproduction through distanciation, literalization and montage suggests the form a Brechtian practice of cinema would take in its relation to reality against 'the mirror of vision' (the privilege of the cinema) and for the 'distance of analysis' of images and sounds (rather than speak of cinema or television, Godard defined them materially as images and sounds) (Heath 1975: 38). Godard described *Two or Three Things I Know About Her* (1967), starring Marina Vlady, as an analytical essay on modern living, 'the vast mutation which our civilization is undergoing at the present', which expressed his concerns with social research and documentary.

The role of segmentation in Godard's film actualizes it as 'epic', which does not possess a final meaning that positions the subject, but in a state of difference, demands articulation and assembly by the spectator. The 'critique of the continuum', Barthes comments, 'is a constant one in Brecht' (1989: 217). His critical art lacerates and fissures 'the crust of language', distancing 'representation without annulling it' (ibid.: 213). However, for MacCabe, although fissured and discontinuous as Barthes describes Brecht, *Two or Three Things* ultimately encourages a spectator's passivity. Despite demonstrating 'the fundamental heterogeneity of the filmic material', it searches nostalgically for the adequate articulation of sound and image that defines aesthetic ideology (MacCabe 1975: 54). The observation that separation, segmentation and discontinuity characterize critical art is expressed in Rancière's commentary on *La Chinoise*; Guillaume (Jean-Pierre Léaud) and Yvonne (Juliet Berto) – members of a Marxist-Leninist cell and student revolutionaries – offer a lesson on the Vietnam War, which they re-enact almost comically through children's plastic toys – fighters, machines guns, battleships and tanks – as props.

Figure 2.1. Godard, *La Chinoise* (1967). Screen capture from Jean-Luc Godard (DVD, May 2005, Optimum Home Releasing).

The 'continuum of image-meaning' (Rancière 2006: 147) is increasingly fragmented as the scene develops its analysis of just and unjust war, flashed close-ups of the students' faces looking and speaking straight to camera alternating quickly with shots of war fought with toy weapons. *La Chinoise* widens the gap between image and object, between signifier and signified, so that it becomes impossible to read through the filmic image as if it were transparent.

Rancière's Critique of Political Aesthetics

Montage is particularly representative of the critical tradition in art. The Soviet avant-garde valued the facticity, authenticity and expressiveness of montage over drawing and painting, which Benjamin called its 'revolutionary attitude'. For the Soviet avant-garde, different forms and techniques possessed different effects: photographs, montages and placards displaced autonomous easel painting. The aesthetic method of montage interrupts the action into which it is inserted, destroying the illusion of reality. For Eisenstein, montage is the essence or 'the nerve of film', but he opposed the view that montage involved assembling or the building up of successive shots. Eisenstein (2004: 26) argued that montage was the conflict between and the collision of two independent shots that when juxtaposed '*explode* into a concept'. The avant-garde recognized montage's capability to reveal hidden causal relations between apparently different worlds. Godard used techniques of montage to combine the disparate worlds of high culture and the commodity to produce alienating and therefore critical effects: in discussing a model of critical art, Rancière (2010: 142) refers to the scene from *Pierrot le fou* (Godard 1965), in which against lurid red and blue monochrome backgrounds dinner party guests communicate the merits of cars, deodorant and hairspray through the language of advertising; the resulting heterogeneity of sound and image 'is intended to reveal the forms of self-alienation and of estranged social relationships that are produced by the language of commodities'.

The clash on the same surface of heterogeneous or discontinuous elements in Dada and Surrealism is at the root of its aesthetic and political success. In the way it assembles photographic fragments of the real, montage allows the spectator to perceive the relations between apparently unrelated realities and therefore perceive the world differently. For Rancière (2009b:

27), photomontage has rendered palpable 'the violence of the class domination concealed beneath the appearances of quotidian ordinariness and democratic peace'. John Heartfield's photomontage *The Meaning of the Hitler Salute: Little man asks for big gifts. Motto: Millions Stand Behind Me!* (1932) reveals the relationship of fascism to capitalism. The photomontages made by the U.S. artist Martha Rosler reveal the reality of imperialist violence beneath the enjoyment of goods and images. Her series *House Beautiful: Bringing the War Home* (1967–72) combines images of the Vietnam War with images of comfortable and glamorous domestic interiors. The production of representations that alienate their subjects to make them unfamiliar is characteristic of Brecht's techniques of alienation. Political art – Godard's cinema, Brecht's theatre or the photomontages of Heartfield and Rosler – reveals relationships that should be obvious to the spectator but which he/she does not want or is unable to see. It presupposes a straightforward relationship between the spectator's understanding and his/her intervention. Rancière questions the political efficacy of this critical tradition in art: there is no necessary reason why the experience of art should induce intellectual and ultimately political awareness. It is uncertain that the typical juxtapositions of Godard's films, 'an advertising image, a printed slogan, newsreels, an interview with a philosopher, [Francis Jeanson in *La Chinoise* and Brice Parain in *Vivre sa vie* (Godard 1962)] and the *gestus* of this or that fictive character will be put back together by the spectator in the form of a message, let alone the right message' (Jameson 1991: 191).

The power of bourgeois communications is in their naturalness, their power to transform culture into nature; what are historical results, the consequences of class struggles, are presented as being a matter of course. This mythical language evolves from and depends upon the continued synthesis of signifier and signified, and in the cinema, of sound and image, which results in convincingly natural representations. The political efficacy of Godard's cinema rests on alienating mythical or ideological representation: it is arguable that an attempt to de-reify cultural representations can underpin practices of political film. Although in *Le Petit Soldat* (1963) Godard intended to realize a 'concreteness' and realism, a 'true picture' of the era that was absent from *A Bout de Souffle* (1959), its theme 'of a French secret agent who refuses to carry out a mission' was ultimately 'not real but news-reel' (Godard 1986: 164).[3] Godard speaks as a modernist, saying that artworks can possess some truth or epistemological value, that they can express some authentic vision of the world. However, in the artistic and cultural allusions and frequent literary and political quotations that structure, and that as digressions increasingly come to destabilize their narratives, Godard's films are 'resolutely postmodernist'. They can appear as 'sheer text, as a process of production of representations that have no truth content [as] sheer surface and superficiality' (Jameson 1981: 112). This conception accounts for the reflexivity of Godard's film in its destructive treatment of any 'binding or absolute status' of the photographic image. However, Godard is unable to stave off the ultimate and inevitable reification or the institutionalization of a system of figuration that different modernisms suffered at the hands of the culture industry. Godard's structural analysis in which sound is pitted against image, his relentless and corrosive dissolving, can itself develop its own inertia or become reified to become the characteristic or recognizable style of his films.

Rancière (2009b: 47) contrasts the critique of illusory, mendacious and seductive images and the consumer society developed by Brecht and in Barthes' *Mythologies* (1957) and Debord's *The Society of the Spectacle* (1967), which is how the politics of art is still usually understood, to another principle of emancipation: 'the dismantling of the old distribution of what could be seen, thought and done' and the experimentation with new forms of life. In sharp distinction to social critique and the strategies of radical art, Rancière assumes that 'the incapable are capable', rejecting the view that 'imbeciles' confuse images for realities and the necessity to educate them in the art of recognizing the reality beyond the image. Indeed, Brecht (1964: 187) described spectators as 'somewhat motionless figures in a peculiar condition... They scarcely communicate with each other; their relations are those of a lot of sleepers... these people seem relieved of activity and like men to whom something is being done'. Pleynet (1978: 157) remarked that a film spectator – 'a bloke sitting in the dark looking at an image' – could only 'master' its scenes 'through the fiction' of the film determined by the 'sovereign will' of the director. And for Baudry (1974–75: 44): 'Projection and reflection take place in a closed space and those who remain there, whether they know it or not, (but they do not), find themselves chained, captured, or captivated'. Rancière (2009b: 2) summarizes the strategies and positions elaborated in the polemics of *Cahiers du Cinema* and *Cinéthique* that suggest it is 'bad' to be a spectator: 'viewing is the opposite of knowing' and the spectator is ignorant of the how appearances are produced and of the reality they conceal; spectating is the opposite of acting; the spectator is merely a passive voyeur seduced by images; the spectator possesses an illusory mastery over the spectacle. The answer is a different practice of theatre or film, one without spectators, which would undermine the passive optical relationship. Those in attendance learn from, rather than being seduced by, the spectacle; they become active participants within it rather than merely passive voyeurs. The spectator must no longer be the calm witness to the spectacle: this is the basic attitude of Brecht's epic theatre and the Marxist theorization of political art and film. For Rancière, this is indicative of the Romantic idea that associates theatre and then film with aesthetic revolution that will change human experience. In the Brechtian paradigm, spectators will be taught not to be spectators and so become agents of social change. Rancière questions this understanding of the spectator and challenges the opposition between passively taking pleasure in images and actively learning from them. In place of this approach to emancipation, Rancière (2009b: 49) affirms 'scenes of dissensus', which suggests new configurations and possibilities of what 'can be perceived, thought and done'. Spectators are active and creative for Rancière, engaged in selecting, comparing, and interpreting images; spectating is nothing like a passive condition of Brechtian aesthetics.

The historical avant-gardes of the earlier twentieth century attacked art as an autonomous institution of bourgeois society and the production of autonomous and expensive objects for passive contemplation. They refused to accept the separation of art and life or the spheres of aesthetics and politics, and desired to reconnect them, to negate the institutional autonomy of art.[4] Rancière, however, explores the political character of aesthetic autonomy through an example of a worker's journal that was published during the 1848 revolution. For Rancière, social emancipation involves a specific aesthetic experience that is exemplified in the account of a worker enjoying a 'spacious view' of a garden or 'picturesque horizon' from the window of the room in which he worked. This aesthetic experience seems to disrupt the way his body is supposed to fit its usual function or purpose and social destination. The worker's 'distracted gaze' introduces 'a new configuration of the sensible' and is indicative of the possibility of a redistribution of unexpected 'capacities and incapacities' in society. The appropriation of a uniquely aesthetic experience separate from his labour represents his refusal to identify with his supposed and expected way of being or condition. For Rancière (2010: 139), aesthetic experience allows the individual a divorce from their prescribed function within the social relations of production. It is therefore political: politics 're-frames the given by inventing new ways of making sense of the sensible ... new bodily capacities'. As such, the worker enters into 'the aesthetic regime of art' or 'play'. Following Schiller, Rancière (2009a: 30) defines play as 'any activity that has no end other than itself, [any activity] that does not intend to gain any effective power over things or persons'. He describes an experience of the Greek statue of the Roman goddess Juno Ludovisi; she is radically indifferent and self-contained, without any care, responsibility or designs; she is aimless and idle. The spectator does nothing before the goddess, and statue and viewer become absorbed in a circle of 'inactive activity', cancelling the opposition of passivity and activity. The experience of the work of art is an entirely autonomous one of 'free play'; it evokes 'an autonomous form of life', which can become a different basis of politics and political aesthetics.

Notes

1. The group made the 'anti-films': *British Sounds, Pravda, Vent d'est, Struggle in Italy, Vladimir and Rosa, Tout va bien* and *Letter to Jane.*
2. See 'Better Fewer, But Better' (1923); 'On Co-Operation' (1923); 'Our Revolution' (1923).
3. The story of Brecht's *Kuhle Wampe* began not with 'a rough piece of reality' but with the media's report of that reality (see Eisenschitz 1974: 65).
4. Peter Bürger's influential *Theory of the Avant-Garde* (1974) discussed autonomy in terms of art's 'independence in the face of demands that it be socially useful', that is, its detachment from 'the praxis of life and the accompanying crystallization of a special sphere of experience (i.e. the aesthetic)'.

References

Arvatov, B. 1977. 'Film Platform (*New Lef* no. 3, 1928)', in J. Ellis (ed.), *Screen Reader 1: Cinema/Ideology/Politics*. Society for Education in Film and Television, pp. 311–14.
Barthes, R. 1972. 'The Tasks of Brechtian Criticism', in *Critical Essays*. Evanston, IL: Northwestern University Press, pp. 71–76.
———. 1989. 'Brecht and Discourse: A Contribution to the Study of Discursivity', in *The Rustle of Language*. Berkeley and Los Angeles: University of California Press, pp. 212–22.

Baudry, J.L. 1974–75. 'Ideological Effects of the Basic Cinematographic Apparatus', *Film Quarterly* 28(2): 39–47.
Bontemps J., et al. 1968–69. 'Struggle on Two Fronts: A Conversation with Jean-Luc Godard', *Film Quarterly* 22(2): 20–35.
Brecht, B. 1964. 'The Literarization of the Theatre', in J. Willett (ed.), *Brecht on Theatre: The Development of an Aesthetic*. London: Methuen.
Carroll, K.E. 1972. 'Film and Revolution: Interview with the Dziga-Vertov Group', in R.S. Brown (ed.), *Focus on Godard*. London: Prentice Hall.
Cahiers du Cinéma. 2001. 'Cinema, Ideology, Politics (for Poretta-Terme)', in N. Browne (ed.), *Cahiers du Cinéma: 1969–1972: The Politics of Representation*. London: Routledge, pp. 287–90.
———. 2001. 'Editorial: Politics and Ideological Class Struggle', in N. Browne (ed.), *Cahiers du Cinéma: 1969–1972: The Politics of Representation*. London: Routledge, pp. 334–42.
———. 2001. 'Editorial: Russia in the 1920s (I)', in N. Browne (ed.), *Cahiers du Cinéma: 1969–1972: The Politics of Representation*. London: Routledge, pp. 112–15.
Comolli, J.L. and J. Narboni. 1977. 'Cinema/Ideology/Criticism', in J. Ellis (ed.), *Screen Reader 1: Cinema/Ideology/Politics*. Society for Education in Film and Television, pp. 2–12.
Eisenschitz, B. 1974. 'Who Does the World Belong To? The Place of a Film', *Screen* 15(2): 65–73.
Eisenstein, S. 2004. 'The Dramaturgy of Film Form [The Dialectical Approach to Film Form]', in L. Braudy and M. Cohen (eds), *Film Theory and Criticism: Introductory Readings*. New York: Oxford University Press, pp. 13–40.
Fargier, J.P. 1977. 'Parenthesis or Indirect Route', in J. Ellis (ed.), *Screen Reader 1: Cinema/Ideology/Politics*. Society for Education in Film and Television, pp. 23–35.
Godard, J.L. 1986. '*Le Petit Soldat*', in T. Milne, (ed.). 1986. *Godard on Godard*. New York: Da Capo Press.
———. 1986. 'Towards a Political Cinema', in T. Milne, (ed.). 1986. *Godard on Godard*. New York: Da Capo Press.
Harvey, S. 1978. *May '68 and Film Culture*. London: British Film Institute.
———. 1982. 'Whose Brecht? Memories for the Eighties', *Screen* 23(1): 45–59.
Harvey, S., et al. 1985. 'The Other Cinema – A History: Part I, 1970–77', *Screen* 26(6).
Heath. S. 1975. 'From Brecht to Film: Theses, Problems', *Screen* 16(4): 34–45.
Jameson, F. 1981. '"In the Destructive Element Immerse": Hans-Jürgen Syberberg and Cultural Revolution', *October* 17: 99–118.
———. 1991. *Postmodernism, Or, the Cultural Logic of Late Capitalism*. London: Verso.
Leblanc, G. 1977. 'Direction', in J. Ellis (ed.), *Screen Reader 1: Cinema/Ideology/Politics*. Society for Education in Film and Television.
———. 2005. 'What Avant-Garde?' in D. Scheunemann (ed.) *Avant-Garde/Neo-Avant-Garde*. Amsterdam and New York: Rodopi, pp. 273–82.

MacCabe, C. 1974. 'Realism and the Cinema: Notes on some Brechtian Theses', *Screen* 15(2): 7–27.
———. 1975. 'Brecht Event IV: The Politics of Separation', *Screen* 16(4): 46–61.
Macherey, P. 1989. *A Theory of Literary Production*. London and New York: Routledge.
Marx, K. 2010. 'The Eighteenth Brumaire of Louis Bonaparte', in *Surveys from Exile: Political Writings Volume 2*. London: Verso, pp. 143–250.
Narboni, J. 2001. 'Towards Impertinence', in J. Hillier (ed.), *Cahiers du Cinema: Vol II The 1960s New Wave, New Cinema, Re-Evaluating Hollywood*. London: Routledge, pp. 300–03.
Orton, F. 1991. 'Action, Revolution, Painting', *Oxford Art Journal* 14(2): 3–17.
Pleynet, M. 1978. 'Economical-Ideological-Formal', in S. Harvey, *May '68 and Film Culture*. London: British Film Institute, pp. 149–64.
Rancière, J. 2006. 'The Red of *La Chinoise*: Godard's Politics', in *Film Fables*. Oxford: Berg.
———. 2009a. 'Aesthetics as Politics', in *Aesthetics and its Discontents*. Cambridge: Polity Press.
———. 2009b. 'The Emancipated Spectator', in *The Emancipated Spectator*. London: Verso.
———. 2010. 'The Paradoxes of Political Art', in *Dissensus: On Politics and Aesthetics*. London and New York: Continuum, pp. 134–52.
Stark, T. 2012. '"Cinema in the Hand of the People": Chris Marker, the Medvedkin Group, and the Potential of Militant Film', *October* 139.
Tretyakov, S. 2006. 'Our Cinema', *October* 118: 27–44.
'We are Searching (Editorial, *New Lef*, no. 11/12, 1927)'. 1977. In J. Ellis (ed.), *Screen Reader 1: Cinema/Ideology/Politics*. Society for Education in Film and Television, pp. 298–99.
Wollen, P. 1972. 'Godard and Counter Cinema: *Vent d'Est*', *Afterimage* 4: 6–17.
———. 1976. 'The Two Avant-Gardes', *Edinburgh '76 Magazine*: 77–86.

Filmography

Battle of Algiers (*La battaglia di Algeri*). 1966. Gillo Pontecorvo.
Battleship Potemkin (*Bronenosets Potemkin*). 1925. Sergei Eisenstein.
Belle de Jour. 1967. Luis Buñuel.
A Bout de Souffle. 1959. Jean-Luc Godard.
British Sounds. 1969. Jean-Luc Godard.
La Chinoise. 1967. Jean-Luc Godard.
The Confession (*L'aveu*). 1970. Costa-Gavras.
Kuhle Wampe (*Kuhle Wampe oder: Wem gehört die Welt?*). 1932. Slatan Dudow.

The Meaning of the Hitler Salute: Little man asks for big gifts. Motto: Millions Stand Behind Me! 1932. John Heartfield.
Persona. 1966. Ingmar Bergman.
Le Petit Soldat. 1963. Jean-Luc Godard
Pierrot le fou. 1965. Jean-Luc Godard.
Strike (Stachka). 1924. Sergei Eisenstein.
Tout va bien. 1972. Jean-Luc Godard.
Two or Three Things I Know About Her (2 ou 3 choses que je sais d'elle). 1967. Jean-Luc Godard.
Vivre sa vie. 1962. Jean-Luc Godard
Z. 1969. Costa-Gavras.

CHAPTER 3
Marker, Activism and Melancholy
Reflections on the Radical '60s
in the Later Films of Chris Marker

Jon Kear

Though best known for the dystopian time travel sci-fi film *La Jetée* (Marker 1962), his only purely fictional film, Chris Marker was first and foremost a cine-essayist. In a career that stretched through one of the most turbulent political periods in history, Marker's films offered a visual archive of and critical commentary on the changing political landscape from the Second World War to the present day. From the beginning, the volatile politics of this period shaped both his life and his filmmaking. Marker fought in the French resistance and with U.S. armed forces in the Second World War, after which he became associated with the current of left wing intellectuals on the Parisian left bank, initially as a writer and critic working on the journals *Travail et Culture, Cahiers du Cinéma* and the neo-catholic, Marxist journal *Esprit*. These literary aspirations were to continue to guide his work, even though in the late 1950s filmmaking eventually took precedence.

Marker's characteristic style gradually surfaced in films such as *Dimanche à Pékin* (1956) and *Letters from Siberia* (1957), both of which consciously rejected the conventions of objective documentary in favour of a more hybrid, literary and subjective cinema. In these films his experimental, self-reflexive approach to image making, in which he used original and found materials in a dazzling dialectical montage style, was matched with a commentary style that combined wit and guileful word play with farsighted critical analysis of the image and the role it plays within our culture. *Letters from Siberia* also saw the emergence of the politically engaged filmmaking that was to dominate his work in the next decade. Described by Bazin as 'a documentary film essay at once historical and political but written from the point of view of a poet' (Bazin 1983: 179), *Letters from Siberia* charts Marker's impressions of the technological and economic modernization of Siberia in the aftermath of

Stalin's death. Though funded by the periodical *France-USSR* and the Foreign Ministry of the Soviet Union, it implicitly critiqued the documentary style of Soviet socialist realism in which all images of the state had to be, in Marker's own words, 'above suspicion' and 'positive until infinity' (Marker 1961: 43). While the film makes no mention of the Gulags to which Stalin sent countless political dissidents to their death, it maintains a wry and ironical view of the process of renewal and renovation, continually undermining conventional wisdom about the region and undercutting the official dictats of progress through modernization.

As this indicates, while Marker aligned himself with Marxism, it was always in a dissenting form. Marker never joined the French Communist Party (PCF) and was critical of the legacy of Stalinism and the contemporary Soviet model of communism. Like many left wing intellectuals of his generation he was increasingly drawn to the struggles in Latin America, Asia and Africa as holding the possibility of a new internationalist left coalition. In the films of the next decade, such as *¡Cuba Sí!* (Marker 1961), a joyously partisan celebration of the Cuban revolution, and *Le Joli Mai* (Marker 1962), a groundbreaking piece of cinéma vérité chronicling social attitudes of Parisians in the shadow of the Algerian war, Marker established a reputation as one of the most radical filmmakers of his generation, one whose works continually encountered problems of state censorship. The trajectory of his work in the mid to late 1960s paralleled in certain respects that of Jean-Luc Godard in searching for new forms of political cinema that engaged the social questions of the day, though, as will become clear, the public altercations and bitter rivalry between them pointed to significant differences in their relationship to their audience and in particular to the possibility of a proletariat cinema. The development of his understanding of the potential scope of militant cinema radically expanded over the period. Initially, Marker's cine-essays had focused on intervening into public debates, by providing alternative leftist perspectives about international and ideological conflicts of the day from those presented by official state or mainstream media. Though this internationalism continued to be an integral part of his filmmaking during the mid 1960s, in a period of rising social and political unrest in France, he began to focus his attention on the social and political forces shaping the country, involving himself in leftist workers collectives.

Toward a New Activism in Cinema:
SLON, ISKRA and The Groupe Medvedkin 1967-74

Though rejecting classical Socialist realism, the model for all this was in many respects the work of the great early Soviet Marxist filmmakers, in particular Aleksandr Medvedkin and Dziga Vertov – the opening sequence of Marker's *Sans Soleil* (1983) is a homage to the beginning of Vertov's *Man with a Movie Camera* (1929). Vertov's theory of *kinopravda,* and more generally Soviet discourses about factography, undoubtedly influenced Marker's conception of the role that cinema could play in reaching beyond the most immediate audience for his films, the French left intelligentsia, to reach a broader, more proletariat audience and to act upon that public by raising its political and ideological consciousness. Yet it was arguably Medvedkin whose work was to leave the most indelible impression on his filmmaking, suggesting ways in which new agitational forms of cinema drawing on Soviet models could be renewed in a contemporary context.

One of the characteristics that made Marker's films so unorthodox was the way that, in addressing political issues of his time, his works continually made references to the films and directors he most admired, most notably to Medvedkin, a pervasive influence on Marker from the time he saw *Happiness* (1935), in 1961 at a film festival in Brussels (Alter 2006: 139–44). Marker's arbitrary references to animals, particularly owls and cats, a signature feature of his movies, refer back to Medvedkin. Marker later met and befriended Medvedkin in 1967 while working on *À bientôt j'espère* (1967–68). Long conversations and extensive correspondence between them followed, leaving a lasting impact on Marker's work. Marker was eventually to make two films dealing with Medvedkin's career, *Le Train en marche* (1971) and the more ambivalent *Le Tombeau d'Alexandre* (1993), which reveals a secret history of Medvedkin's complicity with Stalinist propaganda.

Arguably Medvedkin's most important influence on Marker was in further encouraging his involvement with militant cinema in the mid 1960s. Marker later wrote that his encounter with Medvedkin's work was to provide him with an alternative to the 'corporatism and professionalism' that prevented 'cinema from falling into the hands of the people' and subsequently named his collaborative Groupe Medvedkine de Besançon in tribute to his friend (Marker 1971: 4). The group initiative itself represented an attempt to rethink in a contemporary setting the interventionist aesthetic and ideals of the Soviet model of the agitprop trains that Medvedkin began his career working on and the kinopoezd, or cine-train, pioneered by him in 1932 (Widdis 2005: 2; Leyda 1983: 286–87; Stark 2012: 28–133). Medvedkin's work on the cine-trains encouraged Marker to re-envisage radically the scope of his activities as a filmmaker by directly going into workers' factories and establishing a context in which films could be produced that reflected the experiences and points of view of the workers rather than simply to produce topical political cine-essays about them (Stark 2012: 127–33). This would lead him to become directly involved in workers' cultural associations and develop collaborative programmes that would facilitate workers to become active producers of their own culture and through such interventions deepen their consciousness of the nature of class conflict. As we will see, this entailed a significant rethinking of the terms of Marker's earlier conception of the role of film as a mechanism for consciousness raising. These new collaborations would involve him in acting not so much as a filmmaker but as a facilitator and advisor whose expertise could enable workers to acquire the skills of filmmakers and make films that represented and offered self-conscious reflection on themselves.

Although Marker had periodically collaborated with other filmmakers, in the late 1960s he became increasingly involved in collaborative and collective film initiatives that were aligned to the protest movement and the events of May '68. In 1967 he organized *Loin de Vietnam,* a landmark in political cinema and collective filmmaking (directors included Joris Iven, William Klein, Jean-Luc Godard, Claude Lelouch, Alain Resnais, Agnès Varda and Marker himself), explored various aspects of the Vietnam War, ranging from media coverage and public indifference to the war, to the longer history of western imperialism in Vietnam, not least France's own involvement, and the wider global implications of the war.

While editing the film Marker formed the left wing film directors' collective SLON (Société pour le Lancement des Oeuvres Nouvelles), later renamed ISKRA (Images son Kinescope, Réalisations Audiovisuelles), named after Lenin's political newspaper, in 1974 (Stark 2012: 117–50; see also Lupton 2005: 109–48; Muel 2000: 15–35). Its members included among others, Valérie Mayoux, Jean-Claude Lerner, Alain Adair and John Tooker. SLON's objectives were to produce films and train industrial workers to establish filmmaking collectives of their own. As Marker himself later described it as an attempt 'to give the power of speech to people who don't have it, and, when it's possible, to help them find their own means of expression' (Marker 2003: 39).

The first SLON production, À bientôt j'espère (1967–68), depicts the strike action at the Rhodiacéta textile factory in Besançon in March 1967 that was to have important repercussions for the évènements of '68. What encouraged Marker's interest in the Rhodiacéta strike was that workers were not simply reacting against the working conditions and pay at the factory; their demands exceeded their immediate grievances with their employers to embrace the question of access to culture as a political demand, a demand that was itself to become a radical gesture in the context of growing social and political tensions in France. The centrality of the claim to culture signalled in speeches, interviews, posters, publications and placards, recognized the role of culture in socially maintaining hierarchical class divisions. In calling into question the access to culture, the workers were extending their struggle outward beyond the level of basic economic demands to a broader political struggle, and as such the dispute became a potent symbol of class conflict. These aims were facilitated by the CCPPO (Centre Culturel Populaire de Palente les Orchamps), founded on 9 September 1959, and whose first president was Pol Cébé, one of the workers at Rhodiacéta. In collaboration with René and Micheline Berchoud, Cébé established an ambitious cultural programme of education for workers that included screenings of films by Godard and Ivens among others, lectures on Picasso and performances of Brecht plays. Brecht's theories were particularly important in orienting the enterprise, encouraging the presentation of challenging work that dealt with concrete situations. Cébé also stocked the library, which had fallen into disrepair, with poetry, art monographs and classic Marxist texts. Yet Marker's involvement with the Besançon factory quickly led to a shift in the initiative from initially acting as a forum of cultural dissemination and education to the active formation of a workers' film production group, the Groupe Medvedkine de Besançon, designed to turn workers from cinematic spectators to active producers of films that explored their world from their own class position.

It was under this cinéma ouvrier collective that Marker predominantly continued to work for the next seven years, before returning to personal filmmaking. Many of the later critical accounts of this collective have assumed that Marker was the director or co-director of nearly all the films, though Marker made no such claims on them and the ethos of these group initiatives explicitly rejected the idea of the auteurist tradition in favour of collective co-operation. While some films do bear the imprint of Marker's commentary and editing, others are clearly more independent, though establishing to what extent and in what ways in making these films the filmmakers were under the influence of Marker's direction is not always clear from the scant retrospective testimony that has survived. Although Marker was involved in an advisory capacity for many of these films, the aim was to create the conditions that would allow workers to take control of the production process, thereby breaking down customary class divisions between those who, as Jacques Rancière has put it, are assigned 'the privilege of thought' and those assigned to 'the world of industrial labour' (Rancière 2004: 93). Workers received technical training in using cameras and other aspects of film production. The results would then be screened in the factories and workers' clubs and be followed by group discussion.

SLON was to make a remarkably varied group of films dealing with both national and international social, political and economic factors, including *Le Train en marche,* which was shown in conjunction with the re-release of Medvedkin's *Happiness* and *Classe de Lutte* (Marker 1968), the first of the workers' collective films by the Groupe Medvedkine de Besançon. Many of the films dealt with the specific conditions of class struggle, the dehumanizing conditions of industrialized labour and the manufactured consensus of media reporting. Some followed the lives of actual workers, allowing them to reflect on the relationship between labour, leisure and culture in their own milieu.

Despite its successes, the model SLON offered of a culturally proactive and self-defining proletariat met with scepticism and resistance from those on the left who saw the proletariat as merely the raw material of social change. Godard, whose Vertov group was by contrast conceived as a critical vanguard, criticized Marker's 'romanticism' in believing in the capacity of the working classes' to fully rationalize their own material position, or to find their own 'authentic' language of expression, arguing that such filmmaking would inevitably produce 'false consciousness' and even reification of the class struggle.

Similarly, relations between SLON and union representatives associated with the PCF and the Confédération Générale du Travail (CGT) were fraught. Both were obstructive, viewing Marker's initiative with deep suspicion; local PCF delegates demanded the group to cease its activities. Regarding their own hierarchical position at the vanguard of radical politics as undermined by contemporary events, both the PCF and the CGT sought to reassert their

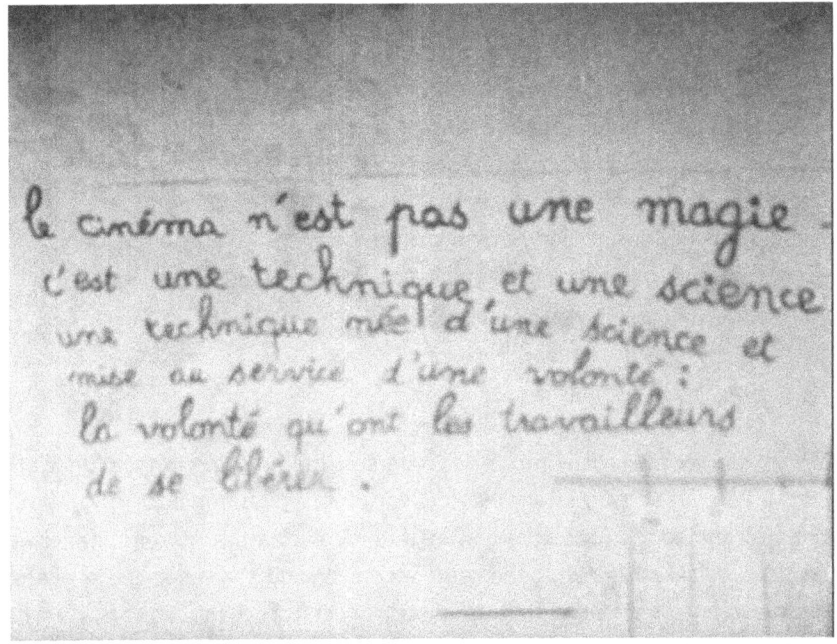

Figure 3.1. Cinema is not magic, it is a technique, a science born in the service of will: the will of workers to free themselves. Screen capture from Groupe Medvedkine de Besançon, *Classe de Lutte*, Société pour le Lancement des Oeuvres Nouvelles (1968).

authority, undermining any such unofficial rapprochement between the workers, intellectuals and the student protest movement, which they dismissed as romantic and unserious (Debord: 1981). After Mario Marret was left to work on parallel film projects associated with the Communist Party, Marker was vocally critical of the films with their fetishization of labour, doctrinalism and worker's ventriloquism of the party's *langue du bois,* which contrasted sharply with the freer aesthetic of liberty of expression of the Groupe Medvedkine films (Marker 2006; see also Stark 2012: 149).

However, eventually virulent institutional, bureaucratic and factional tensions led to the dissolution of the Groupe Medvedkine in 1971 (Stark 2012: 148–49). While Marker was to continue to develop initiatives out of the newly formed ISKRA, in 1973 notably collaborating with Valérie Mayoux, Jacqueline Meppiel and the Belgian sociologist Armand Mattelart on *The Spiral* (1975), which dealt with the rise and fall of the Allende government in Chile, a film that signals Marker's increasing tendency after 1968 to look beyond Europe for struggles that would offer renewed hope for rekindling the ashes of Europe's failed revolution. During the early 1970s Marker would return to working on the individual cine-essays that would define his later work. Though sharing many of the themes and even much of the film stock of his collaborative work of the 1960s, these would be very different in tone and character. The films Marker began working on in the 1970s, as the Groupe Medvedkine floundered under its internal divisions, provide a metacommentary on the frustrated ideals and aspirations that had spurred his involvement with the Besançon initiative.

1968 and its After Images

When Marker eventually returned to personal filmmaking in 1974, his work showed a marked shift of emphasis (Kear 1999: 45; Lupton 2005: 109). If his films during the previous decade were intended as partisan commentaries on the ideological struggles of the post-Second World War period, these later films examined the failure of the revolutionary culture of this era to achieve its ideological aims and the repercussions of this for the present political climate. Films such as *Sans Soleil* (Without Sun) (Marker 1983) and *Le Fond de l'air est rouge* (Grin Without a Cat) (Marker 1977) combine political reflections with increasingly experimental and idiosyncratic forms of filmmaking that make full use of cinema's capacity for interweaving imagery of the past and present together. Despite their stylistic differences, these two films can be seen as companion pieces, the latter extending the former's analysis to deal more in depth with the struggles against imperialism in Asia and Africa.

In these films, original and archival footage from the political struggles of the 1960s, including images of political conflicts and struggles for independence and liberty from colonialism in Africa, Asia and Latin America, but also the revolutionary struggles against hegemonic capitalism in Europe and the United States, is dialectically intercut with images from the present to highlight, among other ends, the continuities and discontinuities between the political landscape then and now, probing how the burden of the political fallout of the 1960s continues to leave its imprint on the present. This history collectively represented in Marker's films offers a melancholic but nevertheless critical account of the political and ideological expansion of capital through imperialism and globalization. It is a history that also amounts to a personal coming to terms for Marker, as he intermittently reflects on his involvement as a filmmaker and activist in the political struggles of the 1960s and their aftermath. In *Sans Soleil,* for instance, the unnamed traveller, whose letters make up the commentary, reflects on the social situation of contemporary Japan in light of the experience of modernization and U.S. occupation in the aftermath of Second World War. These reflections are interwoven with the memories of Marker's many visits to the region, but also interspersed with reflections on the revolutionary struggles in Europe and the United States, and the receding fortunes of the radical left in the present. Past and present are continually interspersed as Marker comments aphoristically and undogmatically on the causes that led to the crushing of the ideals that spurred a generation of political protest, giving weight not only to the way this movement was met with intransigent force but also to the contradictions, ideological quarrels and rampant factionalism within these revolutionary movements.

Sans Soleil derives its title from Mussorgsky's song cycle *Sunless,* the film establishing a common range of imagery with Mussorgsky's lament for lost love, sharing its melancholic, even bitter and regretful, musings on the past and the present, which, as in the Mussorgsky piece, are also addressed to an unnamed female correspondent. But the object of lost love here is not a person but a period, the decade of the 1960s, with its aspirations for liberty and desire to overthrow the existing social order and, to borrow one of its romantic slogans, 'to bring the imagination to power'.

In his essay *Mourning and Melancholia,* Freud writes that while mourning is the conscious acknowledgment of the loss of a love object and the gradual withdrawal from this object, melancholy results from an individual's inability to break the narcissistic identification that formed the basis of the original attachment to the lost person or an abstraction or ideal that has taken the place of one (Freud 1957: 243). While, as Isaac Balbus remarks, 'Freud's confinement of ambivalence towards, guilt over, and identification with, the "lost object" to the category of the pathological' means it cannot serve the foundation for the theory of political mourning, it nevertheless authorizes a way of understanding how an abstract object can become the subject of prolonged cultural mourning and how that process can in turn create an atrophying of the political imagination (Balbus 2000: 41–42; see also Klein 1984). The lost object in question is the lost ideal of the left depicted in Marker's later films, crushed under the grief of intersubjective losses almost too painful for memory; the trauma of violence that stains the earth with the red blood that *Le Fond de l'air est rouge*'s title refers to, and to which the cold, bleak world of *Sans Soleil* alludes. In the latter, images of violence appear so suddenly and unexpectedly as to intrude upon the viewer's consciousness without preparation, as if to simulate the unpreparedness Freud associated with experience of trauma, or as though these memory images were recalled to the memory of *Sans Soleil*'s protagonist by some compulsion to return to the original traumatic image (Freud 1957: 3, 189–221 and 20, 77–172; Kear 1999: 20–46).

Sans Soleil's melancholic reflections on the lost ideals of the 1960s are ambivalent ones. Marker expresses exasperation with the naivety of the ideals and the ideological fault lines in its thinking; its utopian uniting in a common cause of the dispossessed and those revolting against their own privilege, and how easily many in the movement adjusted to a new era of opportunism and pragmatism. As he sardonically comments many of 'the militants who studied capitalism so thoroughly in order to fight it, now provide it with its best executives' (Marker 1982). Yet, there is genuine admiration for the outrage and collective ideals that impelled a generation to revolt and a nostalgia for the sentiments encapsulated in Che Guevara's statement: 'I tremble with indignation every time an injustice is committed in the world'. As Marker observes, the defeat of the spirit of '68 nevertheless brought with it a new understanding on which to rebuild its fractured culture: if the ideals that had driven the protesters onto the streets had concretely failed, nevertheless 'all they had achieved in their understanding of the world could have been won only through the struggle' (Marker 1982).

Sans Soleil's melancholic reflections on the 1960s build upon and reprise many of the themes taken up in greater detail by the film that preceded it, *Le Fond de l'air est rouge,* an epic two-part four-hour film that charts in detail the global revolutionary struggles of the left in the late 1960s and 1970s (Marker later edited the film down for a three-hour version that included updated references in the commentary to later events). Filmed almost a decade after the events of May '68, a central motif of the film, it came at a point of heated debate in France about the meaning and legacy of those days of revolt.

In comparison with Marker's more elaborate filmic essays, the film is largely devoid of the aphoristic style and wit that became the signature Marker style and, except at the beginning, the dazzling editing of some of his later films. In contrast to the epistolary mode of much of his filmmaking, Marker lets the images and the words of others (many of which are uttered by left wing intellectuals involved in the struggles) speak, as far as possible, for themselves. *Le Fond de l'air est rouge* is arguably the Marker film most open therefore to the viewer's interpretation. The film's dialectical style avoids any rapprochement between speakers in favour of pairing alternate political perspectives in order to create a third voice for the spectator:

> *Each step of this imaginary dialogue aims to create a third voice out of the meeting of the first two, which is distinct from them. I don't claim to have succeeded in making a dialectical film. But for once I've tried (having abused the voice-over narration a fair bit in my time), to give the spectator, by means of the montage, their own commentary, that's to say their own power. (Marker 1978: 7)*

Yet, this is not to say the film has no narrative, or that Marker's presence is entirely absent. The intermittent voiceovers set a tone of sombre reflection that leaves the viewer in no doubt about the significance of what they are witnessing.

This is the Marker film above all that comes closest to the realization of that strand of his filmmaking that oriented itself to the archive. The film is composed of a diverse array of images drawn from newsreels, film libraries, militant films and l'Institut Nationale de l'Audiovisuelle (the French national broadcasting archive) and exemplifies Marker's way of addressing his own epoch through the cultural amnesia that occurs as 'one event is swept away by another, living ideals are replaced by cold facts', and the past ultimately 'descends into the collective oblivion' (Marker 1978: 5). Marker's late films seek to preserve the fragility of history from this process of forgetting. In *Level Five* (1997), for instance, Marker recalls the events of the U.S. invasion of Okinawa during the Second World War, an event largely forgotten in the history of the war, but one whose bloody resistance encouraged the U.S. bombing of Hiroshima. Likewise, in *Sans Soleil*, recalling the dispiriting aftermath of the war of independence in Guinea-Bissau, Marker laments: 'Who remembers all this? History throws its empty bottles out the window' (Marker 1982).

While the epochal subject of the *Le Fond de l'air est rouge* cannot be said to be consigned to oblivion in any literal sense, it has, as Kristin Ross in her study of the students/workers revolt in France remarks, been overwritten by the subsequent representations that make up its many afterlives (Ross 2002). These afterlives are marked not only by its many contradictions, but inflected by the projection back onto the period of contemporary fears, dilemmas and fantasies. Paradoxically, in the past forty years, the events of May '68 have been:

> *buried, raked through the coals, trivialized, or represented as a monstrosity... an enormous amount of narrative labor – and not a shroud of silence – has facilitated the active forgetting of the events in France. Memoirs, self-celebrations, recantations, television commemorations, abstract philosophical treatises, sociological analyses – May has not suffered from too little attention ... Discourse has been produced, but its primary effect has been to liquidate – to use an old '68 word – erase, or render obscure the history of May. (Ross 2002: 3)*

May '68 has commonly come to signify a period of rupture that swept away a patriarchal and disciplinary society with a strong sense of national identity, replacing it with the ephemeral, hybrid identities, multiculturalism and globalization of the present. But contemporary popular narratives and debates about '68 are increasingly caught up in a web of contradictions, suspended between the desire to give the moment a definite form and the ever-shifting kaleidoscope of impressions that desire gives rise to; its interpretation caught between a process of normalization and an insistence on them as unique, aberrant and unclassifiable, a social revolt whose significance could not be properly ascertained in the present and whose force could not be adequately related (Webber 2000).

May '68 now serves as an increasingly chimerical reference point in contemporary discourses about the limits of democracy, the crisis of the liberal state and other teleologies of the present. The events, alternately regarded as an inexplicable social irruption or dismissed as a pseudorevolution, as a last ditch resistance to an oppressive disciplinary social order or a necessary stage in the development of late capitalism, as a critical reaction against modernism, or as the last vestiges of modernism as it gives way to postmodernity (Mathy 2011: 26; Ferry and Renaut 1990: 64). Its failures, in particular, are made over into a natural and inevitable course of events, an object lesson of the impossibility of change and the irresistible force of capitalism as a natural state of things (Fukuyama 1996). May's calls for equality and liberty are reduced to the spurious equality of access to consumerism, freedom of choice and the plethora of other empty slogans of late capitalist libertarianism. The 1960s are now increasingly packaged as retro-chic fashion, revolt disarmed and reconfigured as simulationist commodity consumption.

The specific causes, discourses and the underlying historical conditions that spurred the events of May '68, the uneasy alliance between the student protest movement and the workers' strikes and the crisis of Gaullism, the particular socioeconomic and political conditions that encouraged radical revolt increasingly recede from view as the events themselves are reduced to a form of reified historical knowledge, albeit one marked by a certain elusiveness.

As Jean-Phillipe Mathy remarks, in an age of instant information and fading historical consciousness, May '68 has become a marker against which the present measures itself: 'The events of May have become... a site of recollection that the press, television and intellectuals go and visit at the end of each decade to revive the memories of a temporal rupture suffused with nostalgia' (Mathy 2011: 25). This process is also symptomatic, not only of the forms of knowledge production that have overtaken the events they represent, but also the disappearance of a kind of radical praxis and critical questioning that characterized the period:

> The paradox of May's memory can be simply stated. How did a mass movement that sought above all ... to contest the domain of the expert, to disrupt the system of naturalized spheres of competence (especially the sphere of specialized politics), become translated in the years that followed into little more than a 'knowledge' of '68, on the basis of which a whole generation of self-proclaimed experts and authorities could then assert their expertise? The movement swept away categorical territories and social definitions, and achieved unforeseen alliances and synchronicities between social sectors and between very diverse people working together to conduct their affairs collectively. How did such a movement get relocated into defined 'sociological' residences: 'student milieu' or 'the generation'? (Ross 2002: 6–7)

Of course *Le Fond de l'air est rouge* extends far beyond the riots on the Paris streets of May '68, but as such the point is only amplified. If Ross' account risks its own form of idealistic nostalgia, constructing an image of solidarity that erases the high degree of conflict that existed within the radical left, it points nevertheless to the way historical oblivion is not simply achieved by way of neglect. Memory and forgetting, as Marker remarks in *Sans Soleil,* are not oppositions but two sides of the same coin (Marker 1982).

The constituent materials of *Le Fond de l'air est rouge* exemplify the mode of historical salvaging typical of much of Marker's later filmmaking; the montage is in large measure made up of recycling of discarded visual history. While sorting through cans of rushes and outtakes of SLON and ISKRA productions in the ISKRA office, Valérie Mayoux said to Marker, 'There's a film to be made here, a collage film that would use these fragments to tell a story' (Mayoux 1997: 94). What intrigued Marker was what this footage would reveal about the editorial practices of militant filmmaking (Marker 1978: 4). In the introduction to the film's published script Marker remarks on how these outtakes revealed a more complicated story than the ideologically correct version the original films told, and offered the possibility of another narrative, one that might capture better the internal struggles of leftist activism of the period and point thereby to the role these played in the left's defeat. Such a film would offer a more accurate and more sobering picture of the political events of the time. One of the predominant themes of the resulting film is the way the bitter conflicts between the variants of orthodox, militant and reformist Marxism, Trotskyism and Maoism patently undermined and deflected inward the face of revolt.

While the film was not composed only from these discarded fragments, they serve to augment, recontextualize and reframe the more familiar footage Marker includes, as such allowing for the reinterpretation of the original bulletins. One such example is where Marker uses footage he had previously used for a rare fictional short film *La Sixième Face du Pentagone* (1968), which shows protesters breaking through police lines and running towards the front entrance of the Pentagon, a symbolic victory or so it appeared at the time when Marker filmed it. But Marker's retrospective commentary poses questions about how we should interpret it in the light of what we later learned about the tactics of dealing with the protest movement:

> I filmed it, and I showed it as a victory for the Movement … but when I looked at these scenes again, and put them alongside the stories the police

told us about how it was they who lit the fires in the police stations in May '68, I began to wonder if some of the victories of the '60s weren't cut from the same cloth. (Marker 1982)

The problems of interpreting images, of understanding what they conceal within them has long been a preoccupation of Marker, but in these later works hermeneutical uncertainty resurfaces with renewed force and poignancy. In *Sans Soleil*, re-viewing footage from Cassaca of the weeping General Nino being decorated for his part in the African nationalist struggle against Portuguese colonialism, Marker remarks:

We will learn that behind this ceremony of promotions, which in the eyes of visitors, perpetuated the brotherhood of the struggle, there lay a pit of post-victory bitterness, and that Nino's tears did not express an ex-warrior's emotions, but the wounded pride of a hero who felt he had not been raised high enough above the others. And beneath each of these faces, a memory, and in place of what we were told had been forged into a collective memory, a thousand memories of men who parade their personal laceration in the great wound of History. (Marker 1982)

In each of these films Marker, who continued to practice as a photographer and cameraman alongside his filmmaking, treats the image as an enigmatic message, which has the power to create illusions and myths (Kear 2009: 180–92). Detached from the original moment in time in which they occur, these surviving images from history, far from simply reconstituting the past, become the raw material through which the image of the past is continually reimagined and becomes the bearer of legend. In *Sans Soleil* we see Marker the collector and consummate deconstructor of the lives of images, but while this is a feature of his earliest works, here it acquires a renewed poignancy. Whereas earlier films saw Marker engaged with raising awareness of contemporary struggles, here he adopts the role of a historian attempting to preserve for the future the receding memory of the radicalism of the 1960s. Moving away from the more direct, interventionalism of his earlier films, *Sans Soleil* might be seen as expressing an archival desire for preserving for future reference the memory of contents of the past from a present that has been either oblivious or even hostile to them.

Though in many ways its companion piece, *Le Fond de l'air est rouge*, might be seen as less of a mood piece. It is a film that more analytically seeks to demythologize the afterlives and the spectres of its surviving images of the 1960s, though one that is all too aware of the problems of attempting to do so, cognizant that the very form of such an epic and over-reaching film poses it own problems of myth making. Additionally, to make such a film on such a panoramic historical scale is inevitably to periodize and make priorities in a way that at some level must risk repeating the distorted abstraction and totalizing logic that the film seeks to critique. The film's way of resisting this is largely waged on the level of form. *Le Fond de l'air est rouge,* as Paul Arthur has remarked: 'in its rhythms and editing structures ... tries to embody the very shape and textures of historical transformation, rendering the abstraction of change as an amalgam of rapid, plurivocal, uneven, and, at times, contradictory forces aligned in provisional symmetries encompassing past, present and future perspectives' (Arthur 2002: 34). Nevertheless, in terms of its content, the film offers a selective history that has notable omissions. *Le Fond de l'air est rouge* underplays the involvement of women in the events of May '68, barely touches on the conflict in Northern Ireland and says nothing about the struggles in Palestine, Cambodia and Angola (Fargier et al. 1978: 46–51; Richard 1977: 9–15; Lupton 2005: 145). Nor does the film consider the question of the living legacy of those times. The film finds no place for an analysis of what was hard won by the civil rights movements of the period and the political and cultural changes and debates that emerged out of the protest movement. It thus falls into a mode of mourning and melancholy that finds no place to question, whether, as Isaac Balbus remarks, the remarkable longevity of this death of the sixties unwittingly testifies to the survival of its subject' (Balbus 2000: 39).

As Derrida argues in *Specters of Marx*, it is not only the political left that has been afflicted by this melancholy. Despite their triumphalist rhetoric, discourses of the political right reveal an anxiety and nostalgic preoccupation with the demise of communism that continues to inflect its (mis)perception of world politics and ways of thinking about ideological and political conflict. The spectre of Marx and of May '68 continue to act as revenants (Derrida 1993: 10). Sarkozy's 2007 presidential campaign platform to destroy the legacy of the 1960s is only one of many such examples of the haunting of this spectre. But the repeated pronouncements of the death of Marxism and the radical left, the assertive declarations of the 'end of history', conceal within them a profound disenchantment, a paradoxical bereavement for the opponent that gave its struggle meaning and simultaneous anxiety that the spirit of Marx may return. Neoliberal triumphalism, as Derrida argues, contains the consciousness of the persistence of resistances to it and consequently the recognition that the grand narrative of neoliberalism has itself failed (Furet 2000: 20). The pervasive sense of living in what Walter Benjamin called the 'empty time of history' inhabits and inhibits the contemporary political imagination in almost its entirety.

Writing in the interwar years, in a similarly elegiac moment for the left, Benjamin had attacked the way left wing intellectuals' attachment to the abstract ideological dogma of the past and failure to respond to the changing realities of its time, which had effectively severed the relationship between political ideals and corresponding action and resulted in a dangerously 'negativistic quietude' (Benjamin 1999: 2, 425; Brown 1999: 19–27). For Benjamin, leftist melancholy expressed a mournful politics, excessively conservative, tending to the regressive and paralysed from taking action and moving on. The history of the period Marker relays is one similarly permeated by pessimism and an overwhelming sense of loss. As such these films might be regarded as repeating the 'recurrent pattern on the left of both nostalgia for and denigration of the 1960s [that] is at the same time a sign of, and a defense against, a profound political-cultural loss from which we have yet to recover' (Balbus 2000: 42). However, to do so would be an error, for both films offer a critical history that both contests neoliberal accounts of the period by pointing to the causes, both from the state and from within the left, that led to the defeats of '68, while presenting an imagery that offers a potent testimony of why new forms of left wing politics and cultural contestation are so urgently needed. The graphic presentation of state violence in these films serves to defamiliarize official accounts of the radicalism of the 1960s, and in this way show how the conditions of the political present are a direct outcome of those events. Its critique of the factionalism within the left constitutes more than an account of its divisions, but rather a critical reflection on the naïve optimism of progress, hubris and teleological mission that distorted the left's perception of the actual course of history. In this respect Marker's later films point to the need to learn from the limitations and fault lines of that political culture, to confront that history fearlessly and honestly, without losing sight of its political ideals. Seen in this light the sombre account of history of the period provided in these films represents a necessary stage in the process of working through the fraught legacy of the 1960s, rather than an expression of the kind of paralysis and pessimism of political nostalgia that Benjamin had warned against.

Le Fond de l'air est rouge, more than any other of Marker's films, allows the viewer no retreat from the procession of disarray and violence it charts, presenting a harrowing spectacle of conflict, oppression and bloodshed. The procession of images from the period that flow across the screen relay the aspirations and experiences of the left in the late 1960s and 1970s and the brutal repression they were met with. This is immediately evident from the start, in an extraordinary montage in which a series of clips from *Battleship Potemkin* (1925), focused on Eisenstein's detailing of the lexicon of political gesture, are combined with the actual footage of left wing protesters. This semiotic fascination with the political lexicon of gestures is carried through the course of the film, alluded to in the poignant subtitle of the first part, '*les mains fragiles*', which gathers poignant associations as the film progresses. The complex ricochet effect of this political lexicon from life to cinema and back again is one rehearsed in a number of Marker films, but here it leads us from reflection on an iconic moment in the history of cinema, a film that in the popular imagination has most quintessentially served to stand for revolutionary Soviet and Marxist cinema, one that invented in the Odessa steps sequence, an extraordinarily powerful originating myth for revolution, jarringly back to the world of actual leftist revolutionary culture on the streets of France and the United States in the 1960s. What seems momentarily to be a film about a nostalgic, personal reminiscence of the powerful impression of seeing Eisenstein's film quickly becomes the prelude to a wide ranging examination of the impact of the Vietnam War, the aesthetics of leftist politics and the transformation of a once-revolutionary film into a museological curiosity that turns revolutionary culture into cultural tourism. Shortly after we see clips of *Battleship Potemkin,* we see crowds of tourists being lectured to by a guide at the site of the Odessa steps, where Eisenstein invented his most enduring myth. The allusive juxtaposition of the events of the 1960s with clips from Eisenstein's film continues periodically throughout *Le Fond de l'air est rouge,* Eisenstein's film acting like a spectre revisiting the scene of an endless catalogue of actual carnage, strife and political defeats to which the bloodied air of Marker's title alludes.

But this transition from the heroic revolutionary propaganda of *Battleship Potemkin* to the more fraught revolutionary culture of the 1960s does not simply serve to associate the promise of the Russian revolution, with the événements of the 1960s. Through this juxtaposition Marker shows too the separation in time between these two moments of revolt. For while the 1960s seemed to offer a moment where a counter culture discovered its own 1917, the film shows how the rise of the New Left, born from a struggle as much within the divisions of the left as from its opposition to the status quo, paralleled a less visible phenomenon, the rise of the New Right. The film progresses quickly from the elated optimism of radical solidarity, symbolized in the semiotics of clenched fists, peace signs and revolutionary slogans, to the military training camps of U.S. forces as they prepare troops for the implementation of techniques of interrogation and torture against North Vietnamese soldiers and provide training and military logistics for Latin American counter revolutionaries. What follows is a dispiriting historical panorama that shows how the ideals of the marching protesters and striking workers of 1968 were to be crushed by the resurgence of the French right post-de Gaulle, and how the emergence of leftist liberation movements in Latin and South America were, with few exceptions, successfully put down by military dictatorships heavily backed by the cold war foreign policies of the United States.

Figure 3.2. Peace signs featured as part of the imagery of revolt. Screen capture from Chris Marker, *Le Fond de l'air est Rouge* (1977; Icarus Films, 2001).

In his introduction for the published script, Marker designates 1967, the film's main departure point, as the beginning of the declining fortunes for the international leftist movement at the precise point it was gathering momentum. This was the year Che Guevara was captured and executed in Bolivia by CIA assisted forces in a campaign that highlighted the conflict on the left between the 'official model' of the deterministic economic model Marxism adopted by the Bolivian Communist Party and the interventionalist military tactics of Che's guerrilla fighters (Tulchin 1973: 402). The failure of Guevara to gain the support his combatants needed left his campaign doomed to failure and Cuba, which was desperate to open a new Latin American front in order to maintain its independence, ever more economically and politically dependent on the Soviet Union. The result of the failure of the Bolivian campaign, combined with the CIA orchestrated overthrow of Salvador Allende's socialist administration six years later, would see the stifling of hopes of a genuine alternative leftist coalition in Latin America to that offered by the Soviet model. Che Guevara's death at the beginning of the film and Allende's suicide close to the end mark the film's trajectory and point to the weight Marker places on Latin America as a key battleground for the left in realizing aspirations that had long ceased to remain possible in the Eastern Communist block (Lupton 2005: 112–13). One of the film's most poignant moments comes in the footage of Castro, with Cuba isolated and the expansion of the revolution in Latin America thwarted, forced to defend the indefensible invasion of Prague.

Yet, while *Le Fond de l'air est rouge* graphically depicts the ruthless actions of the state in repressing the radical movements on the left, it is as much about the ultimate inability of the left to find common ground and solidarity, and the fragility of those fleeting forms of solidarity, that spurred on the protest movements of the period. The deep divisions caused by the PCF's lack of support for the student protesters period was to be a significant watershed for French intellectuals, given the prominence of the party and more generally Marxist theory in French intellectual life. The events of May, and especially their aftermath, brought to the fore longstanding antagonisms within the radical left, particularly between the orthodox Marxism of the PCF and the variety of reformist and militant *gauchistes* who sought to initiate, in Régis Debray's phrase, 'the revolution within the revolution' (Debray 1967). The disenchantment that followed the failure of the events of May led to deep political turmoil, leading many to repudiate Marxism.

Much of the film turns on the strife and conflict within the left and in particular the resistance of institutionalized forms of the left, whether the Soviet, Chinese or French Communist Parties, to new reformist and revisionist tendencies, and the split between the orthodox Marxist parties in Latin America and the guerrilla liberation movement led by Che Guevara. The division between those that believed in an increasingly institutionalized classical Marxism and those who sought to force an open-ended revolution through vanguard activism is a central motif; Marker's sympathies for the student movement and the radical new forms of unorthodox leftism it gave rise to do not blind him to the political shortcomings of those tendencies, or the conflicts and contradictions within them. The consequences of these divisions were profound: the disappearance of the PCF's status as the vanguard of opposition and the widespread repudiation of Marxism by many on the left, opening onto the era of the post-political and the post-revolutionary.

By the film's conclusion the viewer may have begun to understand the Eisenstein footage with which the film opened in a new light. It is less the images of hope and solidarity that fuelled the October Revolution that now resonate, but rather those of mourning and loss that these passages from *Battleship Potemkin* more discreetly encapsulate; loss of the revolutionary ideals that spurred the revolution, loss of those who died in the name of those ideals.

Epilogue

Beyond its sombre portrayal of unaccountable loss and crushed ideals, in many ways *Le Fond de l'air est rouge* provides the kind of coming to terms with the magnitude of this loss that Balbus sees as necessary to begin to rebuild a left coalition to rival that of the right; the need to confront the sorrow, ambivalence and anger aroused by the failure of the movements of the 1960s to realize their aims, the loss of the political enchantment that Walter Benjamin associated with 'the time of now', as well as the sense of guilt and betrayal of a movement that ended up often repeating the forms of domination it sought to bring to an end (Benjamin 1969: 261; Mathy 2011: 23). *Le Fond de l'air est rouge* rejects the association of mourning and melancholy with acquiescence and regressive quietude, and moves beyond Benjamin's separation of the pure tradition of the oppressed and the tainted official past of the oppressive order, in order to come to terms with a more ambivalent historical understanding of the period that finds a place for its contradictions. It attempts 'to counter the modern assault on memory without mobilizing the noxious weapons of nostalgia' (Balbus 2000: 41).

If Marker's late films indicate the failure of the imagination of the left to establish a new political imaginary, the desire for new forms of democracy, cosmopolitanism and a new relationship between the state and civil society is nevertheless vividly conveyed, as is the recognition that the future of the left rests in neither forgetting its past nor remaining wedded to it. The questioning, deconstructive character of these films and their refusal of inherited dogma points to the need to open up an as yet unnamed new concept of the political. Nor, despite their importance, should these films be seen in isolation. While working through the memory of the failures of '68 Marker, despite his advancing age, continued to seek out new collaborations, writing texts, providing film footage or offering production advice on a variety of film projects, while also producing many short films that have continued to engage with issues of workers' rights and international conflicts, including a series of unfinished portraits of the Kosovan conflict. His studio, with its vast filmic recordings of contemporary events, represents a significant image archive of our times. Though perhaps the most enduring feature of his late work may be its experimentation with the possibilities of new intermedial forms of technology, including CD Rom, web-based and installation work, with a strongly decentred and interactive basis. *Level Five* (Marker 1997), his last feature length film, which deals with the cultural amnesia of the significance of the history of the battle of Okinawa, imagines a form of interactive post-cinema where historical testimony can be continually reconfigured to form new historical matrixes of knowledge. The forms of these works, he hoped, would provide the platform for contemporary cultural expressions of new forms of imaginative, democratic and progressive left-wing politics.

References

Arthur, P. 2002. 'Making History', *Film Comment* xxxviii(3): 34–51.
Balbus, I.D. 2000. 'Mourning the Movement', *Soundings* 14: 39–52.

Bazin, A. 1983. 'Chris Marker, Lettre de Sibérie', in *Le Cinema français de la Libération à la Nouvelle Vague. Cahiers du cinéma,* pp. 179–181.
Benjamin, W. 1969. 'Theses on the Philosophy of History', in H. Arendt (ed.), *Illuminations: Essays and Reflections.* New York: Schocken Books, pp. 253–64.
———. 1999 [1931]. 'Left-Wing Melancholy', in M.W. Jennings (ed.), *Walter Benjamin: Selected Writings 2.* Cambridge, MA: Belknap Press, pp. 313–55.
Brown, W. 1999. 'Resisting Left Melancholy', *Boundary 2* 26(3): 19–27.
Cooper, S. 2010. 'Montage, Militancy, Metaphysics: Chris Marker and André Bazin', *Image [&] Narrative* 11(1): 16–28.
Debord, G. 1981. 'The Beginning of an Era,' in K. Knabb (ed.), *The Situationist International Anthology.* Berkeley, CA: Bureau of Public Secrets, pp. 512–76.
Debray, R. 1967. *Révolution dans la révolution?.* Paris: Maspero.
Derrida, J. 1993. *Spectres de Marx: L'état de la dette, le travail du deuil et la nouvelle Internationale.* Paris: Éditions Galileé.
Dreyer, S. 2010. 'Autour de 1968, en France et ailleurs: Le Fond de l'air était rouge', *Image [&] Narrative* 11(1): 47–63.
Fargier, J.P., et al. 1978. 'Table ronde sur Le Fond de l'air est rouge de Chris Marker', *Cahiers du Cinéma* 284: 46–51.
Ferry, L. and A. Renaut. 1990. *French Philosophy of the Sixties: an Essay on Antihumanism.* London: University of Massachusetts Press.
Freud, S. 1957 [1917] *The Standard Edition of the Complete Psychological Works of Sigmund Freud.* J. Strachey (ed.). London: Hogarth Press.
Fukuyama, F. 1996. *The End of History and the Last Man.* New York: Free Press.
Furet, F. 2000. *The Passing of an Illusion: The Idea of Communism in the Twentieth Century.* Chicago: University of Chicago Press.
Kear, J. 1999. *Sunless.* Trowbridge: Flicks Books.
———. 2007. 'A Game That Must Be Lost; Chris Marker's Level 5', in F. Guerin and R. Hallas (eds), *The Image and the Witness: Trauma, Memory and Visual Culture.* London: Wallflower Press, pp. 129–49.
———. 2009. 'The Melancholy Image: Chris Marker's Cine-Essays and the Ontology of the Photograph', in J. Torney and G. Whiteley (eds), *Telling Stories.* Cambridge: Cambridge Scholars Press, pp. 180–92.
Leyda, J. 1983. *Kino: A History of the Russian and Soviet Film.* Princeton, NJ: Princeton University Press.
Lupton, C. 2005. *Chris Marker: Memories of the Future.* London: Reaktion.
Marker, C. 1961. *Commentaires.* Paris: Editions du Seuil.
———. 1971. 'Le ciné-ours', *La Revue du cinéma/ Image et Son* 255: 4–5.
———. 1978. *Le Fond de l'air est Rouge: Scènes de la troisième guerre mondiale. 1967–1977,* Argos Films, Paris.
———. 2003. 'Marker Direct', *Film Comment* 39(3). http://www.filmcomment.com/article/marker-direct-an-interview-with-chris-marker.

———. 2006. 'Pour Mario,' in *Les Groupe Medvedkine: le cinéma est une arme*. Paris: Éditions Montparnasse, pp. 11–19.
Mathy, J.P. 2011. *Melancholy Politics: Loss, Mourning, and Memory in Late Modern France*. University Park: Pennsylvania State University Press.
Mayoux, V. 1997. 'Dossier Chris Marker', *Positif* 433: 93–95.
Muel, B. 2000. 'Les riches heures du groupe Medvedkine (Besançon – Sochaux 1967–1974)', *Images Documentaires* 37(38): 15–35.
Philipe, A. 1971. 'Medvedkine, tu connais? Interview avec Slon et Chris Make', *Le Monde*, 2 December 1917.
Rancière, J. 2004. *The Philosopher and His Poor*. Durham, NC: Duke University Press.
Richard, S. 1977. 'Un beau rouge, un peu noir … avec des "blancs"', *L'Unité*, pp. 9–15.
Ross, K. 2002. *May '68 and its Afterlives*. Chicago: University of Chicago Press.
Stark, T. 2012. '"Cinema in the Hands of the People": Chris Marker, the Medvedkin Group, and the Potential of Militant Film ', *October* 139: 117–15.
Tulchin, J.S. (ed.). 1973. *Problems in Latin American History: the Modern Period*. New York: Harper and Row.
Webber, H. 2000. Que reste-t-il de Mai 68? Essai sur les interprétations des 'Événements'. Paris: Seuil.
Widdis, E. 2005. *Alexander Medvedkin*. London: I.B. Tauris.

Filmography

Battleship Potemkin (*Bronenosets Potemkin*). 1925. Sergei Eisenstein.
À bientôt j'espère. 1967–68. Chris Marker.
Classe de Lutte. 1968. Chris Marker.
¡Cuba Sí!. 1961. Chris Marker.
Dimanche à Pékin. 1956. Chris Marker.
Grin Without a Cat (*Le Fond de l'air est rouge*). 1977. Chris Marker.
Happiness (*Schaste*). 1935. Aleksandr Medvedkin
La Jetée. 1962. Chris Marker.
Le Joli Mai. 1962. Chris Marker.
Letters from Siberia (*Lettre de Sibérie*). 1957. Chris Marker.
Level Five. 1997. Chris Marker.
Man with a Movie Camera (*Chelovek s kino-apparatom*). 1929. Dziga Vertov.
Sans Soleil. 1983. Chris Marker.
La Sixième Face du Pentagone. 1968. Chris Marker.
The Spiral (*La Spirale*). 1975. Valérie Mayoux, Jacqueline Meppiel and Armand Mattelart.
Le Tombeau d'Alexandre. 1993. Chris Marker
The Train Rolls On (*Le Train en marche*). 1971. Chris Marker.

CHAPTER 4
Marx Immemorial
Workers and Peasants in the Cinema of
Jean-Marie Straub and Danièle Huillet

Manuel Ramos-Martinez

Marx reached the following conclusion in *The Eighteenth Brumaire of Louis Napoleon*, words that have excited a myriad of appropriations and polemics:

> *Insofar as there is merely a local interconnection among these small-holding peasants, and the identity of their interests begets no community, no national bond and no political organisation among them, they do not form a class. They are consequently incapable of enforcing their class interest in their own name, whether through a parliament or through convention. They cannot represent themselves, they must be represented.* (Marx 1963: 124)

The distinction between communication and isolation functions here to make a distinction between the political (worker) and the nonpolitical (peasant). Michael Hardt and Antonio Negri have argued that for Marx political subjectivity is 'fundamentally' a matter of 'internal communication' (Negri and Hardt 2004: 123). In the context examined in *The Eighteenth Brumaire*, Marx understands that 'peasant' does not function as a political name because the peasants are isolated, because there are no collective relations to sustain the politicality of the name. 'Proletariat' functions as a political name because Parisian workers cooperate and communicate with each other, a relationality that allows them to become a collective subject of action. Marx posits here communicability as the criterion to make a distinction in the drama against capitalism between the professional actor and the supporting role, the extra.

Hardt and Negri understand that the major lines of Marxist thought have essentialized the subordination of the peasant to the industrial worker that Marx prescribes in *The Eighteenth Brumaire*. For them the 'rich debate' between different Marxist readings around the peasant has simply 'conceived of the peasantry as a class that could have revolutionary potential only by following the urban industrial proletariat' (ibid.). The figure of the peasant has been situated in these debates at the periphery of the political. 'Peasant' has functioned as a name without a proper referent, as an ambiguous name that can designate on demand a class and a non-class to be represented or not by a professional, communicative, leading actor (proletariat, industrial worker, worker). The figure of the isolated peasant signals the limits of dominant readings of Marx that equate political agency with the powers of the communicative men of action. The isolation of the peasant has operated the quarantine necessary for further examination and debate on the sense(s) of the political.

The cinema of Jean-Marie Straub and Danièle Huillet constitutes a chance to see the relation worker/peasant in a different audiovisual configuration, a chance to imagine another communism. Their cinema, both yesterday and today, has cultivated an untimely force, a marginal éclat that refuses the validity of normative partitions between the obsolete and the contemporary, between the active and the passive. In 1968, when their colleagues were filming factories, protests in the streets and discussions around a little red book, Straub and Huillet filmed baroque executions of Johann Sebastian Bach's compositions (*The Chronicle of Anna Magdalena Bach,* Straub and Huillet 1967), revisited a play by Pierre Corneille with a complex plot of political intrigue in imperial Rome (*Othon,* Straub and Huillet 1970) and examined the conflict between monotheism and polytheism (*Moses and Aron,* Straub and Huillet 1974). In 2000, in the context of a systematic erasure of the figure of the worker from the political stage, they film the relation between a group of workers and a group of peasants, the organization and resistance of a popular commune and the lyrical account of a worker's life (*Workers, Peasants,* Straub and Huillet 2000; *Il ritorno del figlio prodigo – Umiliati,* Straub and Huillet 2003; *Sicily!,* Straub and Huillet 1999). There is an anachronistic obstinacy in the practice of Straub and Huillet, more than this, an experimentation with modes of obsolescence that defy the very objectivation of time into a timetable charting the passage of historical progress.

Theirs is a rare experiment of 'peasant cinema'; a cinema that works to be 'anchored in the lived experience, the space-time of peasants' (Daney 1982). More precisely, their cinema has been engaged, since *From the Clouds to Resistance* (Straub and Huillet 1979), in what could be called an immemorial communism that rejects the worker/peasant hierarchical distinction operating in canonical Marxism. Very different from the Soviet faith in the laws of history and progress, Straub and Huillet manifest in their work the power of a communism 'not as a future objective, not as an episode from the past, but as still present, in a way as always already present' (Lafosse 2007: 143). Their work, since the eighties, has consistently investigated with profound attentiveness the material world of nature, from 'the fate of insects' to 'the wind in the trees', and discovered another temporality, an anti-progressive one, for revolutionary politics (Rosenbaum 1983). Timeless Marxists, their cinema is not preoccupied with the communicative modes of revolutionary agitation but with making perceptible class struggle as a telluric phenomenon. As Badiou puts it, for Huillet and Straub 'the question of power, class relations, is much older [and] much more powerfully structured than [the militant left's] agitation believed' (Badiou 1998: 14).

This chapter focuses on their film *Workers, Peasants* (2000), a key case in their late production, to examine how their cinema reworks the audiovisuality of worker and peasant to affirm a Communist people as present. This film, like most of their recent Italian films, has received little attention in the English-speaking world. This is partly explained by the resistance of Huillet and Straub to subtitle in English, a hegemonic language, all of their films. However their Italian films are key to understanding the fidelities and changes that have occurred throughout their long career. Various thinkers, from Jacques Rancière to Badiou, have emphasized the significance of *Workers, Peasants* and others of their Italian films as cases with which to reinvent the protocols of political cinema (see Rancière 2003, 2011; Badiou 1998). This reinvention includes fidelities and innovations with their films of the sixties, complicating the habitual interpretation of their cinema as exemplarily Brechtian (Walsh 1981). In this sense, Deleuze, writing decades before *Workers, Peasants*, appreciated Straub and Huillet as the greatest political filmmakers of modern cinema because 'they know how to show how the people are what is missing, what is not there' (Deleuze 1985: 216). For him, the task of modern political filmmaking is not to address itself to a predetermined people but to recognize its absence. I argue here that Straub and Huillet have worked in the last two decades of their career not so much to elaborate a critical distance in which the people is absent, but within another aesthetical and practical paradigm to affirm a people as always already present.

In their late filmography, Straub and Huillet defy canonical models of modernization by intensifying the obsolescence of names such as 'worker' or 'peasant'. This intensification makes these names resonate together, it affirms them as having immemorial powers. It is a militant obsolescence that questions the order of the present and its determination of proper and improper relations between specific names, ways of speaking and visibilities. In *Workers, Peasants* there is no activation of the peasants to equate them to the workers but a reconfiguration of the image and sound of both figures. Workers and peasants are immersed in an intense audiovisual conjunction of coincidences and ruptures: a montage dividing and uniting them, nonprofessional actors versifying prose, lyrical politicizations of everyday conflicts and joys. These associations and disassociations do not activate these names by adapting them to the demands of a communicative present. It is a reconfiguration that resists normative communication by making these names both present and immemorial.

Collective Encounter with a Text

The films of Straub and Huillet are always based on literary texts by European authors: Cesare Pavese, Friedrich Engels, Marguerite Duras. In *Workers, Peasants* they work with the complex novel *Le Donne di Messina* (*Women of Messina,* 1949) by Elio Vittorini, a Communist author known as the major literary inspiration of the Italian neorealist movement. In *Women of Messina* there is no incapacitation of the figure of the peasant; the narrative does not respect the precepts of orthodox Marxism. One of the main narrative strands of the novel, the one that interests Huillet and Straub, tells the adventures of a group of workers and peasants engaged in the reconstruction of a semi-destroyed village after the Second World War. Both workers and peasants contribute to the enterprise and discuss the government of the common (the cultivation of the land, the production of electricity, the distribution of food). In *Workers, Peasants* Straub and Huillet are going to audiovisually radicalize the narrative of equality between workers and peasants at work in *Women of Messina.* This radicalization starts with the way they organize the encounter between the actors of the film and the text.

Straub and Huillet reject the idea of doing literary adaptations. As Straub sentences: 'One cannot adapt a literary work. Television does it, and it is like fabricating sausages. The film only exists if there is an encounter between the text and the author of the film' (Straub and Huillet 2008: 13). Against sausage-like literary adaptations Straub and Huillet develop modes of collective engagement with a text:

> *Who is able to read a text? No one, none of us. To read a text one has to live with it for three, four months, and that is the work with the actors. One has to listen to them reading, re-reading, learning by heart, reciting well or badly to finally know how to discover a text we were not able to discover at the starting point. (ibid.: 87)*

The encounter with a text practiced in the cinema of Huillet and Straub is very different from an expert adaptation concerned with qualitative historical reconstruction, from an exercise where the knowledge of the director guides the virtuosity of the good actor. It is a collective adventure between filmmakers and actors to know the text in ways unknown before reading it together.

The actors working the text and interpreting the workers and peasants in the film are what the conventions of cinema call nonprofessional actors. The term nonprofessional actor is an elastic one, used to describe different circumstances: actors who are filming their first film, an amateur who does not regularly work as an actor or an actor who has received no proper training. Nonprofessional actors can have a more or less close contact with cinema: they could be interested in pursuing an acting career; they could have a profession in the culture industry. In the case of *Workers, Peasants,* as Jacques Rancière has observed, Straub and Huillet work 'not only with actors who are non-professionals but with people who are outside the academic and cultural worlds' (Lafosse 2007: 157). The actors of *Workers, Peasants* are two times unqualified, two times illegitimate actors: as nonprofessionals and as outsiders of the cultural world. There is a coincidence between these actors-outsiders and the roles they play in the film, Robinson Crusoes creating a rural commune outside Italian society (Bonsaver 2000: 163). How does this coincidence operate in *Workers, Peasants*?

From a neorealist perspective this coincidence between the nonprofessional actors and the characters of Vittorini's novel authenticates the enigma of workers and peasants. Nonprofessional actors have a double part to play, or rather to be, within the poetics of neorealist cinema. Nonprofessionals contribute to the realistic effects of the films: their accents, their vocabulary, their faces without makeup. Roberto Rossellini, for instance, changed the scripts of his films according to the nonprofessional actors' phrasings and their life experiences. Nonprofessional actors are sources of an authentic reality, of life. But also, nonprofessional actors are to contribute to the mystery of reality. For the theoreticians of neorealism, nonprofessionals contribute to this mystery precisely because they do not act; they are themselves. They are a pure, non-acting, mysterious presence. For Bazin, in neorealist performances, 'it calls upon the actor to *be* before expressing himself [sic]' (Bazin 1971: 65). He understands that in neorealist cinema nonprofessional actors do not act but they are 'a silhouette, a face, a way of walking' (ibid.: 65). Nonprofessional actors are 'living creatures' that echo with their natural voices and movements 'the ontological ambiguity of reality' (ibid.: 66). A congratulatory Bazin notes in passing 'how much the cinema owes to a love for living creatures' (ibid.: 72). This humanistic love for living creatures incapacitates nonprofessional actors as enigmatic non-actors.

In *Workers, Peasants* it is not a matter of authenticating the representation through equivalent beings, but of making perceptible a powerful acting presence. The opposition between the simple enigmatic being of nonprofessional actors against the deceptive art of professional actors is not operative in the practice of Straub and Huillet. Rancière rightly distinguishes their work with nonprofessional actors from any form of ontological love: 'Straub and Huillet do not want to use the bodies of the actors as instruments but to create a new relation between *ordinary beings* and a text' (Lafosse 2007: 157). There is no proper way of reading the text; there is no natural way of reading the text. What matters to Straub and Huillet is to affirm the acting capacity of every 'ordinary being'. The work with the text is to activate every member of the cast through singular and disciplined readings. It is a practice verifying the capacity of anyone to encounter a text. Nonprofessional actor, 'worker' or 'peasant' are not sociological identities with determined properties and (in)capacities, but rather names open to the anonymity of different audiovisual inhabitations. The coincidence between the actors/outsiders and their roles does not work to validate an appropriate representation in the film but rather it affirms the acting presence of anyone to break with a sociological destiny and construct other relations between names and capacities.

This collective experience with the actors is the base of the scene of equality between workers and peasants at the core of *Workers, Peasants*. Huillet and Straub focus the film on four specific chapters from *Women of Messina* (chapters XLIV, XLV, XLVI and XLVII), which are significant within the structure of the novel because in them each character, peasant or worker, narrates from their own point of view the events that occurred in the commune during a specific time (the winter and spring of an unspecified year). The chorus of characters displaces the God-like voice of the narrator, who only intervenes to introduce the different characters as follows: 'The things that happened there until February … are told by the village's inhabitants during the long summer evenings, to refresh their memories or to inform now one and now another, a friend or a new acquaintance who asks about what went on' (Vittorini 1973: 132). These four chapters juxtapose without further explanation the different narratives, each intervention always preceded by the proper name or nickname of the character speaking: Widow Bilotti, Elvira La Farina, Whistle, etc. The multiple voices construct a fragmented narrative about the differences that separate workers and peasants.

Vittorini's text emphasizes a conflictual opposition between workers and peasants. Their conflicts around milk and defection, energy and goats, the cold winter and love stories oppose two distinct socioeconomic groups. The different voices corroborate the sociological division between workers and peasants dear to orthodox Marxism. Everything in their lifestyles separates them. They inhabit different temporalities: peasants do not work during the winter; workers do not work on Sundays. Workers are the energetic people of the machine and peasants are the invariable people of the land. They have different temperaments; peasants are melancholic, workers are enterprising. The text formalizes these oppositions; the different narratives are punctuated by formulas such as 'we, the peasants' and 'we, the workers'. And yet, at the same time, this scrupulous opposition constructs a formal equality between workers and peasants; an equality to discuss what has happened in the commune. Furthermore it is an opposition constantly decentred by different versions, excursus, individual anecdotes, repetitions and poetical images.

In *Workers, Peasants* Straub and Huillet make palpable the opposition between workers and peasants at work in the narrative, but also the musicality of the different voices. The music of the text is intensified by the singular readings of the text offered by the different actors. Speaking these lines is not here an occasion to celebrate the naturally flawed acting of amateurs; rather it is practised as an anonymous capacity of fellow strugglers: workers, peasants, first-time actors. This shared capacity gives a common ground to the division between workers and peasants. As Rancière puts it: 'The debates between workers and peasants … are not dramas of division … these conflicts are not factors of dissociation; on the contrary for the Straubs these are factors of consistency. This Communist people exists, it exists in its division and because of its capacity to affirm this division' (Lafosse 2007: 144). In *Workers, Peasants* the opposition between workers and peasants is radicalized into a scene of conflictive equality, a common that defies sociological partitions. The dispute is not performed as a space of separation between communicative workers and isolated peasants, but rather as an occasion to verify an earlier commonality of struggle and speech. This common makes two names that everything separates resonate together in a conflictive co-presence, a Communist people.

The Workers/Peasants Parliament

The juxtaposition of different voices in the novel *Women of Messina* has been compared to a series of interviews that produce 'a kind of collective self-presentation' (Bonsaver 2000: 165). In *Workers, Peasants* these multiple voices appear not so much as a collection of interviews but rather as a formal discussion between two opposing groups. The different stories told by the village's inhabitants during the long summer evenings become the formal speeches of lyrical orators. The formality of the discussion insists on the division between workers and peasants and at the same time on their shared capacity to dignify and poeticize their separation, their conflicts, aspirations and joys. Huillet, Straub and the actors transform the dispute into a formal and poetic discussion in a parliament.

It is an open-air parliament, situated in an unspecific forest. It is a dateless but absolutely present forest. Together with the formal declarations we hear birds chirping, running water, even insects buzzing. Workers and peasants are orators illuminated by the impressionistic sunlight the trees filtrate. Between the formal discussion, the lyricism of the voices and the sounds of the forest there are continuous passages and isolations, visual accords, overflows and obstructions. The murmurs of the forest contrast with the formality of the discussion and coincide with the affirmation of a lyrical capacity common to workers and peasants. These agreements and dissociations, coincidences and emphases orchestrate an obsolete and lyrical formality undoing the order of proper, modern parliamentary communication. This parliament of workers and peasants, trembling with this intense audiovisuality, makes visible and audible an alternative world to the protocols of parliamentary democracy.

A Formal Division

In *Workers, Peasants* Huillet and Straub choreograph visually the division at work in Vittorini's text between workers and peasants. The audiovisual organization of the film emphasizes the opposition the different voices of the text articulate. The oppositional narratives and their audiovisual organization strictly coincide in the film. The coincidence underlines the division between workers and peasants but it also constructs mathematically their audiovisual equality. The equality of workers and peasants is not represented as a result of their discussion, as a compromise; but rather as already there, from the first frame of the film, in the blunt coincidence between the text and the audiovisual distribution of workers and peasants. The formalization of the discussion constructs a parliament not so much for workers and peasants to exchange ideas and reach agreements, but rather a parliament to demonstrate sensuously and mathematically their equality in the acts of enunciation. The formalization of the discussion happens at three levels: the oppositional framing of equals, the body postures and the mode of speaking.

Straub and Huillet do not frame workers and peasants together; but they frame two clearly distinct groups. Workers occupy the frame only with workers, peasants with peasants (see figures 4.1 and 4.2). In the first movement of the film when a worker or a peasant starts to speak he or she does it, in the first place, as the member of a visually distinct group. The peasant Pompeo Manera speaks first in the name of the peasants, the worker Cataldo Chiesa speaks first in the name of the workers.

For orthodox Marxism, as we have seen in the introduction, an oppositional scheme is used to construct a hierarchical relation between the active worker and the passive peasant. The result of this opposition is the need to transform the peasants into communicative subjects. The oppositional logic of *Workers, Peasants* very differently underlines an arithmetical equality. The opposition

Figure 4.1. Group of peasants. Screen capture from a television broadcast of *Operai, Contadini* (*Workers, Peasants*, 2000, Capricci Films) by Jean-Marie Straub and Danièle Huillet.

happens through a quasi-symmetrical representation of workers and peasants. In the first movement of the film the group of workers is formed of three people (two standing, one sitting down) opposed to the group of peasants formed of three people (two standing, one sitting down). There is also an equitable distribution of the use of speech. The characters/groups occupy the frame and say their lines in strict turns, following a formal rotation. Workers and peasants are represented in geometric equilibrium; they are equals in the oppositional representation.

The postures of the bodies in the film are in accordance with the formality of the discussion. In the first half of the film the actors representing the workers and peasants are perfectly straight and almost immobile. Furthermore the characters are positioned facing the camera; there are no profiles in the first movements of the film. Frontality is an ancient convention used in the representation of kings and emperors; it has been used to convey the idea of a commanding presence. The script of the film repeatedly describes this fron-

Figure 4.2. Group of workers. Screen capture from a television broadcast of *Operai, Contadini* (*Workers, Peasants*, 2000, Capricci Films) by Jean-Marie Straub and Danièle Huillet.

tality as follows: 'they [the actors] look in front of them: to a judge? To the spectator? To God?'. There is a double effect created by the rectitude of the bodies and the frontal representation, in that the division between workers and peasants is emphasized. They do not look at each other but in front of them to a third, invisible party. In this sense the different speeches are visually organized as monologues. And yet, the narratives respond to each other. The division functions, defying their conventional division, both as a collection of monologues and a dialogue, as communication and isolation. Moreover, the frontality and the rectitude represent in the same manner workers and peasants as honourable and powerful bodies. It is not simply a matter of appropriating the ancient visual language of power; the straight, frontal position of the king's body. Straub and Huillet are not only interested in creating a contrast between workers and peasants who are wearing casual clothes and the conventional visual code of absolute, premodern power. The bearing and position of the body function here not so much as appropriated attributes for inappropriate bodies, but rather as the manifestation of the common capacity of workers and peasants to stand and face, without trembling, a judge (the spectator? God?).

Their voices do not tremble either, in these declarations in front of an invisible judge. The actors say but also read their lines. Reading does not function here as a tool to help the actors remember their lines; it is a perfectly choreographed gesture, a gesture indicated in the script. The actors do not read when they hesitate; to read is part of the performance and its formalization. These disciplined performances transform the narratives into formal declarations. The emphasis on the pronouns 'I' or 'we', the careful diction applied to every word or the formidable weight of the voices formalizes the different narratives and constructs them as declarations in the strange immemorial present of this parliament. In *Workers, Peasants,* as Rancière has remarked, 'every narrative becomes live speech', 'the film is always in the present' (see Lafosse 2007: 151). The formalization of the text through the performances is therefore twofold. The declarative quality of the performances formalizes the distance between workers and peasants and at the same time it represents as present their capacity to declare their division.

The audiovisual construction of this parliament differs greatly from how critical narratives of communication habitually use processes of formalization. Firstly, the discussion is not simply constructed as a balanced space of communication where workers and peasants exchange information and reach an agreement about what is common in their situation; the mathematical opposition of workers and peasants does not simply work as a formula to construct a fair geometry of representation. Rather, the quasi-symmetrical opposition functions to construct common conditions from where to emphasize equality before division.

Secondly, the strict formality of the discussion peasants does not operate as a simple critique of the limits of parliamentary communication. In the film *Triple Agent* (2004) by Eric Rohmer, for instance, there is a similar formalization of political discussions. The use of speech is also equitably distributed between the different characters and their conflicting argumentations. But in the case of *Triple Agent,* the formalities of the discussion are used to manifest the lack of real communication between the different characters. The respectful rotation in the discussion is the occasion to ironically underline the limits of the formal discussion, the limits of democratic etiquette. In *Workers,*

Peasants the formalities of the discussion do not caricature the parliament of workers and peasants as a system of incommunicability, but function to obstinately represent a scene of division and equality where communication is not a means to an end but the affirmative demonstration of a co-presence.

The mathematical equilibrium of the representation, the honourable posture of the bodies and the declarative tone of the voices are powerful elements stating audiovisually the common of the division between workers and peasants. It is the unreasonable, stubborn common of two collectives that everything separates. The film defies sociological orders separating, systematically and hopelessly, workers and peasants, and creating hierarchies between capacitated and incapacitated names/actors. It defies the social programme laid out by orthodox Marxists to transform peasants into the industrial workers of the countryside. The audiovisual division workers/peasants functions not as the appropriate representation that confirms their sociological separation but as the common capacity of workers and peasants to declare, stand and face. In *Workers, Peasants*, declaring, standing, facing do not belong to the sociological and communicative proper of the name 'worker' or the name 'peasant'; these are constructed as anonymous capacities obstinately defying naturalized protocols of distinction and action.

Lyrical Declamations

The prose style of *Women of Messina* has been criticized for its combination of colloquialisms and poetic images. In his monograph about Vittorini, Guido Bonsaver corroborates the argumentation behind the negative critical response the novel received when first published in 1949. Bonsaver argues that the amalgamation of colloquial and poetic registers contributes to the novel's 'relative failure' (Bonsaver 2000: 161–73). The use of poetic images and the repetition of words explain the novel's 'overall artificial tone' (ibid.: 167). For Bonsaver, the use of colloquialisms is appropriate for a novel that narrates the story of a group of workers and peasants, but to amalgamate the way workers and peasants speak with poetry can only result in a confusing and false representation. Straub and Huillet's reading of *Women of Messina* is very different from this sociological logic, equating identities and ways of speaking.

In the chapters from *Women of Messina* used for *Workers, Peasants* the different characters often use an elegant or poetical language to narrate their everyday life. Pompeo Manera describes the dispute between workers and peasants as follows: 'Now I took offence, and that is how the ill will there had been during the past month between us peasants on the one hand and the various workers on the other grew into open discord' (Vittorini 1974: 147). Or Siracusa remembers a night she and her lover slept in the open with the following imagery: 'We saw lights above us. The sky was free and the lights were stars twinkling in a faraway wind' (ibid.: 177). The language workers and peasants use in these chapters is not a vernacular proper, but a language with colloquialisms, formalities, repetitions and poetic metaphors. *Workers, Peasants* does not correct these artifices, but Huillet and Straub intensify the lyrical and formal registers at play in Vittorini's prose through the actors' performances.

The actors of *Workers, Peasants* (with Straub and Huillet) rework the narratives of workers and peasants and transform their prose into verses. The process of versification of Vittorini's prose starts, following the usual practice in the cinema of Straub and Huillet, with the detonation of the original punctuation of the text. Huillet equates this practice of detonation and re-accentuation to poetry in the following declaration of love/aggression to language: 'There is nothing complicated about this [their work with the texts]: it is the same kind of thing that poets do with language. They take a language which has become rigid, that has become a system of habits, almost a dead language and they suddenly try to do things that have not been done before or have long been forgotten' (see Böser 2004: 213). The detonation of the original punctuation allows the actors to musicalize with another rhythm the text. There is a correspondence between how the characters of *Women of Messina* poeticize their narratives and how the actors of *Workers, Peasants* intone, or rather de-tone, the prose. The capacities of workers and peasants to speak a formal and poetic language, capacities the critics of Vittorini judged confusing, are doubled by the actors' *detonation* of their lines into verses. The film co-relates the lyrical capacities of the workers and peasants from the novel and the non-professional actors who interpret them. This is not a sociological convergence confirming the appropriateness of using nonprofessional actors to act like, or rather be, the workers and peasants of the film; it is the correspondence of two lyrical transformations that invalidate the opposition between the being of nonprofessional actors, peasants, workers and the acting of proper actors. It is a correspondence that speaks of a common capacity of the names 'worker', 'peasant' and 'nonprofessional actor' to trouble the determination of their social ethos and its prescription of idiosyncratic vocabularies, enunciations and actions.

Furthermore in *Workers, Peasants* the actors de-tone the text with an intonation that is at the same time formal and lyrical. The actors do not simply narrate, more or less convincingly, what has happened in the commune. The actors perform their lines like declarative verses, according to a usage of language that emphasizes the formal and poetic dimensions of the text. The formal discussion in the parliament of workers and peasants combines at the same time the musical tonalities of a declarative and a lyrical intonation. There is a grandiloquent intonation that operates at the same time as declamation and operatic aria.

The actors of the film do not have the tired voices Bertolt Brecht appreciates in proletarian actors. Brecht admires proletarian actors because they cannot but convey the fatigue of a life divided by work in the factory during the day and being on stage at night: 'the way these people act does to some extent betray their lack of surplus energy' (Brecht 1964: 148). Their exhaustion is for Brecht one of the main acting skills of these workers, who unintentionally perform through it the capitalist class division of time and energy. In *Workers, Peasants* the intonation is, very differently, energetic and grandiloquent. This intonation transforms the narratives of workers and peasants into a vehement oratory. It is a process of formalization and intensification of the narratives that distinguishes them from a colloquial conversation.

At the same time, each character delivers the verses following a repetitive rhythm, like a regular *ritournelle*, or jingle. Rancière (Lafosse 2007: 143) has noticed that there is 'a kind of overarticulation' in the way the actors deliver their lines/verses in the film. Each word is pronounced with extreme precision, and each syllable is accentuated and given a dramatic magnitude. The meticulous articulation usually works in a dialogue as a strategy of clarity, as a procedure to make what is being said understandable to the listeners, but the overatiiculation at work here also functions as a glorification of each syllable, as an exaltation *à la lettre* that goes beyond the needs of communication and intelligibility. The overarticulation of each syllable produces a potent eloquence and a solemn incomprehensibility.

The use of a lyrical register in the workers/peasants parliament contradicts the conventions about the appropriate language for political debate and communication. Prose is conventionally 'the language of discursive, positive, scientific reason, the language of everything that is opposed to Art' (Durosoir 2000: 35). Prose is the appropriate language, the naturalized language in the democratic order of things, for negotiation, debate and deliberation. Prose, from the Latin *prosa* meaning 'straightforward', is the language workers and peasants should use to solve the fact, the social fact, of their difference. However the cinema of Straub and Huillet is not interested in articulating an audiovisuality where the differences between workers and peasants are debated and/or solved; rather it organizes as a common their capacity to appear and declare. These capacities do not simply demonstrate the competence of workers and peasants to communicate and expose their quarrel in the forest parliament. The lyrical dimension of the performances in the film insists on inventing an obsolete language, 'a language that does not separate prosaic speech and chant' (Lafosse 2007: 148).

The language of workers and peasants does not oppose poetry as the language of sentiments, mystery and nature, and prose as the language of argumentation and debate. Félix Guattari has observed about the privilege of prose in politics that 'it always comes back to the idea that if you abandon the discourse of reason, you fall into the black night of passions, of murder, and the dissolution of all social life' (Guattari 2009: 244). In the case of *Workers, Peasants* there is a formal and lyrical practice of language that breaks with this logic and its hierarchical equations. In this sense in *Workers, Peasants* it is not so much that workers and peasants appropriate a language that is not theirs, the language and intonation of poets, but that their use of the lyrical disrupts the logic of proper registers that divide and normativize the use of language. The lyrical is not so much here a register but a practice undoing the equation between a vocabulary, a pronunciation, a syntax and a communicative purpose. It is a power to undo the equation between a vocabulary, a pronunciation, a syntax and a social name. In this process the peasants do not learn the communicative skills of the workers. In *Workers, Peasants* the lyrical, a practice of both workers and peasants, functions to break the logic of appropriate registers and construct as a common power the strange capacity of workers and peasants to speak the murmur of an obsolete language, a language that appears as unheard since immemorial times.

The poet and essayist Paul Valéry has also favoured the lyrical when he defined prose, poetry and song as the three distinct states of language. In his text 'On Speaking Verse', he writes:

In short we note that in song the words tend to lose their importance as meaning, that they do most frequently lose it, whereas at the other extreme, in everyday prose, it is the musical value that tends to disappear; so much so that song on the one side and prose on the other are placed, as it were, symmetrically in relation to verse, which holds an admirable and very delicate balance between the sensual and intellectual forces of language. (Valéry 1958: 164)

In this summary of his thesis, Valéry organizes a gradation between prose, poetry and song in relation to signification. Poetry is the privileged register of this gradation. For Valéry, prose, everyday speech, ordinary discourse are not without musicality, but their musicality is subdued to their function of communication and signification. Song would function inversely: signification almost disappears; words tend to lose their meaning and function simply as 'the carriers of *flatus vocis*' (Durosoir 2000: 59). Valéry positions poetry in a position of mediation between these two opposite tendencies towards signification and non-signification. This gradation operates a clear-cut distinction between these three states of language (he talks of extremes), while at the same time there is a certain amount of ambiguity (he talks of the fragility of the distinction). Poetry is for him the privileged and yet fragile state of language where to equilibrate signification and music. Valéry resolves this ambiguity by understanding that poetry is the negotiation of an agreement.

The lyrical in the practice of Huillet and Straub, the lyrical as a practice, does not simply follow this prosaic gradation between different levels of signification. Their cinema does not follow a politics of negotiation, but it stubbornly practices the construction of other possible assemblages between language, names and capacities. In *Workers, Peasants* it is the stubbornness of a series of performances verbalizing an unreasonable correlation between a declarative prose and a singing intonation. This strange language does not simply communicate one or various messages but makes audible and visible the configuration of another relational order between speakers; one where a strangely lyrical and formal language does not need the sociological competence of appropriate names to function.

The discussion about the commune is neither a process where workers and peasants learn how to communicate properly through the prosaic language of politics, nor a process where workers and peasants avoid the traps of signification through the musical effacement of the text. And it is not the negotiation of these two strategies. The formal and lyrical performances make audible and visible the strange power of workers and peasants to act and verbalize a language that is at the same time sensuous and intellectual, passionate and mathematical. The performances operate the obstinate co-incidence of lyrical and formal capacities that ignore the logic of the good communication of the men of action. To listen to the vocal performances of the actors in *Workers, Peasants* is to listen to an affirmative ensemble bustling with contrasting equations between linguistic registers, rhythms, significations and communication. The names worker and peasant are not updated into the names of communicative actors participating in a modern parliamentary discussion, rather they are activated as the anonymous names of actors defying the logic of their sociological definition through the construction of a common, powerful, immemorial parliament.

Workers, Peasants is a significant case to rethink conventional regimes of efficacy between cinema and the political. It is a lyrical film where texts, bodies and voices resonate in unison to radically affirm a common very different from the social planning of orthodox Marxism. 'Workers' and 'peasants' are not the names of revolutionary subjects promised by a five-year plan of modernization, but the names of orators declaring a conflictive common. Montage, acting and framing are here tools to question protocols of sociopolitical action and to reconfigure the sound and image of these names. The relations between the names 'worker' and 'peasant' and different formal and lyrical capacities, form a cinematic material consistency to visualize a common power. Against dominant ideologies in contemporary discourse insisting that communism is a historical episode with a beginning and an end, the cinema of Huillet and Straub makes communism visible and audible as a stubborn presence, the presence of an immemorial equality.

References

Badiou, A. 1998. 'Penser le surgissement de l'événement', *Cahiers du Cinéma (hors-série): Cinéma 68*: 10–19.

Bazin, A. 1971. *What is Cinema?* 2, trans. H. Gray. Berkeley and Los Angeles: University of California Press.

Bonsaver, G. 2000. *Elio Vittorini, The Writer and The Written*. Leeds: Northern Universities Press.
Böser, U. 2004. *The Art of Seeing, The Art of Listening, The Politics of Representation in the Work of Jean-Marie Straub and Danièle Huillet*. Frankfurt: Peter Lang.
Brecht, B. 1964. *Brecht on Theatre, the Development of an Aesthetic*. London: Methuen Drama.
Daney, S. 1982. *Cinemetorology*. Paris: Libération.
Deleuze, G. 1985. *Cinéma 2: L'image-temps*. Paris: Minuit.
Durosoir, G., ed. 2000. *Parler, dire, chanter*. Paris: Presses de L'Université de Paris-Sorbonne.
Guattari, F. 2009. *Chaosophy*. New York: Semiotext(e).
Lafosse, P., ed. 2007. *L'etrange cas de Madame Huillet et Monsieur Straub*. Toulouse: Editions Ombres.
Marx, K. 1963. *The Eighteenth Brumaire of Louis Bonaparte*. New York: International Publishers.
Negri, A. and M. Hardt. 2004. *Multitudes, War and Democracy in the Age of Empire*. New York: Penguin.
Rancière, J. 2003. 'La parole sensible: à propos d'Ouvriers, paysans', *La Revue Cinéma*: 68–78.
———. 2011. *Les Ecarts du cinéma*. Paris: La Fabrique.
Rosenbaum, J. 1983. *Film: The Front Line 1983*. Denver: Arden.
Straub, J.M. and D. Huillet. 2008. *Rencontres avec Jean-Marie Straub et Danièle Huillet*. Paris: Beaux-arts de Paris, les Editions.
Valéry, P. 1958. *The Collected Works of Paul Valéry 7*. New York: Pantheon Books.
Vittorini, E. 1973. *Women of Messina*, trans. F. Frenaye and F. Keene. New York: New Directions Books.
———. 1974. *Le Opere Narrative 2*. Vicenza: Mondadori.

Filmography

The Chronicle of Anna Magdalena Bach (*Chronik Der Anna Magdalena Bach*). 1967. Jean-Marie Straub and Danièle Huillet.
From the Clouds to Resistance (*Dalla Nube Alla Resistenza*). 1979. Jean-Marie Straub and Danièle Huillet.
Il ritorno del figlio prodigo – Umiliati. 2003. Jean-Marie Straub and Danièle Huillet.
Moses and Aron (*Moses und Aron*). 1974. Jean-Marie Straub and Danièle Huillet.
Othon. 1970. Jean-Marie Straub and Danièle Huillet.
Sicily! (*Sicilia!*). 1999. Jean-Marie Straub and Danièle Huillet.
Triple Agent. 2004. Eric Rohmer.
Workers, Peasants (*Operai, Contadini*). 2000. Jean-Marie Straub and Danièle Huillet.

CHAPTER 5

In the Heat of the Factory
The Global Fires of *The Hour of the Furnaces*

Bruce Williams

Lauded in such festivals as Pesaro and Cannes, Fernando Solanas and Octavio Getino's *The Hour of the Furnaces* (*La hora de los hornos,* 1968) drew upon some 180 hours of clandestinely filmed interviews and found footage to document Juan Perón's rise to power, his eventual overthrow and the lasting legacy of peronism in Argentina. This film, referred to as agitprop inasmuch as its structure and ideology reflect Soviet film of the 1920s, has frequently been viewed primarily as a neocolonialist document, particularly by international audiences. Nonetheless, a good deal of its broader theoretical scope is based upon a very local foundation – an extensive examination of the Argentine working class and labour movement. Its depiction of the plight of workers in Argentina promises a high level of authenticity inasmuch as workers, union leaders and labour unions at large were closely involved in the making of the film. Prior to the 1973 release of *The Hour of the Furnaces,* Solanas and Genino presented the film in underground locales, with structured pauses and intermissions designed to foster active discussion among audience members. The subversive power of these screenings cannot be downplayed, and all participants took great risks, not only because of the film's indictment of the ties of the Argentine oligarchy to neocolonialism, but also, and of greater threat to the regime, due to its equation of peronism and the labour movement. Internationally, there was no restriction on such debate, and foreign audiences came to learn of the lives and working conditions of both rural *campesinos* and urban factory labourers. International readings reinterpretated and recontextualized *The Hour of the Furnaces* in diverse ways, allowing non-Argentine audiences to *translate* the film transnationally. Whatever awareness these spectators lacked of the specific context of Argentina was compensated for by their ability to appropriate the film for their own purposes, or for those of international left-wing movements. In terms of the transnational movement of culture and politics, this phenomenon inverts current debates in transnationalism, and can best be described by a term we will coin here: 'functional mediating cultural translation'. Such a concept allows for a partial understanding of the original context coupled with expanded meaning stemming from the new viewing setting.

From an international perspective, the reception of *The Hour of the Furnaces*, as I will explore, has been especially insightful in France and Québec. There, one finds the most probing appropriations of the film in critical discourse, especially with regard to the labour dynamics present. Nonetheless, of equal importance is that *The Hour of the Furnaces* has expanded its meaning in France through the medium of film, most notably in the work of Jean-Luc Godard and the Dziga Vertov Group.

The Hour of the Furnaces: A Revolutionary Project

A great deal of the political and economic backdrop for *The Hour of the Furnaces* can be found in the Argentine labour movement. It was decidedly labour-led coalitions that brought Perón to power, a phenomenon examined at length by María Victoria Murillo, who explores the symbiotic relationship between unions and the political system. She asserts that peronism turned labour unions into 'key players in the political system', and further fostered import substitutions, industrialization and state-led development, all of which had the effect of reinforcing unionization and labour bargaining power (Murillo 2001: 27). Together with Murillo, a number of scholars, including Walter Little (1988) and James W. McGuire (1997), have examined the close ties between the Perón administration and labour union dynamics. McGuire emphasizes the role of the national secretary of labour, who intervened on behalf of workers upon negotiation breakdowns and regularly consulted with union leaders on issues of state policy (McGuire 1997: 52–53). Despite the political and economic chaos that followed the ousting of Perón, the successoral governments failed to efface his impact on workers, and unions remained faithful to peronism, despite official repression. As Murillo asserts, 'Peronist unions learned how to create industrial distress with political objectives and adapt to different political environments to a much greater degree than labour leaders in Mexico and even Venezuela' (Murillo 2001: 48). She further explains that the banning of the peronist party increased union power by turning unions into 'the only legal form for political activities for Peronists' (ibid.: 48). Such a situation ushered in the period of' 'resistance', which Juan Carlos Torre has described as characterized by 'strikes, [and a] general policy of insubordination, including industrial sabotage' (ibid.:129).

Defiantly aligned with peronism, the Grupo Cine Liberación was essentially composed of two individuals, Argentine-born Fernando Solanas and Spanish writer Octavio Getino, the latter having received the literary award of Cuba's Casa de las Américas in 1963. Timothy Barnard clarifies that the filmmakers travelled some 18,000 kilometres around Argentina, with Solanas operating a sixteen millimetre camera and Getino doing sound. They were accompanied by a young assistant and a director of photography (Barnard 1996: 44–45). The work was made midway through one of the most repressive periods of Argentine history under the military government of General Juan Carlos Onganía, and hence the filming was done as clandestinely as possible. Although the filmmakers intended to make a much shorter piece, the resulting four-and-a-half-hour mammoth was divided into three parts: 'Neocolonialism and Violence', 'An Act [or Ceremony] for Liberation' and 'Violence and Revolution'. Issues of work and the labour movement are particularly evident in the film's second part, which visits factories and draws heavily upon interviews with workers and union leaders. In their 1969 essay, 'Towards a Third Cinema: Notes and Experiences for the Development of a Cinema of Liberation in the Third', Solanas and Getino describe their agenda as breaking with both a First Cinema, epitomized by Hollywood, and a Second Cinema, that of the auteur, in favour of a violent, unfinished and proletarianized film. In this much-cited work, the filmmakers draw parallels between their 'guerrilla' cinema of violence and the labour process. They argue:

> Guerrilla cinema proletarianizes the film worker, and breaks down the intellectual aristocracy that the bourgeoisie grants to its followers. In a word, it democratizes … The revolutionary film-maker acts with a radically new vision of the role of the producer, team work, tools, details, etc. Above all, he supplies himself at all levels in order to produce his films, he equips himself at all levels, he learns how to handle the manifold techniques of his trade … Each member of the group should be familiar, at least in a general way, with the equipment being used: he must be prepared to replace another in any of the phases of production. The myth of irreplaceable technicians must be exploded. (Solanas and Getino 2010: 51)

This exploration of the creative process as labour intensive is an inherent component of other movements in Latin America. For instance, it closely mirrors the tenets of Brazilian *cinema novo*, which drew heavily upon Oswald de Andrade's 'Cannibal Manifesto' (1928), a document which argued that Brazilian writers and artists should, in a manner not unlike the Tupinambá Amerindians, consume First World culture, digest it and create a new, uniquely Brazilian product for exportation (Andrade 1928: 7). Such a process, expressed through a cannibalistic metaphor involving consummation, defecation/urination ('Tupi or not Tupi', ibid.: 3) and regeneration, further implies the work process inasmuch as the artist must struggle to synthesize raw material and ultimately distribute it. Artistic creation is thus viewed in terms of production (work) and dissemination (distribution), two processes of which workers engaged in the taking over of factories as explored in *The Hour of the Furnaces*, assuming full ownership.

Given the close alliance between the proponents of cinema novo and the proletariat classes, Carlos Estevam's 1982 discussion of the ideological precepts of Brazil's radical Popular Centre of Culture foregrounds the role of art in the 'material processes that structure social existence' (Estevam 1982: 59). Implicit in these material processes is the notion of work, specifically that of the artist. In a like manner, Glauber Rocha speaks of the 'tri-continental filmmaker' (Asia, Africa, Latin America), and what comes to the forefront in his discussion is the way in which 'technique' is subsumed by overarching ideology. When Rocha defines the technical aspects of film favoured by cinema novo as 'tools' for ideological expression, he, by extension, refers to the workers behind the tools (Rocha 1967: 80). Whether a rural or urban context, *cinema novo* gave workers visibility. Of the seminal works of this movement, it is arguably Paulo Cesar Saraceni's *The Challenge* (*O desafio*, 1965) that most closely allies itself with *The Hour of the Furnaces*. Saraceni's film contains a sequence set in the wake of the 1964 military coup in which the wife of a Brazilian industrialist, herself the lover of a leftist journalist, visits one of her husband's factories and is confronted for the first time with the conditions of labourers. The film, in a manner not unlike *The Hour of the Furnaces*, fell victim to censorship in Brazil, and was initially shown in museum and private screenings, which were followed by discussion and debate among Brazilian writers and intellectuals (Williams 2012).

In a 1969 interview with Gianni Volpi, Piero Arlorio, Goffredo Fifi and Gianfranco Torri entitled 'Cinema As a Gun', Solanas indicts Argentina's 'old Marxist left' as being petit bourgeois and reformist, lacking ties to the workers' movement (Volpi et al. 2010: 19), a stance that parallels cinema novo. Nonetheless, the filmmakers draw upon the work process as a means to explain the delay in the use of film as a revolutionary medium, referencing 'lack of equipment, technical difficulties, the compulsory specialization of each phase of work, and high costs' (Solanas and Getino 2010: 46).

From the standpoint of film production as labour, *The Hour of the Furnaces* allowed its authors and technicians a more absorbing participation in the film process. By creating a mechanism through which crew members and writers could learn of each other's craft and replace each other when needed, greater understanding was fostered for all concerned with the materiality of film. Film production was characterized by increased transparency, and all concerned were better able to contextualize and see the relevance of their own work. Once again, the very filming of *The Hour of the Furnaces,* to a great degree, mirrored the numerous factory takeovers it depicts in which workers gain ownership of their own labour.

Roy Armes has argued that *The Hour of the Furnaces* can be classified as a documentary, 'although it embraces a whole host of forms (film letter, film poem, film essay, film pamphlet, and film report)' (Armes 1987: 100). Such a remark is in conformance with the statements made by Solanas and Getino, however disputed, regarding the open-endedness of such a project. Solanas describes it as 'an open work, designed to stimulate debate' (Volpi et al. 2010: 21–22), yet he notes that the embedded discussions are led by a 'militant' (ibid.: 24). Clearly, despite claims of open-endedness and divergent interpretations, the film was devised to lead audiences in a specific, propagandistic direction. It was, indeed, conceived as a true work of agitprop. To this effect, Shohat and Stam further view *The Hour of the Furnaces* as a reflection of the very contradictions at play in peronism, arguing that the film was 'at once manipulative and participatory, strong-armed and egalitarian … [speaking] the language of popular expression … but also [resorting] to hyperbolic language and sledgehammer rhetoric' (Shohat and Stam 1994: 268–60).

Images of Labour, Slogans of Revolution

The opening credits of *The Hour of the Furnaces* acknowledge the cooperation of workers, countryfolk, militant revolutionaries, intellectuals, union leaders and popular organizations, with labourers and workers receiving top billing. The film's first section, 'Neo-Colonialism and Violence', explores Argentina's political and class struggles from the historical context of neocolonialism and expands the implications of such struggle to Latin America at large. This section, radical in its structure, juxtaposes images of oppression with international pop music, depictions of poverty with slogans advocating violent revolution. One of its first sequences depicts factory labourers punching time clocks and carrying out their daily activities. Voiceovers by activists discuss the repression of union leaders, arrests of workers, etc., while captions argue that 'There Are Countless Political, Economic, and Cultural Resources as Effective as Weapons of War'. A voiceover describes the death of workmen at the hands of the police, and the segment concludes with shots of the flashlights on the hard

Figure 5.1. Debunking the Good Life. Screen capture from *The Hour of the Furnaces* (1968), Grupo Cine Liberación.

hats of miners, which turn into an abstract play of light and dark. A subsequent sequence details the activities of rural labourers as voiceovers decry the paucity of permanent jobs and the eleven-hour day. Extended montages of the opulence of Buenos Aires, showcasing high rises, chic venues and 'La Recoleta', the cemetery of the well-do-do, then ensue. Ties between the Argentine elite and U.S. imperialism are underscored by shots of Jackie Kennedy's visit to Buenos Aires.

An extended sequence presents graphic images from a slaughterhouse alternating with commercial ads for cosmetics, cars and lingerie. Robert Stam describes this sequence as a fusion of Eisenstein and Warhol, in that we have a juxtaposition of slaughter and the advertising of the products of multinational companies. He stresses that, in Argentina, workers can barely afford the meat they produce, but are, nonetheless, bombarded by ads for frivolous products. Stam further explores the role of music in the sequence: 'The vapid accompanying music by the Swingle Singers (Bach grotesquely metamorphosed into Ray Conniff) counterpoints the brutality of the images, while underlining the shallowly plastic good cheer of the ads' (Stam 1990: 209).

The film's second section, 'Ceremony for Liberation: Notes, Testimonies, and Debates on Recent Struggles for the Liberation of the Argentine People', is considerably less radical in its narrative structure. Comprised primarily of found footage and interviews, it offsets aerial shots of the masses celebrating the victory of Perón with fragments of an Eva Perón speech articulating the new regime's solidarity with workers. Images of the funeral of Eva Perón are followed by an interview with the ex-president, who stresses that he should have been more proactive in employing violence against his opponents.

A great deal of the section consists of oral history, inasmuch as unofficial stories are effaced from official histories. Early on, it presents an image of the smokestacks of a factory while a voiceover argues that Perón had not been definitively defeated. We later see union leaders discussing the arrests and forced exile of activists, and asserting that the peronist movement survived, despite the death of its political party, through clandestine meetings, including in jail cells. The simulated discussions are often set in informal contexts; in one case, activists debate in the foreground while workers play pool in the background. The former activists recall that, in the wake of Perón's exile, there were hundreds of disturbances and conflicts between labourers and the police.

Figure 5.2. Factory takeover. Screen capture from *The Hour of the Furnaces* (1968), Grupo Cine Liberación.

'Ceremony for Liberation' proceeds to examine the wave of factory takeovers of the mid 1960s. Former occupants of a textile factory describe the defence strategies they employed, recalling that they were prepared to blow up the plant should the police invade. Workers stress how their own illiteracy forced them from the provinces to the capital and foreground the empowering nature of the factory occupations. In a like manner, factory women recall such takeovers fondly, arguing that they became 'owners' of the factory, needing to at once produce and manage. A voiceover asserts that through the possession of work, the labourers gained possession of their own humanity.[1]

The Reception of *The Hour of the Furnaces*: The Argentine Context

In an 18 December 1968 memorandum banning the release of *The Hour of the Furnaces* in Argentina, Dr Ramiro de Lafuente, general director of the Argentine National Film Institute, describes the film as a 'highly effective piece of

Communist propaganda with a high potential for penetration in all public sectors' (author's translation). Nowhere in the memorandum are there any overt references to peronism or labour. Nonetheless, this context is implicitly present by virtue of the film's ability to penetrate 'all sectors' and by the regime's extreme fears of the rise of peronism or the return of the former leader.

The initial reactions in Buenos Aires to the tremendous success of *The Hour of the Furnaces* downplayed or ignored altogether the problematics of labour that the film presents. In August 1968, an anonymously authored articled published in *Análisis* (Buenos Aires) in the wake of the film's triumph at the Fourth Pesaro International Film Festival of New Cinema emphasizes the film's deconstruction of neocolonialism, but modulates its call to violence ('Después de Pesaro – Solanas: la vuelta al hogar' 1968: 34). Although it skirts the main issues put forth in the film, it describes *The Hour of the Furnaces* as 'an open, inconclusive film that did not depend upon any traditional scheme by virtue of its production as well as its creative method' (ibid.: 34) (author's translation).

A second article, published in *Dinamis* (Buenos Aires) in December 1968, looks back at the film's success, not only in Pesaro, but also in Karlovy Vary, Mérida (Venezuela) and Mannheim. It stresses the fact that, despite the critical admiration the film has seen internationally, Argentina must be content with being the theme and image of the film, with 'no apparent possibility to live the experience of seeing itself reflected in such an audacious form' ('Cine politico sin concesiones': 74) (author's translation). This insightful article makes a couched reference to the importance of labour in the film by explaining that *The Hour of the Furnaces* examined the ten years of the Perón regime and the bursting out of the working class into the Argentine political process. It further describes the film's examination of the 'decade of violence' (1955–1966) and its depiction of the struggle of the working class during this period.

When the film began to circulate at clandestine venues in Buenos Aires, reports on discussions were kept well under rap. Solanas and Getino had envisioned that each projection and discussion would be completely different, and would conform to the specific context. Thus, the entire film was rarely shown in Argentina. Despite a dearth of documentation regarding such screenings, Gilberto Gómez Ocampo has shed light on similar phenomena throughout Latin America in the 1970s, and has described the creation of alternative screening space, especially *cine clubes*. He argues that these initial sessions were political in nature and aimed at showcasing the virtues of communism and even helping recruit supporters (Ocampo 1997: 182). Although Solanas refrained from overtly discussing screenings in Argentina, he referenced the impact of screenings abroad, specifically one at the National Cinémathèque in Venezuela, where the audience left 'demonstrating and singing the Internationale' (Volpi et al. 2010: 24). Similarly, in 'Towards a Third Cinema', Solanas and Getino spoke of student-raised barricades along Montevideo's Avenida 18 de Julio following a projection of the film (ibid.: 46).

Ten months prior to the Buenos Aires release of *The Hour of the Furnaces,* an article in *Clarín* described the work as the most important political film made in Latin America. It contextualizes it among the works of those filmmakers in Bolivia, Mexico, Uruguay, Cuba, Chile and Argentina, who went against the grain of all cinematic infrastructure to both witness and participate in reality. Quoting Solanas, who categorizes his work as a film of the masses rather than one of mass distribution, the article describes the initial showings of *The Hour of the Furnaces* in union halls, schools and universities, and how it constituted 'an attempt to render a *tabula rasa* the taboos of production and distribution of the cinema industry' ('Una película puesta al servicio de una ideología' 1973: 7) (author's translation). The article stresses that through these alternative distribution circuits, the film could reach five hundred or one thousand people who would, in turn, mobilize the rest. It posits that the international acclaim the work received in Pesaro provided it with a sort of 'protection' at a time when Argentina had the least (to date) degree of freedom of expression. Viewing *The Hour of the Furnaces* as 'the most important ideological diffusion that peronism had had' (author's translation), the article stresses that *The Hour of the Furnaces* had been seen by forty million viewers in thirty-two countries and by 140,000 Argentines (ibid.: 7). The positioning of the review on the entertainment page of *Clarín* is not without irony. It is flanked on the left by an ad for Leo Fleader's *Titanes en el ring (Titans of the Ring)* (1973)[2] and on the right by an ad for *The Godfather* (Coppola 1972). Below it, on the left, is an ad for the latest James Bond film, *Diamonds are Forever* (Hamilton 1971). In stark contrast, on the bottom right, is an ad for a release of the latest complete copy of *The Battle of Algiers* (Pontecorvo 1966). The latter is described as a 'unique film, an ode to liberty' (ibid.: 7). One notes that this article fails to provide any information as to an eventual Argentina release of *The Hour of the Furnaces*. Perón would only return to power on 12 October 1973, and the film would be released slightly over two weeks later, on 1 November.

International Critical Reception

Firstly, let us begin with a surprising, and perhaps, structuring absence. Although one might have expected the film to travel to the Soviet Union, there is no evidence thereof. Research at the Mosfilm archives has produced no references to Soviet or Russian screenings of the film. The fact that its title, *The Hour of the Furnaces,* has been translated into Russian as either *Chas pechyei* ('The Hour of the Stoves') or *Chas ornyei* ('The Hour of the Fires') (Vyetrova 2010) suggests that there was most likely no officially authorized print in the Soviet Union. Had there actually have been a screening, the film's title would most likely have been given a single Russian translation. Moreover, had Solanas authorized Part I, which lacks explicit reference to the call for violent revolution, to be released in the Soviet Union, as he had done for commercial release in the United States, it is likely that there would have been nothing controversial to the Soviet government. Thus, the lack of evidence for the release of *The Hour of the Furnaces* in the Soviet Union is most surprising, and suggests that the work was of much greater consequence to progressives in Europe and the United States.

In contrast to journalistic pieces published in Argentina at the time of the film's initial appearance in festivals, the Peruvian press engaged more directly with the topic of labour. An interview with Solanas made during the festival of Latin American documentary film held in Mérida, Venezuela, and published in the Lima-based *Hablemos de Cine,* discusses at length the making and political agenda of *The Hour of the Furnaces.* Exploring the gains of peronism, Solanas unravels British colonialism in Argentina, devoting special attention to the complete lack of rights for workers, *campesinos,* and the proletariat at large (González Norris 1969: 9). Equating peronism with the working class, he argues that, during the mid-fifties to mid-sixties, labour unions filled the gap left by the lack of a political party (ibid.: 10). Solanas further highlights the importance of factory takeovers: 'In Argentina in 64, 11,000 factories were taken over with bosses being taken as hostage, a movement in which two and a half million workers took place' (ibid.: 10). The interview is followed by a boxed, bold-faced dedication to the workers, *campesinos,* militants, revolutionaries, intellectuals and popular union organizations that took part in the making of *The Hour of the Furnaces.* Solanas was free to draw the equation between the working class and peronism in the Peruvian interview, a parallel that would have been squelched in contemporaneous Argentina. Overt references to labour and unions would have been inflammatory for a regime fearful of the return of Perón. The growth of the left during the late 1960s eventually turned this fear into reality and provided a context in which *The Hour of the Furnaces* could enjoy a theatrical release.

Two screenings of *The Hour of the Furnace* in New York City, separated by some forty years, attest to a rather superficial appropriation of the film. When Part I of *The Hour of the Furnaces* was released theatrically on 25 February 1971, *The New York Times* ran a fairly uninsightful review in which Vincent Canby describes the film as a 'vivid, angry, indoctrination lesson' and foregrounds how it depicts the 'balkanization' of Latin America that resulted from U.S. and British economic interests. On 4 April 2010, a screening held at 16 Beaver, a New York City art space dedicated to artistic, cultural, economic and political projects, attempted to recreate the original clandestine Argentine projections, questioning 'what does a film from 1968 mean to us in 2000?', and, more broadly, 'what is the function of a political film, a revolutionary cinema, in our contemporary cultural landscape?' A zine/reader compiled by DocTruck and Red Channels and distributed to participants contained appropriate writings by José Martí and Che Guevara; interviews with Solanas; the transcript of a discussion between Godard and Solanas; an essay from the *Cahiers du Cinéma*; the original *New York Times* review upon its U.S. commercial release and a text of 'Towards a Third Cinema'. The invitation to the event, nonetheless, was far less politically engaged and referenced the ecologically friendly health foods that participants should bring to the all-day event. The invitation, moreover, was cautionary in nature, reminding us that *The Hour of the Furnaces* 'has also become a relic of a long-since-passed *Zeitgeist*. The danger comes from the potential of presenting a memorial service; that the ceremonial structure of such an event will be an acting out, an anachronism' (16). Following the screening, a discussion of the event by Colin Beckett published in the online magazine *Red Current* described it as 'politics as a fetish ... underpinned by the desire for films about which we can say interesting things rather than the desire to make the world more humane'. Beckett expressed his doubt that viewers can continue to find social meaning in their passion for films and stresses his confidence that such debate is 'no longer useful for doing so'.

From a much more politicized perspective, Zuzana Pick describes two opportunities on which she was able to view *The Hour of the Furnaces*, one in

Montréal in the spring of 1971 and the other in London in the winter of 1977. Pick assesses the collective experiences, implicitly contrasting them with the early screenings of the film in Argentine union halls, intellectual circles, etc. She explains that the London screening was attended by mostly Argentines and Latin Americans, who 'during the breaks, debated the ideological value of the film's position on peronism, one year after the military coup in Argentina' (Pick 1993: 207).

The British viewing was undertaken from a highly Latin American perspective, and thus spoke to Argentines some seven years subsequent to the film's original release. Despite the time lag, with regards to labour, the same common denominators were present, the atrocities committed by the military regime of the mid-seventies against workers and unions being the most salient. The Latin American spectators in London, however, viewed the film from a perspective not foreseen by the original audiences of *The Hour of the Furnaces*. In the new context, the need to argue for the return of peronism had been replaced by the necessity to reassess, in retrospect, the outcomes thereof, changes in Juan Perón's political stance and events leading to the military coup.

As stated previously, the reception of *The Hour of the Furnaces* in the Francophone world has been especially insightful. Regarding the March 1971 Montréal screening referenced by Pick, it essential to contextualize the event in terms of the labour and independence movements in Québec, which William D. Coleman views to be interrelated. Coleman stresses that factory layoffs and closures caused Québeckers to feel a lack of control over their own economy. Tensions mounted, and in October 1970, two cells of the Front de Libération du Québec kidnapped the British Trade Commissioner James Cross and the Province's Minister of Labour Pierre Laporte, who was subsequently assassinated. The Canadian government imposed martial law, and the events became known as the 'October Crisis'. The screening took place some five months later. Pick explains:

> Although no provisions were made for discussion, the breaks between each section gave rise to all kinds of debates. In Montréal, the denunciation of neo-colonialism, the first part of The Hour of the Furnaces, elucidated debates on the status of Québec in view of the events of October of 1970 and the suspension of human rights by the government of Canada. (Pick 1993: 207)

An anonymous article covering the event and published in *Relations* briefly alludes to the original Argentine context, yet quickly transits to what the film means for Québec, as suggested by its title, 'Un Film plus québecois que bien d'autres' (A Film More Québecois than Many Others). Montréal and Buenos Aires are compared inasmuch as, at that time, not only were they home to half of the population of the respective nations, but moreover, they were 'true epicentres of neo-colonialist politics' ('Un Film plus québecois que bien d'autres' 1971: 90) (author's translation). Nonetheless, the article stresses that one should not stop at interesting comparisons, but rather, must take the final moments of the film to heart and 'add our own pieces to the dossier and find a Québecois path to our own liberation' (ibid.: 90) (author's translation). Among the concrete steps that must be taken, the article identifies: 1) the recoupment of collective memories of such events as important strikes and social conflicts, given that these usually differ greatly from official accounts, and 2) the affirmation that that socioeconomic liberation, which ultimately will confront unemployment, regional disparities and language issues, must go hand in hand with national liberation.

In 1982, the French journals *CinémAction* and *Tricontinental* jointly published a 222-page special issue entitled *Le Tiers Monde en films*. The second section of the collection features brief commentaries on two hundred films from thirty countries. The Argentine entry, authored by Paulo Antonio Paranagua, focuses primarily on *The Hour of the Furnaces*. Paranagua foregrounds the dynamics of mass struggle as presented in the film and explores the role of organized labour in mobilization. He describes the left wing of the peronist movement as 'strongly influenced by the Cuban revolution and radicalized by the rich trajectory of the Argentine workers' movement' (Paranagua 1982: 99) (author's translation). Paranagua stresses that, even in 1982, the narrative of mass factory takeovers as narrated by female textile workers is 'striking and full of suggestion' (ibid.: 99) (author's translation). He further states that it is understandable how such events terrified the Argentine bourgeoisie and military, eventually leading to the repressive events of the subsequent dictatorship.

Paranagua's essay echoes back to a mutual interview between Solanas and Jean-Luc Godard recorded in Paris in 1969 by the Third World Cinema group. In 'Godard by Solanas! Solanas by Godard!', the French director stresses his profound respect for the Argentine filmmaker and his radical work, and draws parallels between the events depicted in *The Hour of the Furnaces* and the events of May '68. He foregrounds the necessity to give voice to workers and to express what 80 per cent of the French population wants to say. He argues, 'This is why I do not want to make films with film people but with the people who constitute the great majority of humanity' (Third World Cinema Group 1969). He discusses his intent to make a short film entitled *The Strike,* in which a woman, from her home, relates the events of a strike and explores the relationship between work and sex. 'When you work 10 hours a day, intellectual or manual work, you can't make love', Godard argues. He articulates his intent to make the film with a small television camera, without having to depend on a laboratory, etc. The film would be made in one place; 'The work will be in the dialogue' (ibid.). Godard's plan was to disseminate the film at neighbourhood cafés and in industrial areas. One notes through this interview how quickly Godard transits from the Argentine context of *The Hour of the Furnaces* to the labour struggles of contemporaneous France.

Transformation through Film

Later in 1969, the Dziga Vertov Group, comprised primarily of Godard and Jean-Pierre Gorin, reconceived the planned film, *The Strike,* into one of the primary narrative threads of *Le vent d'est* (*Wind from the East*) (Godard 1970), a structurally complex work. The film opens on an eight-minute static shot of man and a woman lying in a meadow with their hands chained. The woman is clad in a white petticoat suggestive of the nineteenth-century French bourgeoisie. In a voiceover, two women recall, from the perspective of the factory management, a strike at the Alcoa Company near Dodge City, Kansas, recalling that the union representative essentially sold the workers out to management. This sequence is but one in which the women's voices relate incidences of maltreatment of workers by the bourgeoisie. *Wind from the East* subsequently details a letter written by Suzanne Monet to *Le Figaro,* which argued that striking workers in the Gare Saint Lazarre were interfering with her husband's ability to paint. As Julia Lesage (1974) has pointed out, this discussion is juxtaposed with images of a woman in a pink dress holding a parasol and a man, purportedly a union official, clad in a black jacket, the pair appearing as figures in a Monet painting. Throughout the film, moreover, spoken references to striking workers are juxtaposed with images of cavalrymen, a device which references the exploitative spaghetti westerns Godard abhorred.

Wind from the East is far more hermetic and challenging than *The Hour of the Furnaces*. As Lesage has argued, 'In practice, Godard and Gorin, who owned copies of their films, were accessible to French radicals to whom they liked to show and "discuter" their work on a high political level' (Lesage 1973). She recalls that Godard felt that only one or two companions would actually view the films of the Dziga Vertov Group. Lesage asserts that the filmmakers were rejected by the French, British and U.S. left for their intellectualism. In 1972, Godard and Gorin brought forth similar concerns in a more accessible, yet highly Brechtian manner in *Tout va bien* (Godard 1972). The film stars Jane Fonda and Yves Montand as an U.S. journalist and her French husband, a filmmaker, who become entangled in a workers' seizure of a sausage factory. This theme was further explored in France by Marin Karmitz's *Blow for Blow* (1972), a fiction film focusing on the takeover of a textile factory, of which the cast consists of both actors and actual workers. Godard and Gorin, nonetheless, rejected Karmitz's film because of its bourgeois form and lack of political analysis (ibid.). In contrast, Dominique Dubosc acknowledges the support of Godard in *The LIP Conflict* (1973–74), a documentary focusing on striking workers who overthrow a watch factory in the French city of Besançon. The strike sought to ameliorate working conditions rather than to seek increased compensation. This film, which returns to a discourse similar to that of *The Hour of the Furnaces*, intersecting interviews, footage of the strikes and slogans, is far less heavy-handed in its didactic mission. *The LIP Conflict*, moreover, reveals Continental solidarity with the strikers by including footage of a solidarity meeting in Eindhoven, Holland, in which Dutch workers perform a musical based on the French strike.[3]

The dynamics of labour that define *The Hour of the Furnaces* have thus been recouped transnationally in divergent contexts, but not always through the paradigms suggested by recent debates in film and transnationalism. In her discussion of transnational cinema, Nataša Ďurovičová causes us to reflect upon a translation theory known as 'functional equivalent translation', which draws upon language translation to describe how a text can be moved in its entirety from one context to another. Such a process has as its goal the effacement of all evidence of both the site of production and of the translation process, and provides, as Ďurovičová asserts, a 'reassuring for-me-ness'

(Ďurovičová 2010: 112). Ďurovičová implies that the ramifications of functional equivalent translation can well be extended to cultural and political processes. The New York City screening at 16 Beaver appears largely reflective of this; the U.S. audience found more relish in the natural foods they brought to the screening rather than in the harsh realities of fifties/sixties Argentina. They appropriated the film to their own privileged time and space, dismissing the possibility of a true political film today. In contrast, reception in both Québec and France revealed quite another phenomenon, which, as stated early on in this essay, can be described as a functional mediating cultural translation, one that allows for partial understanding of the original context coupled with an expanded meaning. The exploration of work in a national context relatively unknown to France or Québec was obviously understood in its general terms. Yet audiences and filmmakers deployed the labour dynamics of *The Hour of the Furnaces* to undertake a probing analysis of labour in their own national settings. The film thus crossed borders and was remoulded, re-forged to align with the social and political arenas that followed May '68.

Notes

The author graciously acknowledges the research assistance of Tamara Amirkhanova and Aliy Berzegov in the preparation of this manuscript.

1. The final section of *The Hour of the Furnaces* presents few images directly related to the notion of work or organized labour. Nonetheless, it underscores the importance of violent revolution as the only viable solution to the neocolonialist plight described in the preceding sections.
2. *Titans of the Ring* is a pop-culture cult film that portrays wrestling from the circus-like perspective of Armenian wrestler Martín Karadagian.
3. The Dutch performance recalls the spirit of the pageant presented at Madison Square Garden in New York City by the striking workers of the Paterson, New Jersey silk strike in 1913.

References

16 Beaver. 2010. 'Resurrecting a Revolutionary Cinema: *The Hour of the Furnaces*'. Retrieved 12 November 2012 from http://www.16beavergroup.org/monday/archives/003083.php.

Andrade, O. 1928. 'Manifesto antropófago', *Revista de Antropologia* I: 3-7.
Armes, R. 1987. *Third World Film Making and the West*. Berkeley: University of California Press.
Barnard, T. 1996. 'La hora de los hornos', in T. Barnard and P. Rist (eds), *South American Cinema: A Critical Filmography 1915-1994*. New York: Garland, pp. 44-50.
Beckett, C. 2010. 'Overcoming Silence: Some Thoughts following *The Hour of the Furnaces*', *Red Channels* 9. Retrieved 4 December 2011 from http://redchannels.org/writings/RC003/RC003_furnaces.html.
Canby, V. 1971. '*La hora de los hornos*: Argentine Epic', *The New York Times*, 26 February. Retrieved 12 December 2011 from http://movies.nytimes.com/movie/review?res=9906E0DB1530E73BBC4E51DFB466838A669EDE.
'Cine politico sin concesiones'. 1968. *Dinamis* 3: 74-75.
Coleman, W. 1984. *The Independence Movement in Quebec, 1945-1980*. Toronto: University of Toronto Press.
De Lafuente, R. 1969. 'República Argentina, Instituto Nacional de Cinematografía: Memorándum N. 15/127', Buenos Aires, 21 April.
'Después de Pesaro – Solanas: la vuelta al hogar'. 1968. *Análisis* 386: 34-35.
DocTruck 006/Red Channels 001. 2010. 'Resurrecting a Revolutionary Cinema: *The Hour of the Furnaces*'. New York: DocTruck.
Ďurovičová, N. 2010. 'Vector, Flow, Zone: Towards a History of Cinematic Translatio', in N. Ďurovičová and K. Newman, *World Cinemas, Translational Perspectives*. New York and London: Routledge, pp. 90-120.
Estevam, C. 1982. 'For a Popular Revolutionary Art', in R. Johnson and R. Stam (eds), *Brazilian Cinema*. Austin: University of Texas Press, pp. 58-63.
Gómez Ocampo, G. 1997. 'The Persistence of Vision: Going to the Movies in Colombia', in A. Stock (ed.), *Framing Latin American Cinema: Contemporary Perspectives*. Minneapolis: University of Minnesota Press, pp. 174-85.
González Norris, A. 1969. 'La violencia y la liberación: entrevista con Fernando Solanas', Lima: Hablemos de Cine.
Lesage, J. 1973. 'Godard-Gorin's *Wind from the East*: Looking at a Film Pollitically', *Jump Cut* 4. Retrieved 20 November 2012 from http://www.ejumpcut.org/archive/onlinessays/JC04folder/WindfromEast.html.
Little, W. 1988. 'La organización obrera y el estado peronista, 1943-55', in J.C. Torre (ed.), *La formación del sidnicato peronista*. Buenos Aires: Legasa.
Murillo, M.V. 2001. *Labor Unions, Parisan Coalitions, and Market Reform in Latin America*. Cambridge: Cambridge University Press.
Paranagua, P.A. 1982. 'Argentine', in G. Hennebelle and J. Euvrard (eds), *Le Tiers Monde en films*. Paris: François Maspero, pp. 97-99.
Pick, Z. 1993. *The New Latin American Cinema: A Continental Project*. Austin: University of Texas Press.
'Protesta la embajada argentina por la exhibición de un film en Cannes'. 1969. Buenos Aires: *La Razón*, 16 May.

Rocha, G. 1967. 'The Tricontinental Filmmaerk: That Is Called Dawn', in R. Johnson and R. Stam (eds), *Brazilian Cinema*. Austin: University of Texas Press, pp. 76–80.

Shohat, E. and R. Stam. 1994. *Unthinking Eurocentrism*. New York and London: Routledge.

Solanas, F. and O. Getino. 2010. 'Towards a Third Cinema', in DocTruck 006/Red Channels 001, *Resurrecting a Revolutionary Cinema*: The Hour of the Furnaces. New York: DocTruck, pp. 36–57.

Stam, R. 1990. '*The Hour of the Furnaces* and the Two Avant-Gardes', in J. Burton (ed.), *The Social Documentary in Latin America*. Pittsburgh, PA: University of Pittsburgh Press, pp. 251–66.

Third World Cinema Group. 1969. 'Godard by Solanas! Solanas by Godard!', *CineFiles*. University of California, Berkeley Art Museum and Pacific Film Archives. Retrieved 22 October 2012 from http://www.mip.berkeley.edu/cinefiles/DocDetail?docId=11299.

Torre, J.C. 1998. 'The Ambivalent Giant: The Peronist Labor Movement, 1945–1995', in J.P. Brennan (ed.), *Peronism and Argentina*. Wilmington, DE: Scholarly Resources, pp. 125–37.

'Un Film plus québecois que bien d'autres 1971'. 1971. *Relations* March: 90

'Una película puesta al servicio de una ideología'. 1973. Buenos Aires: *Clarín*, 11 Enero: 3.

Volpi, G., et al. 2010. 'Cinema as a Gun: An Interview with Fernando Solanas', in DocTruck 006/Red Channels 001, *Resurrecting a Revolutionary Cinema*: The Hour of the Furnaces. New York: DocTruck, pp. 18–29, 36–57.

Vyetrova, T.N. 2010. *Kinematogfraf Latinskoi Amyeriki. Vyersha svoyu sud'by*. Moscow: Kanon+.

Williams, B. 2012. 'Simultaneous History: *Translatio* and Memory in Paulo César Saraceni's *The Challenge*', European Network of Cinema and Media Studies, June 2012. Lisbon (unpublished).

Filmography

Battle of Algiers (*La battaglia di Algeri*). 1966. Gillo Pontecorvo.
Blow for Blow (*Coup pour coup*). 1972. Marin Karmitz.
The Challenge (*O desafio*). 1965. Paulo Cesar Saraceni.
Diamonds are Forever. 1971. Guy Hamilton.
The Godfather. 1972, Francis Ford Coppola.
The Hour of the Furnaces (*La hora de los hornos*). 1968. Fernando Solanas and Octavio Getino.
The LIP Conflict (*Le conflit LIP*). 1973–74. Dominique Dubosc.
Titans of the Ring (*Titanes en el ring*). 1973. Leo Fleader.
Tout va bien. 1972. Jean-Luc Godard.
Wind from the East (*Le vent d'est*). 1970. Jean-Luc Godard.

PART II
Present Activism

CHAPTER 6

Contemporary Political Cinema
The Impossibility of Passivity

William Brown

In this chapter I shall argue that *Tropa de Elite*, or *Elite Squad* (José Padilha, 2007), and *Un homme qui crie*, or *A Screaming Man* (Mahomet-Saleh Haroun, 2010), both offer a more or less explicit rejection of Gilles Deleuze's film-philosophy, in particular his notion that the time-image, a type of cinema characterized by passive 'seers' who are overwhelmed by the optical and sonic power of a situation, is a cinema better equipped for political resistance. In drawing out how and perhaps why these films do this, I shall argue that various shortcomings in Deleuze's film-philosophy impede us from understanding not just these films, but contemporary political cinema on a more general level – assuming both *Elite Squad* and *A Screaming Man* be allowed to exemplify contemporary political cinema in spite of their different styles, subject matter and production contexts. The reason for pursuing this line of argument is not simply to say that Deleuze's theory is now outmoded or wrong (for this is far from being the case). Indeed, were Deleuze entirely irrelevant, there would be no need for *Elite Squad* explicitly and *A Screaming Man* implicitly to snub Deleuze's work. The reason for pursuing this line of argument is, rather, to demonstrate how the concept of value, as elaborated in the work of Karl Marx, manifests itself in Deleuze's work. For it is Deleuze's tendency to attribute value to different films that arises as a potential shortcoming in his work on cinema. And it is value, for Marx, which lies at the core of capital, and which, broadly speaking, itself defines the system against which contemporary political cinema struggles. In using Marx to critique Deleuze, then, we can perhaps also deconstruct the concept of value in relation to cinema, thereby gaining a richer understanding of *Elite Squad* and *A Screaming Man* in particular, contemporary political cinema more widely, and perhaps also cinema as a whole.

Crossing out Deleuze: *Elite Squad*

Elite Squad is set in Rio de Janeiro in 1997, just before a visit to that city by Pope John Paul II. It has at its core three main protagonists: Captain Nascimento (Wagner Moura), a father-to-be who works for the Batalhão de Operações Policiais Especiais (Special Police Operations Battalion, or BOPE – the titular 'elite squad') and who is seeking a replacement so that he can spend more time with his family. His two would-be replacements are Neto (Caio Junqueira) and André Matias (André Ramiro). Neto and Matias have been friends since childhood, but Neto is an impulsive character, while Matias is more reflective, with aspirations not always to work for the police but also to become a lawyer.

About fifteen minutes into the film, Matias and fellow students Maria (Fernanda Machado), Roberta (Fernanda de Freitas) and Edu (Paulo Vilela) form a group in their sociology class in order to discuss one of a list of works by various different philosophers and thinkers. On the blackboard in the classroom we see written the names of Sigmund Freud, Claude Lévi-Strauss, Gilberto Freyre, Adam Smith, Max Weber, Emile Durkheim, Friedrich Nietzsche, Michel Foucault, Karl Marx and Gilles Deleuze. As different groups claim the different thinkers that they want to discuss, we see the teacher, Professor Gusmão (Bernardo Jablonski), draw a line through various of the names to indicate that they have been chosen. We see three names and the partial titles of an associated work being crossed through. These include Nietzsche (whose *Genealogy of Morals* is the work to be discussed), Deleuze (one of the volumes, unspecified, of *Capitalism and Schizophrenia*; co-author Félix Guattari's name does not feature in the frame) and Foucault (*Discipline and Punish*).

Although it is *Discipline and Punish* that Maria, Roberta, Edu and Matias will study, it is interesting that the filmmaker also gives over screen time to show Nietzsche's and, in particular, Deleuze's names being effaced (with the erasure of Foucault's name perhaps being justified by the fact that our student protagonists will study him). The scene as a whole is of some narrative importance: it allows Matias to meet Maria, with whom he will briefly have a relationship, as well as Edu, who deals drugs to his fellow students. As we shall see, Maria also works for a charity that helps to educate children in Rio de Janeiro's slum dwellings, or *favelas,* and it is to the Prazeres favela that Edu goes to buy drugs from local gang boss Baiano (Fábio Lago). The connections that both of these characters have with the favelas, in particular Prazeres, will ultimately feed into Matias' work as a policemen, both for the 'regular' police force and, subsequently, for the BOPE, which is charged with ending the drug trade in Prazeres before the Pope's visit.

However, while the scene is important for establishing these links between the characters, the rest of its content is narratively superfluous. Indeed, as a law student Matias need not be in a sociology class, and he could have met Maria and Edu under other circumstances. More particularly, there is no narrative need to include shots of Nietzsche and Deleuze's names being effaced on/from the blackboard – and yet these shots are included in the film, and it is the crossing through of Deleuze's name that I would like in particular to explore here. For the inclusion of the effacement of Deleuze's name seems a deliberate and meaningful gesture, not just diegetically by Professor Gusmão, but also by the film.

Gilles Deleuze: A Film-Philosophy in Two Parts

Over the course of his two volumes on cinema, Deleuze offers up a 'taxonomy' of image types. As per the titles of the volumes, Deleuze sees cinema as being divided – albeit with overlaps – into two major categories: the movement-image and the time-image. In *Cinema 1: The Movement-Image* (1986), Deleuze explores the way in which cinema is defined first and foremost by bodies in movement, or by action. In broad terms, Deleuze sees movement-image cinema as being defined by perception-images, affection-images and action-images. A perception-image roughly corresponds to a point of view shot, even if not literally so: characters identify an object with which they can interact, or a situation that they can modify. This is then followed by an affection-image, or what we might equate to a reaction shot: we see how the character is affected by what they see, and how they move from affection towards carrying out action (via what are referred to as impulse images). This is then followed by action-images: characters performing actions that in turn modify the original object or situation shown in the perception-image.

What Deleuze is describing in his own terms, then, is narrative cinema: it is a cinema in which people do things. While movement-image/narrative cinema is comprised of various different shot types (perception-, affection-, impulse and action-images), this more generally leads to overall arcs of action that are themselves defined by the large and small form of the action-image. In the large form of the action-image, a character identifies a situation (S), then acts (A), and the result is a modified situation (S'). Meanwhile, in the small form of the action-image, a character acts (A), a new situation arises (S), and this in turn changes them (A').

At the end of *Cinema 1,* Deleuze identifies that there is a 'crisis' in the action-image, which will in turn lead towards Deleuze defining a new type of cinema that he elaborates upon more fully in his second tome, *Cinema 2: The Time-Image* (2005). Here, Deleuze identifies various kinds of time-image, but all of which take as their root the crisis of the action-image identified in *Cinema 1*. I do not have space to rehearse his argument in detail, but Deleuze suggests that a crisis in the action-image is brought about for a variety of reasons, the two foremost being the twin horrors of the Holocaust and Hiroshima. The reason why these events are particularly important for identifying a crisis in the action-image is because they challenge the centrality of humanity in the universe and, subsequently, in cinema. The reason for this might conveniently be put in the following fashion. Modernity had perhaps been defined by man taming and coming to dominate nature. This process is writ large in movement-image cinema, and in particular in the classical western, through the defining myth of man's excursion into and civilisation of the wilderness, which is given anthropomorphic form in both the Native American and in the outlaw. After the horrors of the Second World War, however, humanity must acknowledge the essential destruction, rather than the institution of order, involved in the process of modernity, since the world has therein witnessed millions of lives being lost in concentration camps and hundreds of thousands of lives being lost in a single flash of atomic light. Rather than a cinema populated by heroic individuals who tame nature via the SAS' process described above, we have instead characters who are overwhelmed by their situation and who are powerless to change it. This Deleuze sees as the founding principle of Italian neorealist cinema, but it is also worked through in other cinemas, in particular the European new waves of the late 1950s, the 1960s and onwards. Here, the rejection of linear narrative, the confusion of dream and waking states, and the ambiguity and lack of narrative closure respectively reflect a rejection of the anthropocentrism involved in dominating nature, an inability to know what is real after the nightmare of the Second World War, and an understanding that there are forces in the world that are far bigger and more powerful than we are. In short, they ask whether we can or should really achieve mastery/domination, and can we really be sure of what we know?

It is important for this chapter that we acknowledge the way in which Deleuze includes, as part of his analysis of the time-image, something that he terms 'modern political cinema'. This is for at least two reasons. Firstly, it is through the concept of modern political cinema that Deleuze offers his most sustained analysis of non-Western films, including films from Brazil (the work of Glauber Rocha) and from Africa (Ousmane Sembène's films in particular). That is, Deleuze's treatment of modern political cinema potentially speaks most closely to the films under scrutiny in this chapter, namely *Elite Squad* and *A Screaming Man*. And secondly, it is important because Deleuze elides modern political cinema with his concept of the minor, as elaborated in his work on Kafka with Félix Guattari (Deleuze and Guattari 1986). Modern political, or minor, cinema is a time-image cinema because, by and large, it is a cinema that challenges the Eurocentric mythology of the movement-image as civilisation and the imposition of a majority order. Eurocentrism, which is not a term that Deleuze employs, here stands for the belief that all history emanates from or is caused by the developed world, in particular North America and Europe. Minor cinema is political because, in effect, it reveals the mythology of the classical western as a genre to be ideologically Western. And it is a time-image because it shows a temporality that differs from the mainstream Western norm.

Minor cinema does this through various techniques, especially through editing patterns, or how shots of different focal length and duration are assembled, and through *mises en scène* that little resemble Hollywood cinema. In other words, minor cinema has a different time/temporality/tempo/rhythm to Hollywood cinema. What is more, minor cinema often uses 'intercessors' – figures who intercede into the narratives of these films, thereby disrupting our ability to see them as the work of a single author (which would be a Western model of understanding cinematic authorship), meaning that instead we must recognize them as 'collective enunciations'. Furthermore, these intercessors *fabulate*; that is, they tell stories, the truth-status of which is ambiguous. In other words, as other time-image films mix the oneiric with the waking, these films mix fiction and documentary such that we cannot tell them apart. They do not purvey official truths, nor directly do they oppose the official truths, narratives or histories told about a particular people. Instead they demand that we do not automatically accept as true what we are being told, and that we instead think for ourselves (see Deleuze 2005: 196–215). In this sense, minor cinema achieves in its own way what Italian neorealism achieves regarding the crisis of the action-image; as the characters of Italian neorealism can no longer boldly step forward into the world and modify it according to their own ambitions and desires, instead being incapable of action as they are overwhelmed by the situations in which they find themselves, so, too, do the characters and intercessors of minor cinema challenge dominant myths (the ideological equivalent of believing unthinkingly in one's own righteousness and modifying the world), instead encouraging us to stop and think about matters for ourselves.

Deleuze's Hierarchy of Images?

A charge commonly levelled against Deleuze is that his work on cinema is Eurocentric (see, for example, Martin-Jones 2006; 2011). The charge is valid, but one can also defend Deleuze from a variety of perspectives. Firstly, in addition to discussing the work of Rocha and Sembène, Deleuze does in the course of his two books make mention of and analyse films by a variety of other filmmakers from around the world, including Yasujiro Ozu, Yilmaz Güney, Youssef Chahine and Lino Brocka. 'Simply exceptions that prove the rule,' one might say, but this then leads to a second defence: surely Deleuze could only discuss the films that he had seen, and while he may indeed be Eurocentric in his tastes, this arguably only reflects the Eurocentrism inherent in Parisian film distribution and exhibition during Deleuze's lifetime. In other words, one cannot but be a product of one's environment, and so a European is perhaps inevitably going to be Eurocentric, but the issue is to what extent they recognize and take into account their own biases.

More forceful as an argument against Deleuze, then, is that his outlook on cinema is, to borrow a phrase from Ella Shohat and Robert Stam (1994), *unthinkingly* Eurocentric, above and beyond the films he specifically mentions and discusses. In the *Cinema* books, the history of cinema is defined almost exclusively by the United States and Europe, and that which does not conform to it stands directly in opposition to it, thereby reaffirming the former's centrality. What is more, non-Western cinema is in this process read through a Western lens, when alternative frameworks might be more useful for understanding those cinemas. In short, rather than simply fitting easily into either the movement- or time-image categories, other cinemas from around the world might in fact demand new image types – the argument essentially made by Martin-Jones in the above-cited two major works on Deleuze and cinema.

I mentioned earlier that Deleuze's take on minor cinema – implicitly if not explicitly – posits a cinema that challenges the dominant Western myths, narratives, so-called truths and histories involving the areas, regions, nations and, most pertinently, the people from which those modern political films spring. In other words, I would like to offer a further defence of Deleuze's seeming Eurocentrism; his 'modern political' and time-image frameworks may not explain those films that he places under this rubric entirely, but they do explain (from a Eurocentric perspective) how modern political/time-image cinema challenges Eurocentric myths, not least the myth that is key to the movement-image, that the white man is a powerful agent justified in his quest to bring law and civilisation to the uncivilized world, which now extends from the Wild West to Brazil, Africa, Turkey, the Philippines and further afield.

Nonetheless, even if Deleuze is perhaps less (or simply more justifiably?) Eurocentric than various of his critics have argued, I think that there is a separate problem, or shortcoming, to be discussed with Deleuze's categorization of cinema into the movement-image and the time-image, which I should like to highlight here. This is the issue of the seeming hierarchy that emerges between the movement-image and the time-image, with the time-image often perceived as being 'better' than the movement-image. This hierarchy between Deleuze's two main image types has at its core the concept of value. I shall argue that the intrusion of this concept of value into Deleuze's work in part undermines his project, and that *Elite Squad* and *A Screaming Man* in disparate ways both illustrate how this is so.

Richard Rushton suggests that there is no value-judgement regarding Deleuze's different image types; or rather, if one does emerge, 'his intention was not to do so' (Rushton 2012: 73). As much can be seen in the fact that Deleuze regards filmmakers such as Vincente Minnelli as makers of *both* movement-images and time-images. If the time-image were somehow 'better' than the movement-image, in that it induces thought and opens our eyes and ears to different temporalities that otherwise we might only see in an 'automatic' fashion, then Minnelli's films straddle and thus subvert this distinction. However, even though Minnelli does straddle both image-types, and even though Deleuze may not have wanted to draw a qualitative distinction between the image types, he nonetheless, and contrary to Rushton's reading of him, does so. This is seen most powerfully when Deleuze says that, after the so-called crisis of the action-image, Hollywood cinema becomes akin to Hitler (Deleuze 2005: 159–66). That is, movement-image cinema is not only seen in an unthinking or automatic fashion, but it is also a tool for inducing unthinking and/or automatic behaviour in people – a potential in the medium that was realized by Hitler and his propaganda machine in bringing into being the Holocaust. It is hard not to see the comparison between movement-image cinema and Hitler as a qualitative judgement, even if, as Rushton reminds us, this judgement is made within a specific historical context.

However, while this Eurocentrism may be understandable, a hierarchy of value between the image categories nonetheless seems implicitly if not explicitly to emerge in Deleuze's work. In other words, the movement-image is not inherently better than the time-image, but the movement-image becomes problematic for Deleuze after the Second World War. It is perhaps for this reason that Patricia Pisters suggests that the time-image itself is being replaced in contemporary cinema by a new type of image, the neuro-image (Pisters 2012). Without rehearsing Pisters' argument in detail, she suggests temporally what David Martin-Jones suggests spatially regarding Deleuze's work – namely that new types of image emerge if we expand our understanding of cinema beyond a particular place (Europe, the United States) and beyond a particular time (the twentieth century). If the geographical limitations of Deleuze's work makes him Eurocentric, then the temporal limitations of his work in turn make him what we might term 'nuncocentric'. From the Latin *nunc,* meaning now, Deleuze suffers from believing his own time period to be central for understanding cinema, when in fact all that he offers is a means for understanding the cinema of his time period and for understanding cinema more generally from the perspective of his time period.

But even if Deleuze's qualitative hierarchy between the movement-image and the time-image is not atemporal but has an historical context, the time-image is still reckoned by Deleuze and other Deleuzians to be 'the highest point of thought where cinema and philosophy converge' (Rodowick 1997: 207). That is, Deleuze's time-image cinema – the works mentioned in *Cinema*

2 – has become a pantheon of great films, the greatness of which is measured by their ability to make us think. In other words, value judgement creeps into Deleuze's work. Be it Eurocentric or nuncocentric, it is this value judgement that is perhaps most problematic in Deleuze's work.

Now, before turning to Marx, I should like to illustrate three recent and similar critiques of Deleuze. Jacques Rancière, John Mullarkey and I have all argued, in separate places, that the differences between the movement-image and the time-image are not as clear cut as Deleuze implies. Rancière seems simply to suggest that Deleuze's work is confusing since the difference between the two image-types is 'near indiscernible' (a charge that will perhaps curry sympathy with many of Deleuze's readers who find his often-heady prose hard to get through; see Rancière 2006: 122). Mullarkey, meanwhile, suggests that what defines the time-image is not so much any formal qualities pertaining to the image, but rather what the image does, with the time-image in effect being subversive, or 'transgressive', and thus inspiring thought, while the movement-image is conformist and can be read in an unthinking or automatic fashion (see Mullarkey 2009: 103). This means that those formal aspects that are subversive will change over time, as certain types of image become more commonly used, or clichéd, than others, and thus will be read in an unthinking and automatic fashion. I agree with Mullarkey, but I also suggest that any image could be a movement-image or a time-image, or that any image can be read 'automatically' or inspire 'thought' – depending on who is viewing the image and what sorts of image those viewers have previously seen (see Brown 2013: 135). In this sense, I would disagree with Deleuze and say that one cannot hierarchize the time-image over the movement-image since all images have the potential to be new to different spectators, and spectators also have the potential to see new things in 'old' images. In other words, one cannot place value on images, an approach which I should like to explore further now through a brief foray into Marx.

Marx and the Concept of Value

There are various ways in which Marx uses the term value, the most common being the component terms use-value, exchange-value and surplus-value. Use-value is the extent to which something is useful; exchange-value is how much something is worth, or its price; and surplus-value is what arises when labour is more productive than how much it costs. However, Marx also talks about value itself, without the component terms named above, and the meaning of value is perhaps best drawn out by comparing value to price, or exchange-value. Value, for Marx, depends entirely upon labour; an object only has value if labour has gone into it, with use-value being the usefulness of the object and value itself being the cost of the labour. Anything, meanwhile, can have a price or exchange-value. As such, Marx is happy to discuss 'the price of uncultivated land, which is without value, because no human labour has been incorporated into it' (Marx 1999: 63). Marx also teases out this distinction between value and price when he says: 'The name of a thing is something distinct from the qualities of that thing. I know nothing of a man, by knowing his name is Jacob. In the same way with regard to money, every trace of a value-relation disappears in the names pound, dollar, franc, ducat, etc.' (ibid.: 62). Here Marx says that price (however many pounds, dollars, francs or ducats an object is worth) is not only distinct from value, but that it in fact occults value (value 'disappears'). This occultation is in certain respects crucial; for if value is not the same as price, value is nonetheless the concept that allows price to come into being. That is, value is the ground upon which hierarchies of exchange-value are founded. Value is a concept that is intimately linked to the creation of hierarchies as a whole, with hierarchies perhaps understood as systems of value, which can be measured by any criterion and not just price, commercial worth or exchange-value.

Now, it is a hierarchy, or a system of value, that we see emerge in Deleuze's contention that the time-image is 'better' than the movement-image (the movement-image is like Hitler; the time-image is the 'highest point of thought'). It is as if Deleuze has said that the time-image is worth more than the movement-image. That one type of image is better than the other (that it has a different 'price') is not really the issue. Indeed, we know that prices fluctuate and that in different circumstances a movement-image might be 'better' (or have a higher 'price') than a time-image – in effect Mullarkey's contention when he says that what constitutes a time-image changes over time. That the hierarchy between the two image types is historical rather than atemporal affirms as much: there was a time when the movement-image was not only the dominant type of image, but also a time when it was the 'better' of the two image types – hence Deleuze's decision to explore the movement-image in *Cinema 1*. The criterion for 'better' in Deleuze's work is not box office returns; movement-image films have always grossed more than time-image films – in the West and many other parts of the world, if not everywhere and at all times, with the movement-image having also, since soon after the birth of narrative cinema, been and continuing to be today the dominant (i.e. the most common) type of image. Instead, Deleuze's criterion is the capacity to induce thought, with the term 'minor' maybe even suggesting for Deleuze that there is an element of the non-commercial being 'better' than commercial cinema. But both sets of criteria – ability to induce thought and box office returns – are systems of value that in turn lead to hierarchies, even if very different/diametrically opposed ones.

What is important to note is that debating which image type is 'worth' more, be it according to the box office or according to a film's ability to induce thought, at any given moment in time, occults from view the system of value that enables there to be a hierarchy at all. Price, be it a price determined by box office returns or by an ability to induce thought, is simply a surface phenomenon, the fluctuations of which matter little to the underpinning system of value. Lauding the time-image over the movement-image, the movement-image over the time-image, or putting forward new types of image in a hierarchy only reaffirms the system of value that Deleuze cannot help but insert into his work, even if, according to Richard Rushton, he does not intend to.

Interestingly, value as defined here is akin to time as defined in Deleuze's work. For, if value as a system is the process of price coming into being, then value is temporal – and it is perhaps for this reason that Matteo Mandarini brings Marx and Deleuze together in his discussion of money, time and crisis (Mandarini 2006). That is, Mandarini argues that capital demands the homogenization of time so that each unit of time can take on an exchange-value, which in turn is a means of containing labour-power, since all labourers would work at the same tempo. This homogenization of labour-power itself prevents the radically new, or new temporalities, from emerging except in an always already controlled manner.

Having established how the concept of value unthinkingly sneaks in to Deleuze's work on cinema (and perhaps into his work more generally given Deleuze's unremittingly 'good taste', in that he is seemingly well versed in only the most canonical films, painters, writers and musicians), we can now turn our attention to the ways in which *Elite Squad* and *A Screaming Man* challenge this hierarchy in Deleuze – with the former snubbing Deleuze to suggest that the movement-image is every bit as meaningful as the time-image, and the latter arguably creating a time-image film that brings itself to auto-critique, as I shall explain below.

Deleuze under Erasure in *Elite Squad*

With his first child imminent, Captain Nascimento has had enough of the BOPE, but in order to leave he must choose a suitable replacement for himself. Ultimately his choice lies between Matias and Neto. Nascimento initially chooses Neto to replace him, even though Neto has a dangerous tendency to act first and to think later. This is because Neto is, simply put, quite prepared to use force in order to achieve effective results as a police officer. Neto's use of force is something that Nascimento believes Matias is lacking; as a would-be lawyer, he tends to over-think and not to act enough with force in order to prevent crime. However, Neto is killed by Baiano as he is running an errand for Matias (who is Baiano's desired target, after he discovers that Matias is a cop who has been walking around his favela with Maria and who has also told Edu to stop dealing Baiano's drugs or else he will arrest him). Given the death of his friend, Matias finally adopts Nascimento's desired hard line regarding the use of force, and he replaces Neto as Nascimento's successor. Matias' adoption of Nascimento's and the BOPE's hard line is signalled during the film's closing moment when Matias shoots Baiano in the face with a shotgun.

In Deleuzian terms, *Elite Squad* is seemingly a movement-image film. Indeed, as Nascimento manages to quit the force and as Matias manages to defeat Baiano, the film seems to be a large form (SAS') action-image film: both characters find themselves in a situation (S), in which they take action (A), and, in doing so, achieve a new or changed situation (S'). This narrative trajectory is matched by the film's aesthetics: there is much movement onscreen, while the camera also is highly mobile – flying above favelas or following characters handheld around various locations. The film is located in a specific time and place (Rio de Janeiro, 1997), and rarely if at all are viewers confused by the film's narrative.

Elite Squad's 'rejection' of Deleuze via the crossing through of his name might seem to suggest that the film knowingly and consciously sets itself up in contradistinction to his image types in general. I would suggest, however, that the film is also a more specific rejection of the time-image. In referencing Rocha, Sembène and others, Deleuze implicitly identifies modern political, or minor, cinema with the Third World: the time-image functions in this context as an oppositional gesture against the 'Hitlerism' of Hollywood, an aesthetic gesture that is precisely political, because it also implies a post-colonial and/or anti-Imperial stance against, precisely, First World influences – although minor cinema is not a perfect fit with post-colonial cinema, because Deleuze even includes as minor filmmakers U.S. cineastes like Charles Burnett.

In seeming to reject the time-image in favour of the movement-image, it is not that *Elite Squad* wishes to conform wholeheartedly with Hollywood and the political and economic dependence that it symbolizes. Rather the film seems to suggest two things. Firstly, that it can rival Hollywood productions with regard to action and style, a gesture that can be read as defiantly political, and which works beyond the 'simply oppositional' cinema of the time-image as initially conceived by Deleuze; indeed, that 'simply oppositional' cinema can be understood as an affirmation of Hollywood's centrality, as signalled by its containment within the film festival circuit. Furthermore, that cinema has moved beyond a simple Hollywood-non-Hollywood binarism can be seen in

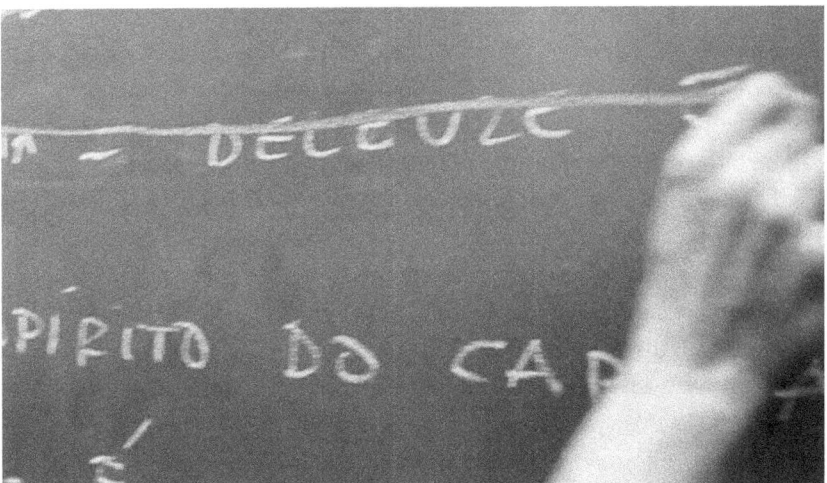

Figure 6.1. Under erasure: Deleuze's name is crossed through on a blackboard in *Elite Squad*. Screen capture from *Tropa de Elite,* or *Elite Squad* (José Padilha, Brazil/Netherlands/USA/Argentina, 2007).

recent analyses of Hollywood cinema by David Martin-Jones (2006; 2011), Patricia Pisters (2003; 2012) and myself (Brown 2013), with all three of us arguing that Hollywood produces time-image cinema or cinema that features a hybrid of movement- and time-images. *Elite Squad* suggests a similar rapprochement – but from the non-Hollywood side of the supposed binarism. Secondly, it is not so much that the movement-image is the 'new time-image' by dint of subverting expectations and inducing thought, but rather that the whole system of value that is drawn out through the Marxist critique offered here of Deleuze's film-philosophy is to be rejected. This can be seen by the way in which *Elite Squad* seems to be a movement-image film, but is only so in a qualified manner.

Roberta Gregoli (2011) has demonstrated how *Elite Squad* means different things to different audiences: some viewers have sympathy for the criminal characters in the film and find the BOPE's authoritarian violence to be unpleasant to watch, while others sympathize with the BOPE and approve its tactics of violence in combating the drug trade and criminality in the favelas. Read through the lens of classic representational theory, the left-leaning bourgeois liberal might find *Elite Squad* hard to like: the film seems happy to characterize the favelas, or slums, of Rio de Janeiro as dangerous places that are swarming with heartless criminals; Nascimento, as a figure of authority and whose voiceover narrates the film, verbally abuses and physically intimidates his wife, blaming her for Neto's death because she had suggested to him that he choose Neto as his successor over Matias (as if Nascimento did not make that choice himself); and Matias, although black and from a poor family, ultimately embraces the predominantly white, middle class values of the BOPE, which include state-backed torture and violence – and murder, as he shoots Baiano in the face with a shotgun (as an act of state-sanctioned personal revenge) rather than bringing him to justice. If the film gives voice to any social group, it is really the BOPE, not the poor of the favelas; and the film is seemingly right-wing in its condemnation of Maria and Edu for being privileged left-wing liberals who think that they can connect with the residents of the favelas via charity work and drug dealing respectively. Instead, they are just endangering themselves because in the favelas live psychopaths like Baiano, who will kill them at the drop of a hat should they step out of his line (which is what happens to Edu, with Maria only escaping when one of Baiano's men turns his back on her). In short, in spite of Gregoli's argument/observation that the film means different things to different audiences, it would seem that *Elite Squad* is a film that is more Hitler than Glauber Rocha in its politics.

Nonetheless, formally the film does have elements that we might consider more suitable to the time-image than to the movement-image. Firstly, the film's fast pace need not be simply an adoption of what David Bordwell (2006) would term the intensification of the continuity editing style, and which would therefore make the film a movement-image film. For the fast pace of the editing, together with moments of intense and suspenseful action, gives to the film an affective quality that can be understood as more transgressive than an easily understood, classical narrative film. Or, as Teresa Rizzo put it, 'by means of fast editing, rapidly alternating multiple camera angles, surround sound, explosive action produces a kind of visual, aural and bodily confusion' (Rizzo 2012: 27). Similarly, the film's multiple characters and plot strands challenge the linear development of classical narrative, and thus arguably of movement-image cinema, suggesting a society that is indeed beyond one's control and which one is struggling simply to survive, not to master, tame or civilize. In other words, rather than an SAS' structure, *Elite Squad* has more what David Martin-Jones identifies in relation to spaghetti westerns as an 'SSSSS' structure: characters never overcome their circumstances or environment, but instead must struggle to survive in the face of the relentless onslaught of obstacles that the globalized world puts in their way (see Martin-Jones 2011: 21–66).

However, where Martin-Jones deems the 'SSSSS' structure of spaghetti westerns as indicative of a new type of image, which he terms the attraction-image, for present purposes *Elite Squad*'s confusion or blend of movement-image and time-image elements not only suggests that the two are not easily separated, but it also serves, in the context of a film in which we see Deleuze's name crossed through on a blackboard, to suggest that neither is better nor worse than the other: a time-image film featuring a blend of dream and reality, long takes and intercessors, is not necessarily better than a movement-image film featuring action. By combining these two aesthetics in a film that specifically erases Deleuze's name, *Elite Squad* challenges the system of value that underwrites Deleuze's work. The ambiguous politics of the film – in that the film means different things to different audiences, as per Gregoli – would seem to affirm this. While it is perhaps most tempting as a would-be liberal European viewer to read *Elite Squad* as politically retrograde (the film endorses state violence), the film perhaps more verily demonstrates state violence without necessarily judging it in a certain way – otherwise all viewers would find it hard not to read the film in the same way. Nominally left-wing viewers might dislike the film for not condemning the violence, while nominally right-wing viewers might believe that the film endorses an appropriate response to real world issues. In both cases, however, what is being revealed is not what the film says, but what the viewers want the film to say. That is, the value system of the viewers is exposed in this process – just as this would-be liberal European's unease with the film only reveals, precisely, my own Eurocentrism and liberal assumptions. In short, then, *Elite Squad* helps to expose the value system underwriting Deleuze's work by subverting not just one type of image, but the whole system of trying to classify and hierarchically to rank all image types.

Sterile Spectators and *A Screaming Man*

A Screaming Man is ostensibly a film that conforms to Deleuze's modern political/minor cinema, as defined in *Cinema 2,* in a much more obvious fashion than does *Elite Squad.* The film tells the story of Adam (Youssouf Djaoro), a former swimming champion ('Champion' is his nickname), who now works as a pool attendant with his son, Abdel (Diouc Koma), at a luxury hotel in N'djaména, Chad. Champion's existence is disrupted, however, when the hotel that he works at is privatized. The boss, a Chinese immigrant named Mrs Wang (Li Heling), fires one of the chefs, a Cameroonian named David (Marius Yelolo), and downsizes the pool attendance team. Champion is demoted from pool attendant to barrier attendant at the hotel's entrance, with Abdel taking on the pool attendant job on his own. Repeatedly Champion tells us, at first in a voiceover that Mrs Wang and other characters may or may not hear, but then out loud to Etienne (John Mbajedoum), the man whom Champion replaces as barrier attendant, that the pool is his life.

Simultaneous to Champion's professional fall is a growing amount of violence in the country, as rebels lead uprisings against the government. Champion owes money for the war effort against the rebels to corrupt local government representative/*chef de quartier,* Ahmat (Emil Abossolo M'bo). In order to get out of the debt that through his demotion he cannot pay, Champion volunteers Abdel to join the government forces – a move that also allows him to get his old pool attendant job back. The rebel cause grows in strength and tourists abandon the hotel, replaced at first by UN soldiers as guests, and then by no one. However, when Abdel's pregnant Malian girlfriend, Djénéba (Djénéba Koné), arrives at Champion's house, Champion begins to regret his decision to send Abdel to war, and so decides to go find him. As many flee N'djaména, Champion makes his way to the barracks at Abéché, about 500 kilometres from the capital. Here Champion finds Abdel severely wounded in a field hospital. Champion puts Abdel into the sidecar of his motorbike and tries to drive him back to N'djaména. Abdel dies en route, and so Champion takes his son to the river, where he lets his body be taken by the water.

With regard to Deleuze's modern political cinema, *A Screaming Man* features 'intercessors' of a sort, particularly through Djénéba, Abdel's Malian girlfriend who is also a singer and whose song at the end of the film constitutes a kind of fabulation, as she stands for a future African people to come (Chad as a multicultural nation, made up of Chadians, Malians, Cameroonians, Chinese people and so on). Furthermore, Deleuze's time-image cinema is full of characters whom he describes as 'seers', characters whose sensory-motor links have been broken and who are incapable of action. This would seem to be the case with Champion, as he seems incapable of action in the face of the changes taking place in Chad: Champion rarely does anything in the film, and we see little from him in the form of emotional responses. Even his decision to have Abdel enrolled in the army takes place off screen. Indeed, his role as seer is made most clear when Abdel is subsequently taken by the army; at this moment, Champion is inside his house when government soldiers arrive in his courtyard and literally grab Abdel, as the latter and Champion's wife, Mariam (Hadjé Fatimé Ngouou), call for his help. Champion does nothing and instead looks through the window, which is lit in a bright white fashion such that it resembles a small cinema screen. This cinema screen effect may not only suggest that Champion is a seer, but perhaps also that Abdel's abduction is a fantasy rather than real, thereby taking us further into the time-image as we find it hard to differentiate the oneiric from the real. This mix of dream and reality is also signalled by imagery that occasionally takes on a surrealist quality, in particular the image of Champion riding his motorbike using a diving mask as a means to keep the dust from his eyes: Champion seems underwater when on dry land, a man out of place with his location and the times.

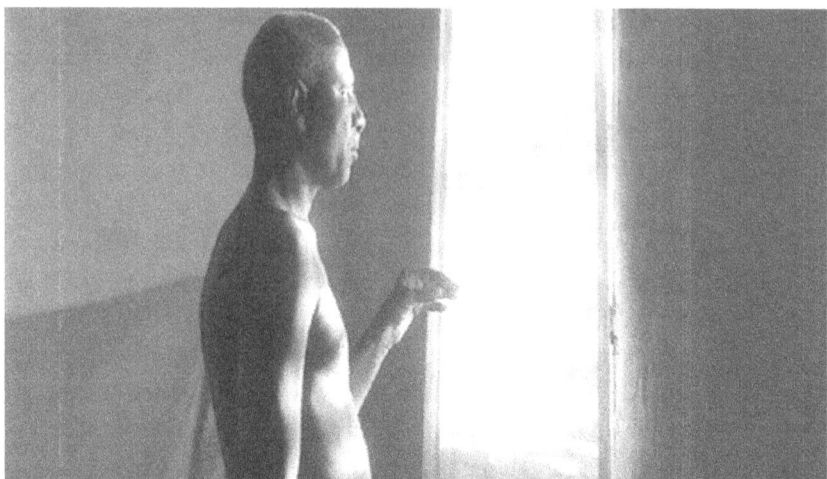

Figure 6.2. The window as cinema screen: Champion watches his son, Adam, being abducted by the army in *A Screaming Man*. Screen capture from *Un Homme qui Crie*, or *A Screaming Man* (Mahomet-Saleh Haroun, France/Belgium/Chad, 2010).

However, it is not just the rebel uprisings and the political conflict of which Champion is a seemingly helpless victim (even though he orchestrates Abdel's abduction). For Champion's demotion at work (together with the firing of David and Etienne) are explained as being the direct result of the privatization of the tourist industry, which is in turn signalled by the presence in the film of Mrs Wang. In other words, the neoliberal economics of globalization result in Champion's demotion, a process that also feeds into the rebel uprisings. Far from being the hero of an SAS' narrative, then, Champion is prey to wider forces that are entirely beyond his control. Unlike *Elite Squad,* which arguably has an SSSSS structure as Matias and Nascimento at least manage to survive in the film, Champion's world instead falls apart.

While we might think of *A Screaming Man* as a time-image film that implicitly critiques the destructive consequences of capitalism in terms of personal job security and political violence, the film has a surprising ending when, after Champion has let Abdel's body drift down the river, we hear Djénéba singing words from Aimé Césaire's *Notebook of a Return to my Native Land* (2001), which are translated in the subtitles as follows: 'Beware of assuming the sterile attitude of a spectator, for life is not a spectacle, a sea of miseries is not a proscenium, a screaming man is not a dancing bear'. Herein we have suddenly not an endorsement of the seer in the time-image, but seemingly a critique thereof, for Champion as seer has in fact failed and caused Abdel's death precisely because he assumed the 'sterile attitude of a spectator'. In this sense, Deleuze might use the time-image as a means of critiquing the capitalist system that underpinned the movement-image cinema of the pre- and post-Second World War period, but *A Screaming Man* implicitly critiques Deleuze for raising a cinema of passivity above a cinema of activism, when action, not passion and distant 'seeing', is required.

In other words, where *Elite Squad* uses movement-image tropes to critique the movement-image/time-image hierarchy, here Haroun does something similar when he makes what is in many respects a time-image film, only then to offer a critique thereof via Césaire – suggesting instead a call to arms. Given the way in which the time-image is usually upheld as 'better' than the movement-image, that Haroun points out the shortcomings of the time-image – it does not involve action at a time when action is perhaps demanded – similarly upsets the perceived hierarchy between Deleuze's image types.

Conclusion: Get up out of the Cinema

That Champion's betrayal of Abdel is figured almost as if Champion were in a cinema (watching the white screen that is the window through which he can see Abdel being taken by the army), the film's viewer is also implicated here: is watching films enough at a time when action is perhaps necessitated if the forces of neoliberal global capitalism are going to be allayed? Is *A Screaming Man* not to be seen as a 'dancing bear', but instead as a genuine cry of anguish?

In rejecting time-image tropes in their own different ways, both *Elite Squad* and *A Screaming Man* upset the perceived hierarchy between the time-image and the movement-image. Given that they do not easily conform to Deleuze's definition of modern political, or minor, cinema, perhaps they combine to constitute a contemporary political cinema, one defined by a critique of passivity and a return to action. Regardless of whether these and other films involve new image-types, elements of both the movement- and the time-image are recognizable, to greater and to lesser degrees, in both films. But in both, the concept of value that underwrites Deleuze's movement- and time-image categories is revealed and upset; and in both films, an exhortation to act seems to take place, which does not mean that the movement-image now simply replaces the time-image as 'better' or more (socialistically) politically committed. Rather, we are invited not only to think for ourselves once again about which political outlook to adopt (if any), but also to consider actively taking part, as best as we can, in the process of life as politics, in the process of living.

References

Bordwell, D. 2006. *The Way Hollywood Tells It: Story and Style in Modern Movies.* Berkeley: University of California Press.
Brown, W. 2013. *Supercinema: Film-Philosophy for the Digital Age.* New York: Berghahn Books.
Césaire, A. 2001. *Notebook of a Return to the Native Land,* trans. C. Eshleman and A. Smith. Middletown, CT: Wesleyan University Press.
Deleuze, G. 1986. *Cinema 1: The Movement Image,* trans. H. Tomlinson and B. Habberjam. Minneapolis: University of Minnesota Press.
———. 2005. *Cinema 2: The Time Image,* trans. H. Tomlinson and R. Galeta. London: Continuum.
Deleuze, G., and F. Guattari. 1986. *Kafka: Towards a Minor Literature,* trans. D. Polan. Minneapolis: University of Minnesota Press.
Gregoli, R. 2011. 'Transnational Reception of *City of God* and *Elite Squad*', *Participations: Journal of Audience & Reception Studies* 8(2): 350–74.
Mandarini, M. 2006. 'Marx and Deleuze: Money, Time and Crisis', *Polygraph: An International Journal of Culture and Politics* 18: 73–97.
Martin-Jones, D. 2006. *Deleuze, Cinema and National Identity: Narrative Time in National Contexts.* Edinburgh: Edinburgh University Press.
———. 2011. *Deleuze and World Cinemas.* London: Continuum.
Marx, K. 1999. *Capital,* trans. S. Moore and E. Aveling. Oxford: Oxford University Press.
Mullarkey, J. 2009. *Refractions of Reality: Philosophy and the Moving Image.* London: Palgrave Macmillan.
Pisters, P. 2003. *The Matrix of Visual Culture: Working with Deleuze in Film Theory.* Palo Alto, CA: Stanford University Press.
———. 2012. *The Neuro-Image: A Deleuzian Film-Philosophy of Digital Screen Culture.* Palo Alto, CA: Stanford University Press.
Rancière, J. 2006. *Film Fablesm,* trans. E. Battista. Oxford: Berg.
Rodowick, D.N. 1997. *Gilles Deleuze's Time Machine.* Durham, NC: Duke University Press.
Rizzo, T. 2012. *Deleuze and Film: A Feminist Introduction.* London: Continuum.

Rushton, R. 2012. 'Rebirth of the World: Cinema According to Baz Luhrmann', in D. Martin-Jones and W. Brown (eds), *Deleuze and Film*. Edinburgh: Edinburgh University Press, pp. 71–87.

Shohat, E., and R. Stam. 1994. *Unthinking Eurocentrism: Multiculturalism and the Media*. London: Routledge.

Filmography

Elite Squad (Tropa de Elite). 2007. José Padilha.
A Screaming Man (Un homme qui crie). 2010. Mahomet-Saleh Haroun.

CHAPTER 7
Cultural Resistance through Film
The Case of Palestinian Cinema

Haim Bresheeth

I hope, therefore, that, together with other nations, the Jews will ultimately become aware – or regain the awareness – of the inadequacy of the nation-state and that they will find their way back to the moral and political heritage that the genius of the Jews who have gone beyond Jewry has left us – the message of universal human emancipation.

—Isaac Deutscher, 'The Non-Jewish Jew'

Zionism, the State and Colonialism

Socialists and Marxists have traditionally preferred large political constellations, beyond the nation state and the supposedly ethnically uniform society, if such ever existed outside the creative imagination of committed racists. This was understandable; for those concerned with class and its iniquities, the bourgeois nation state offered a problem rather than a solution. In the quote above, Deutscher is expressing not just a typical Marxist view, but for many years, a view typical of most Jewish intellectuals before the Second World War. Until the watershed of the Holocaust, most leading Jewish intellectuals were either hostile or indifferent towards Zionism and its simplistic ethnic unity and tribal identity. Zionism, after all, meant the abandonment of class struggle in favour of Jewish identity. Indeed, the ideas of Herzl, and most of those who followed him, were based on the political sway they believed was held by Jewish multimillionaires such as the barons Hirsch and Rothschild, a view shared with anti-Semites.

That Zionism managed to get many Jewish Socialists from Russia to follow its lead was indeed a failure of Russian socialism, partly fuelled by the corrosive effect of traditional Russian Orthodox anti-Semitism, potent even within the Russian left. Herzl always perceived himself, (and also promoted himself to Europe's leaders) as offering an antidote to the 'dangers of socialism' – supposedly spread by Jewish refugees from Russia. Zionism, argued Herzl, will act as a lightning rod, attracting radical Jews away from the false lure of Marxism and revolutionary action, and towards the socially conservative and compliant Zionist camp; aided by the colonial powers, Zionism will repay the debt by preserving the interest of European imperialism in the Middle East. Some of his interlocutors have indeed believed in this potential (in most cases, the result of anti-Semitic propaganda machines that they were responsible for themselves), and it came to pass within his short lifetime.

The conception of Jewish world power, a concept borrowed from anti-Semitism, was not something Herzl kept to himself; indeed, he saw himself as offering a double service to the European empires: firstly ridding them of an unwanted and truculent ethnic minority, to be followed, after the mass emigration to Palestine, by a bulwark for European interests in the Middle East. When planning his meeting with the German Kaiser, he muses interestingly, 'Let the German Kaiser say to me: I shall be grateful to you if you lead these inassimilable people out. (This will lend me authority and make a big impression on the Jews)' (Herzl 1895: 42).

This formative ideological, foundational maxim was crucial to Zionist thought and action. Ever since 1896, when the primary Zionist pamphlet *Der Judenstaat* (1896) was published, the tenor of this close cooperation between political Zionism and Western colonialism has been well established. While in his publications Herzl covered up this thesis with great care, he was very open about it in his diaries; indeed, if the diaries can be seen to have a central theme, it must be this one. Time and again, Herzl conveyed his promise to various Western leaders – the Grand Duke of Baden, the German Kaiser, the Ottoman Sultan, the Russian anti-Semitic Interior Minister, von Plehve – whoever of Europe's leaders was ready to listen to Herzl, heard this thesis and related promises.

Herzl's real follower was Chaim Weizmann, the Zionist who filled most of the important roles in the movement, and became the first President of the State of Israel in 1948. Weizmann inherited his method and principles from his mentor, but managed to greatly improve on Herzl's achievements. Using the same blend of secret diplomacy and intrigue, and choosing the right empire – the British empire at its height, just before it started its fast decline – he managed through long and arduous effort to wrestle the Balfour declaration out of the British government on the eve of its conquest of Palestine, in November 1917, thus establishing the long-term contract between Zionism and the interests of Britain in the Near East.

Since then, *Der Judenstaat* has served as the political manual of Zionist leaders, who would always negotiate with the most powerful Western nation they could muster. Thus, in the 1950s, Israel exchanged Britain for France, with enormous consequences. Not only did France agree to finance and supply the IDF, a relationship which lasted almost two decades, but it also agreed to assist Israel in getting its own nuclear weapons developed and produced, in great secrecy. This close partnership changed again after 1967, and was replaced by the more durable, and even more dependable, much more lucrative relationship with the United States. Israel could always count on the deep-seated orientalism prevalent and dominant in Western political thought and action; thus it assisted France in its war against Algeria, and initiated the neocolonial war against Egypt in 1956, when it supplied the excuse for Britain and France to bomb the Suez Canal and take it over, in a failed attempt to re-establish their colonial control over the canal. The lines of action, and the concepts underlining them, have hardly changed since then, though the arena of intervention has grown, and now includes, in addition to the whole Arab world, also Iran and some African countries.

The Global Context of Cultural Resistance through Film

While the classical left-wing revolutions in the early twentieth century, and up to the 1960s, were taking place in a changing world – a world in which colonialism and imperialism were seemingly on the vane – the same is not true for later political liberation struggles such as that of Palestine. Lenin's understanding of imperialism as the 'last stage of capitalism' and as a phase of 'moribund capitalism', has been generally accepted even by non-Marxists and liberals, and served as the foundation for theorizing imperialism for decades. The cracks in this edifice started to emerge in the late 1970s, as the new pattern of emerging globalism become ever clearer. That imperialism has not disappeared or ossified, as predicted by Lenin, but instead continued to develop, morphing its methods and modus operandi, argues Bill Warren, in a posthumous volume, which opened the landscape to new theorizations of the process of globalization as a form of imperial control (Warren 1980). Warren, a forerunner of thinkers such as Naomi Klein, Michael Hardt and Antonio Negri, has described the emerging order of international control by the existing Western powers, assisted by the new capitalism emerging in Africa, Asia and Latin America, as a dynamic force, rather than the moribund and spent capitalism described by Lenin. Warren has also rejected the old Marxist adage that the development of capitalism in what we term the 'Third World', or the 'South', aided by imperialism, is a progressive development per se, as it builds a strong and organized proletariat in such countries. He denied any easy linkage between the growth of capitalism in the South and the growth of the potential for socialism.

As the growth of the 'means of production' was so important for Marxist theorists, and hailed, supposedly, the growth of the strength of the proletariat class, the other aspects of the new phenomenon have been overlooked, such as the role of consumption in a globalized economy, or the environmental destruction wielded by uncontrolled growth. At the same time, Anthony Brewer was mapping the Marxist historical debate on imperialism, coming to some similar conclusions to Warren when looking at the multinationals that have shaped the financial landscape of the period, finally giving the lie to Lenin's arguments about inter-imperialist rivalry (Brewer 1984a, 1984b, 2004). It is now quite clear that the nationalism that has driven so much of the capitalist development in the Third World, and the neocolonialist theories developed in some of its centres, was composed of straw men, never to drive such societies towards socialism, but rather away from it.

The harsh realities of the new phenomenon would bring about some new theoretical structures, such as those developed around the turn of the century by Naomi Klein (2007) and Micahel Hardt and Antonio Negri (2001), none of them orthodox Marxists, though following strands in Marx's thought. A wealth of information then assisted and enhanced the new approaches, from the role of new technologies to the behaviour of the global players in local crises, and the patterns emerging from such supposedly isolated and unconnected actions. The new forms and new methods of the imperialism of the twenty-first century were now understood in a new context, unforeseen or mainly ignored by much of the traditional Marxist analysis, and certainly by the Stalinist states: the intensifying destruction of the environment on a global scale, the role of global financial institutions in enforcing the new system and its iniquities on local economies, the role of new technologies in intensifying and regulating patterns of global consumption, and new forms of distribution of commodities, crucially including the virtual environment. There were, of course, some clear kernels of Marxist thought on these questions, which would eventually lead to such groupings as eco-Marxism, but for much of the period, these were relatively minority trends.

In this new world, where the Soviet Union (despite all its terrifying faults and crimes) does not exist as a countermeasure, and Third World nations such as India or Brazil, not to mention China or Russia, have fully engaged with the capitalist system with gusto, there seems to be little space for small nations to take a divergent view and counter capitalist measures. Leaders of small nations like Palestine have fully embraced the new, globalized neoliberal world order, despite the fact that it does not benefit their people in any way. In a world where the financial 'shock' experienced by larger countries such as Argentina, Greece, Spain, Ireland or Portugal, a nation in a drastic predicament like Palestine – devoid of territory, its mineral wealth robbed by Israel, even its water confiscated, and its population subject to illegal occupation, mass killing of citizens, a total lack of civil, property or human rights of any sort – can hardly be expected to start countering the new globalized world order on its own.

However, exactly due to its serious predicament under the Israeli occupation – an occupation fully supported by the strongest military power on the planet, which was also its strongest financial power and political force – Palestine had to fight using all means at its disposal; small as they might be, they were not insignificant. This chapter examines the history and future potential of cultural resistance in Palestine, as it seems to be widely accepted that a military struggle against Israel, with the United States and European Union on its side, is bound to fail. This leaves the civil forms of struggle, non-violent direct action and that of the cultural resistance, to lead the liberation effort.

Cultural Resistance's Place in Revolutionary Change

If film was the emerging art of modernity and the urban metropolis in turn-of-the-century Western capitalist society, then its crucial role in society was typically marked by one of the most ardent opponents of capitalism, and at a quite early stage of cinema's development. Interestingly, an early writer on cinema notes its importance not only for capitalism, but also for those who oppose and struggle against it.

The writer referred to is of course VI Lenin. In most publications about the importance of cinema in a social context, the words of Lenin enjoy pride of place: 'of all the arts, for us the cinema is the most important' (Taylor 1979: 29). Taylor points out that cinema is also very useful for capitalism, in Lenin's view; in an article written before the First World War, Lenin notes:

> *The cinema is systematically employed for studying the work of the best operatives and increasing its intensity, i.e., 'speeding up' the workers. A newly engaged worker is taken to the factory cinema where he is shown a 'model' performance of his job ... the worker is made to catch up with that performance ... All these vast improvements are introduced to the detriment of the workers, for they lead to their greater oppression and exploitation* (ibid.: 29).

These lines certainly are prophetic – they presage the cinematic parables of *Metropolis* (1927) by Fritz Lang, and the later *Modern Times* (1936) by Charles Chaplin. In *Metropolis,* this is done in the famous scene where the Master of Metropolis watches his workers through a camera in real time, a kind of early example of CCTV, giving his orders for increasing the speed of production through the same means. Chaplin satirizes this scene in his own recreation of the sequence, from a somewhat different perspective to that of Lang, who was strait-jacketed by a script written by his Nazi wife/screenwriter, Thea von Harbou, whose resolution of the conflict between capital and labour was the Nazi pact[1] between the feuding antagonists, negotiated by the good services of the NSDAP, the Nazi party. For Chaplin, a suspected Communist hounded by Joseph McCarthy and his Un-American House of Representatives Committee in the 1950s, the role of cinema in capitalist production echoes the understanding of Lenin some two decades earlier, though we do not know whether he was aware of Lenin's text.

As an icon of modernity, and as the new technology of the age, the cinema naturally drew the interest of progressive and revolutionary thinkers since its very inception. This was focused on and intensified after the Bolshevik revolution, when its very universal capabilities, unconstrained by the written and, at that point, also the spoken word, were noted and appreciated. In an article by Ippolit Sokolov published in the journal *Kino-Fot* in 1922, the special qualities of the new art form are noted: 'The slow-analytical and rapid-synthetic language of the cinema is the new visual Esperanto of the future' (Taylor 1979: 36). For the Soviet artists, theorists and propagandists, the cinema was indeed the most important art form, and for some sound reasons.

Russia of the post-war period, and immediately following the revolution, was a vast country of illiterate and backward peasantry, ruled by the proletarian elite and the *intelligentsia,* supported by a small group of radical and revolutionary artists, authors and political activists. Their immediate problem was reaching the millions of peasants and persuading them that the revolution was indeed in their interest, and demanding their commitment and support against the invading Western powers in the War of Intervention, which threatened the existence of the proletarian order in the new Soviet Union. Russia of the period is not a country well connected by modern communication systems, and written language was not a solution to this difficulty; the peasantry was for the most part illiterate, meaning pamphlets and books were not much use for spreading ideas.

The Communist Party in Moscow had to resort to the new means of communication, the radio and cinema, and the well-proven and intensely visual poster, if it was to reach the masses of the Russian population in the vast countryside. Hence the role of new technology in the service of the revolution was inscribed and delineated early on. A special early edict by Lenin has led to the nationalization of the film industry and the setting up of VGIK, the Gerasimov Institute of Cinematic Arts, in Moscow in 1919, the first film school anywhere and an important instrument of training the new filmmakers needed by the revolution. The first head of the school, Vladimir Gardin, started his career as an actor, but turned to directing films in 1913, producing some key adaptations of Russian literary classics for the screen. As one of the more experienced film directors in Russia, and politically supportive of the Bolsheviks, Gardin was chosen to lead the crucial new institute.

As we know, VGIK not only produced the genius of Russian revolutionary cinema of the 1920s, but also led to some of the most influential theoretical writings on cinema – Eisenstein, Pudovkin, Kuleshov and many others started their intellectual activity in this protective but demanding elite revolutionary hothouse, and quickly graduated to working as cinematographers on the armoured trains of propaganda and agitation, becoming masters of agitprop, as Mayakovsky termed it. In the following years, these young and inexperienced filmmakers, with limited amounts of short-end film rolls purchased illicitly in France, would change the history of cinema and its means of expression beyond recognition. What was a capitalist tool of production enhancement, not to mention the ideological means of projecting its creed, would become an active vehicle for propagating the Bolshevik revolution to the far reaches of Russia and beyond, through the complex, demanding and beautiful creations of its famous masters.

In hindsight, the fact that early cinema was silent was quite fortuitous, and not only for Russian revolutionaries. The lack of sound, prompting the use of live music to accompany film, was one of the most important characteristics of the new art, which made it universally understood almost immediately. The fact the cinema was limited to the visual means of the black and white emulsion and devoid of spoken language, and almost devoid of written words, meant that its language was to become a new international lingua franca – exactly the new 'visual Esperanto' of Sokolov. It was exactly the lack of spoken or written language that made it understandable everywhere, and this was the background to the refusal by some well-known artists, famously Charles Chaplin, to adopt the sound film introduced in 1927, and thus, by necessity, limiting the international appeal of the films, by now using the more limited spoken language of the country of production. The new cinematic format threw up many solutions to the problem of films in a language unknown to viewers abroad – bizarre and marvellous side-titling, subtitling and over-titling systems emerged everywhere, mainly powered by slide projectors using thirty-five millimetre clear film, on which handwritten, badly translated lines attempted to decipher the spoken language for foreign viewers. As there was no way of synchronizing such devices to the main film projector, their use was limited and incidental, as the roll of translation titles was reeled by hand, forever late or early, never being in real synchronism with the actual spoken dialogue. Until proper subtitles emerged many years later, other solutions, such as dubbing or the live *Benshi* in Japan, standing in front of the screen, freely interpreting the dialogue for the audience rather than translating it, arose in different countries and cultures. As we know, some cultures, such as the large market in the United States, resisted all such systems, including that of modern subtitling, making it most unlikely that a U.S. audience will come in contact with the majority of cinematic productions on this planet, unless the film happens to be in English and in an accent they can accommodate. The great insularity and narrow-mindedness of U.S. politics may well be strongly influenced by such refusal to listen and see the rest of the world on cinema and television screens.

These limitations of the new technology were still some time off when the classics of Soviet cinema were produced, making them immediately accessible to audiences all over the globe, and thus extending their revolutionary message well beyond the vast boundaries of the Soviet Union itself. The establishment of VGIK as the Institute of Cinema, rather than just a film school, meant that a central government arm was in control of all cinematic aspects – production, distribution, exhibition and education – for the first time in history, being the earliest example of public ownership and control of media production, distribution and exhibition. What was once the tool of market capitalism became an important and efficient armament in the service of a large and powerful state, and was used by the political and cultural elite that ruled it, enabling it to communicate with the mass population in Russia and beyond. The cinema was sending a message of liberation, modernism, justice and radical change, as well as assisting in the creation of a new national, socialist identity in Russia, by creating and projecting new ideas, visual icons and new iconic visual sequences, feeding popular imagination. In this way, the cinema in post-revolutionary Russia played a similar role to that of the U.S. cinema, which had also to reach a nation of immigrants speaking a wide variety of languages, and to turn them into the nascent U.S. nation, without the use of spoken language. Eisenstein has been an admirer of David W Griffith for this very reason, despite the very questionable politics of the Griffith films, and especially *Birth of a Nation* (1915). He was not alone, of course. The period saw the importation of much Hollywood cinema into the USSR, very popular with the Soviet masses and, one supposes, also allowing for simmering resentment against the regime. The cinema became the huge and dispersed megaphone of the new regime, enabling a new mode of social control through cultural production rather than the crude means of military or police powers. Soft power had been invented, assisting the harder powers already at work within the USSR.

That this important revolutionary lesson was well learnt can be seen in such different countries such as Cuba and Egypt, where, after the revolutions in both countries, institutes of cinema were set up and the industries nationalized. Both countries also set up film schools, very much modelled on the VGIK in Moscow, and had ample support from the USSR for their nationalizing efforts. Some countries in Africa did so after liberation, such as Tunisia and Senegal, and as a result were able to support important cultural cinematic authors, even if not to set up an industry on the Egyptian model – after all, the film industry in Egypt preceded the revolution by more than a decade (Shafik 1998: 11–15).

The Palestine Liberation Organisation (PLO) also seemingly learnt this important lesson, and set up the photographic department of the PLO in 1968, to become the Palestine Films Unit (PFU, or Wihdat Aflam Filastin) two years later. This outfit, controlled by Fatah, despite the limited resources at its disposal and the very difficult conditions under which it operated, was responsible for almost seventy films before its expulsion from Beirut in 1982, during the Israeli incursion into Lebanon. This also brought the end of the cinema institute and the production unit of the Democratic Front for the Liberation of Palestine (DFLP) (Gertz and Khleifi 2008: 12). The films were seen widely, especially in the Arab world, but some also were screened in Europe and helped to recruit European authors to the Palestinian cause – famously Jean Genet and Jean-Luc Godard, who ended up making documentaries about the conflict and have remained committed to the cause of Palestine ever since. Most of the PFU output was documentary films, with only one narrative fiction film, *The Return to Haifa* (Hawal 1982), ever produced. Even following the forced move to Tunisia, after being ejected from Beirut in 1982, the unit went on making films serving the cause of Palestinian liberation, but at a reduced rate.

An important development took place during the First Intifada, which started in December 1987. The popular resistance through nonviolent direct action (NVDA) captured the imagination of many in the West and beyond, and a large number of documentary films were produced during the first few years of the struggle. While such films were not, in the main, produced by Palestinians, the process introduced many young Palestinians to the medium, through working as guides, fixers and translators for Western crews, and many were to take up media production later on.[2] This was important, as the pendulum of Palestinian film production would then move to Palestine itself, with young filmmakers from both Israel and the Occupied Territories of Palestine (OPT) starting to make their mark on the scene of cultural production – most significantly, through the first Palestinian feature film, *Wedding in Galilee* (1988), by Michel Khleifi, a Palestinian with Israeli citizenship, residing in Belgium. The new filmmakers were working on their own, isolated from the PLO film unit, and had to face the difficult task of raising finance for production on their own – mainly resorting to the sympathetic attitude of some of the EU media funding programmes, as well as the French, German and Belgian television channels. While this could not be termed an industry, there was clearly a new force at play, reflecting similar developments elsewhere (see Naficy 2001).

The point of change is normally seen as the arrival of the PLO in Palestine, after the signing of the Oslo Accords, in 1993. One would have expected that on arrival in Palestine the PLO would not just continue film production, but would increase it by following the VGIK and Cuban models, building a national film institute and a film school in Palestine, and building a support system for the young Palestinian cinema.

The reality, however, was very different. The relationship with Israel, heavily constrained by the nature of the agreements, as well as by the insistent U.S. pressure on the PLO and Palestinian Authority (PA), meant that any act or institution of cultural resistance had to be denied and subverted by the PA, so that no proper support system for the arts was ever built by the PA's ineffectual and corrupt regime. Ironically, it was at the point of returning to Palestine that the PLO work on cultural resistance was abandoned, greatly impairing the struggle for liberation and end of Israeli occupation. This can be understood if one considers that the PLO at the time felt that its own return to Palestine and its working relationship with the Israelis and the United States were more important to it, it seems, than the continued struggle by the population, which, in the form of the First Intifada, brought about that very return of the PLO and, inadvertently, the Oslo Accords. Thus, by institutionalizing the popular struggle of the Palestinian people, the PLO and the then PA started to act as an Israeli adjunct – a security service in the part of Palestine controlled by the PNA, a tiny part of the country – serving Israeli security needs, as conceived in Jerusalem. Cultural resistance and cultural production were left for the free market in Arafat's PNA; after all, Arafat was never a Marxist, neither were any of his lieutenants. In that sense, they saw cultural production as having little to do with 'government', in the same way that most aspects of life in Palestine were excluded from the public domain, and remained privatized to the detriment of society. Hence many of the health, education and welfare systems in

Palestine have never attained the status they enjoy in Western Europe, and have indeed stayed within the market economy of the PA, such as it is. The PA itself was rife with private interests, and conflicts of interest have existed for many of the ministers of the PA administration. The fact that culture was more or less left out of government control was hardly surprising, given the U.S. free-market bias of the administration.[3]

This distance from issues and difficulties of cultural production (and cultural resistance) by the PNA and PLO, after 1993, had some interesting results. The fact that there was hardly any public support for film production by the PNA, and that film culture, like most other areas of cultural production, was overlooked or disregarded by the PNA, was obviously very negative – the fact that lessons were not learnt from other national and anticolonial struggles was deeply damaging to Palestinian society, and its potential for resistance. Clearly, as the PNA was not concerned with resistance or interested in cultural production, and actually played its part in outlawing and policing any such attempts, the culture of resistance was also not one they wished to develop. This means that after only a decade, in 2004, the first hesitant moves to establish a Palestinian Film Festival were undertaken; this, at a time when many capitals in the West already had well-established Palestinian film festivals of their own.[4] Most cinemas in Palestine disappeared around the end of the 1980s, either burnt down or hounded out of existence by Islamic fundamentalists, or closed down due to the financial downturn brought about by the occupation, and their inability to cover costs. The PA did nothing to remedy this disastrous turn of events. This lack of support not just for production, but also for the whole structure of film culture – distribution, exhibition, research and publication – is very striking. The PLO and PNA instead put their propaganda eggs into the faulty basket of PBC, the television arm of the Palestine Broadcasting Corporation, which, despite its name, bears little resemblance to the BBC. PBC is the channel most Palestinians avoid, in favour of Al Jazeera and Al Arabia, recognizing the crude attempts at promoting the PNA, with its poor production values, as culturally useless. This attempt to control the Palestinian public sphere through a 'national' television channel backfired, as the Palestinian public is much too sophisticated for such a manoeuvre. Nonetheless, the abandonment of the cultural sphere in favour of political persuasion bodes ill for the future in Palestine, as the filmmakers and their public were left to their own devices.

This raises a crucial question, arising from the conditions of raising finance for Palestinian cinema. It is true that the Palestinian cinema is impressively lively, for such a small and divided nation, living not just in Palestine, but all around the globe, with 51% of Palestinians living outside of their country. The vivacity and complexity of Palestinian cinema is the envy of larger and more powerful nations, and it now has a global reach, though with small audiences typically made of students and activists in many countries. Many more people view such films abroad than do in Palestine, where most of the viewing is on television screens due to the great shortage of cinemas or cinematheques, resulting from the lack of proper systems of support. Joseph Massad rightly raises the question: 'who are these films targeting?' (Massad 2006: 39).

This is not an idle query. To produce Palestinian documentary or fiction with European funding, the films have to address audiences in these countries, rather than direct themselves primarily to a Palestinian audience per se. There is of course great value in reaching such audiences – with the EU supporting Israel uncritically and decisively, even when Israel is carrying out massacres and war crimes, such as it did more than once in Lebanon and Gaza – as a direct address of European audiences is crucial to make the case for Palestine, tell its story and promote its narrative.

So, in comparison to the earlier, institutional film production, which has targeted mainly the Palestinians and other Arabs, the current spate of Palestinian cinema is largely seen outside of Palestine, premiering at film festivals and shown for the most part on European television channels and some limited, non-commercial screenings for political activists and cineastes. Some Palestinian critics have argued that the leading Palestinian filmmaker, Elia Suleiman, is working mainly towards his overseas audience, for example. While such claims are far from justified, one can quite understand the sentiment, due to the fact that most Palestinians in Palestine are unable to see his films on the large screen they were made for, and clearly deserve. Such criticism may also be caused, to a degree, by the fact that recent filmmakers are not refraining from harsh criticism of their government in Palestine, and also voice strong social critique like filmmakers do elsewhere. Elia Suleiman, Anna-Marie Jacir, Hani Abu Assad, Rashid Masharawi and, more than most, Michel Khleifi are not shying away from their social and political responsibilities in this respect, and their films are not limited to an attack on Israeli policies and actions, but also have much to say about current Palestinian society. In his latest film, *Zindeeq* (Here-

Figure 7.1. The Palestinian girls' choir singing the nationalist Hebrew 'independence' song in Elia Suleiman's *The Time that Remains* (2009). No funding from the Palestine Authority was used, in a film financed by European TV channels and the MEDIA programme, in the main. The image is courtesy of the filmmaker.

tic in Arabic) (2011), Khleifi voices a searing critique of Palestinian society in his hometown of Nazareth, a place seemingly in the grip of criminal gangs, where fear reins every night, totally ignored and maybe even abetted by the Israeli police and other state authorities. This social decline worries and concerns Khleifi, as it does Elia Suleiman, not a stranger to such controversy himself.

It seems that some Palestinians, especially those whose social and political capital lies with the PNA, are enraged by the courage and commitment of such films, and interpret them as 'weakening the fighting spirit'. This, despite the fact that it is exactly such films that continue and extend the political and cultural struggle against the occupation, Zionism and the iniquities meted out to most Palestinians on a daily basis, when it is the PNA that seems to collaborate with the Israeli authorities and do their bidding.

Clearly, such films, harsh and real as they are, seem to reduce the PNA's very weak cultural inclination even further, ironically; the films that gain Palestine adherents and supporters elsewhere, are shunned or ignored in Palestine by its current 'government'. Additionally, the proper support for cinema is still missing, five decades after the setting up of the PLO, and two decades after its return to Palestine. The more prizes are won by such films, the more they seem to be shunned in Ramallah.

While the PNA reaction is not atypical of insecure and authoritarian regimes elsewhere, it is similar to the Israeli government's attitude to its own cinematic crop. In Israel, the Cinema Bill, enacted in 2000 and guaranteeing finance to the film industry, as well as its independence of politicians, has been recently amended to reflect such concerns by the Zionist right wing – too many of the films supported by the legislation enraged right-wing politicians. Thus they have amended the wording of the law to reflect their belief that all films supported by the Israeli public's purse should reflect their nationalistic, racist and exclusivist value system. It is now no longer possible to produce such films, as the wording demands support of the regime and the Jewish State in principle, and one wonders what the new crop of Israeli films is going to look like.

So on both sides of the conflict, in the colonizing nation and in the colonized society, the powers that be are unhappy with their cinematic output, at a time when both Israeli and Palestinian films are praised elsewhere. In Israel, the debate flared up this year due to the fact that out of five documentaries chosen for the Oscar, two came from Israel, at least notionally. These were the stunning *5 Broken Cameras* (2011) by Emad Burnat and Guy Davidi, and *The Gatekeepers* (2012) by Dror Moreh. In their different ways, both films attack and undermine the Israeli consensus, which supports the occupation, and their selection was presented by some in Israel as an anti-Israel plot, even an anti-Semitic plot (Segal 2013). It is clear that such films will not be produced in the future, now that the legislation has been amended. The *Jerusalem Post* daily has even gone as far as speaking of a 'coup d'etat'; the article defined the film by Dror Moreh, in which he interviews six past heads of the security services about the current state of the conflict, as: 'This blurring of their "professional" and "political" opinions feels like an attempted coup d'etat by the retired Shin Bet heads. Wrapping their political conclusions – and those of the director Dror Moreh – in the mantle of credibility they earned while serving the nation in this sensitive position bypasses the political process' (Troy 2013). The film *5 Broken Cameras* received even angrier and more hostile reactions in the Israeli press. On the occasion of the film not winning the Oscar, the same paper reported: 'Bayit Yehudi chairman Naftali Bennett said Monday morning that he "didn't shed a tear" over the loss of what he referred to as an "Israeli anti-Israeli" documentary *5 Broken Cameras*. Fellow Bayit Yehudi MK Ayelet Shaked also expressed her dislike to the film. "There were never so many Israelis so glad [that a movie] didn't win the Oscars," she said' (26 May 2013).

But beyond the rage and incomprehension expressed in Israel, is hidden another, simpler and crucial issue – is *5 Broken Cameras* really an Israeli film? Was its predecessor at the Oscars, the film *Paradise Now* (Hany Abu-Assad 2005), which was nominated in 2006 as a film 'from Palestine', a Palestinian film? Not according to Israel, whose pressure was immediately applied to the Academy members in Hollywood, arguing that there was no country or state called Palestine, hence the film could not be from there.

The case of *5 Broken Cameras* is especially fascinating. The film is a personal tour de force by director Emad Burnat, who not only lost five video cameras in the making of the film (all destroyed by the occupation army; two by actual bullets meant for him), but ended up in hospital after a life-threatening accident, lost his closest friend, who was shot dead by the soldiers, saw all his brothers arrested as well as himself, and faced the sheer desperation of his wife, as he lost more and more of his health in the struggle against the brutal IDF. The text of this film has, in a real and immediate sense, been inscribed on the very body of its director, who received nothing but abuse from Israel and its authorities. The claim that this is an 'Israeli film' rests on a later development – after many years of shooting his documentary on his own, his material was seen by an Israel filmmaker, Guy Davidi, who immediately recognized its

Figure 7.2. Emad Burnat with his broken cameras in *Five Broken Cameras* (2011). The film received no support whatsoever from the Palestinian Authority, like most other films produced in Palestine. The image is courtesy of the film's co-producer, Guy Davidi.

great value and potential and joined Burnat as an enabler of the completion of the project; he was also able to raise funding to finish the film from Israeli sources. Thus, what is probably the most Palestinian of all Palestinian films, has ended up as being defined as 'Israeli'. Asa Winstanley interviewed the Palestinian director, asking him about this definition. Burnat was clear: 'But Burnat today denied this. On his Facebook page,[5] after being alerted as to how the Israeli press is describing it, Burnat said it was actually a "Palestinian film … My story, my village story, my people's story, seven years I was working on the film' (Winstanley 2013). Guy Davidi has supported this, though qualified his wording: 'it's first and foremost also a Palestinian film, as well as an Israeli film' (ibid. 2013).

The irony of such a situation has not failed to interest critics everywhere. One is reminded of the 'Israeli falafel' or 'Israeli humus' that is to be found in so many countries and cookbooks, or the Israeli town of Old Jaffa, or Jaffa oranges, all of which are totally Palestinian, of course. Israel is full of thousands of sites where the destruction of the Palestinian past has spared some homes, houses, gardens, wells, orchards – only to christen them as 'Israeli'. The physical destruction and denial has to be also joined by a denial of identity, memory and history. The two processes have acted together since the very earliest stages of the Zionist project in Palestine.

Thus, as we have seen, the absence of financial and institutional support for Palestinian cinema has meant that filmmakers were able to be more independent, to take a long and hard look at their own society, as well as the Israeli occupation. The lack of support has led, ironically, to greater creative autonomy. In the case of Israel, the support system is now cutting its losses, making sure that filmmakers tow the racist, nationalist line required by all cultural production supported by the state and public funding. In one case, in the colonized nation, the lack of left-wing social support for filmmaking has meant that cultural resistance is alive and well. In the other, in the colonizing nation, the qualified support is leading to the emasculation of the filmmakers' independence. Surely, a lesson worth remembering.

This also raises the question of a possible future in Palestine. As the latest charade of 'peace talks' and 'talks about talks' gets underway in Jerusalem, it is clearer than ever that the so-called 'two-state solution' is dead and buried, mainly due to the Israel settlement programme of the last five decades (Bresheeth 2004). The realities of Palestine mean that both national groups are bound to live together, sooner or later; thus the questions of culture, language and identity loom large. If one considers the possible solutions that will become viable in the next period, which may bring this conflict either to a violent clash or a painful resolution, one wonders about the potential of cultural production in the new, future, united Palestine, whatever it may be called. Can a state that is secular, unitary, democratic and anti-racist be the solution for Palestine? Can a bourgeois national state be that, ever? Can the cinema play a part, as it did in the USSR during the 1920s, in the shaping of new social and political identities, again?

This is not merely an abstract musing. Filmmakers on both sides collaborated well before the current 5 Broken Cameras, and produced remarkable work, showing the great and exciting potential of such collaborations. The most substantial of such projects was no doubt *Route 181*, by Michel Khleifi and Eyal Sivan (2003) – a massive three-part documentary effort lasting some eight hours, dealing with the past as a key to the future of Palestine (see Bresheeth 2012: 138–52).

The joint production in this case is no accident. It is a decision of the filmmakers to work together and defy the destructive forces unleashed by the Zionist project, and especially by the Nakba in 1948. The film is not just a searing picture of the evidence of that trauma, but also a manifesto of sorts – it makes a statement about the future, as well as about the past. By reclaiming the precarious cohabitation that existed for long periods of history between Jews and Arabs in the Middle East (and elsewhere, between Jews and Muslims, in *Andalus* [Andalusia in Spain] or in Sarajevo or Turkey, for example), the filmmakers are building an argument for future cohabitation, coexistence, and cooperation in one democratic society. Perhaps the cinema can be part of the solution.

Notes

1. Of course, this type of pact can also be described as social-democratic, in both the Menshevik sense of the term and in referring to the many social-democratic parties that emerged in Europe.
2. An example from my own experience: while working (with Jenny Morgan) on the BBC documentary *A State of Danger* (BBC2, 1989) we trained a number of Palestinians in film work. I later had the chance to send a several donated video cam-

eras and arrange for production training in the West Bank, based on the links we had established.
3. This can be seen by the lack of any socialist initiative, even of the very mild variety practiced in India or many African states after liberation in the 1950s – capitalism was never questioned, and both social services and the utilities became privatized, and in many cases owned by ministers of the PA; the monopolies of gas, petrol, water, cement and food distribution are few examples.
4. The first call for submissions for the new festival went out in 2003, and the festival took place in 2004. This new initiative was not very successful, and more or less petered out, with little support from the PA.
5. https://www.facebook.com/EmadBurnatOfficial.

References

'Bayit Yehudi Rejoice at "5 Broken Cameras" Oscar Loss'. 2013. *Jerusalem Post*, 25 February. Retrieved 26 May 2013 from http://www.jpost.com/Breaking-News/Bayit-Yehudi-rejoice-at-5-Broken-Cameras-Oscar-loss.

Bresheeth, H. 2004. 'Two States – Too Little, Too Late', *Al Ahram Weekly*, 11–17 March. Retrieved 26 May 2013 from http://weekly.ahram.org.eg/2004/681/op61.htm.

———. 2006. 'The Nakba Projected: Recent Palestinian Cinema', in H. Bresheeth and H. Hammami (eds), *The Conflict and Contemporary Visual Culture in Palestine and Israel* (special issue), *Third Text* 20(3–4): 499–509.

———. 2012. 'Reviving the Palestine Narrative on Film: Negotiating the Future through the Past and Present in *Route 181*', in K. Laachir and S. Talajooy (eds), *Contemporary Cultures of Resistance in Middle Eastern Cultures: Literature, Cinema and Music*. London: Routledge, pp. 138–52.

Brewer, A. 1984a. *A Guide to Marx's 'Capital'*. Cambridge: Cambridge University Press.

———. 1984b. *Marxist Theories of Imperialism*. London: Routledge.

———. 2004. 'Political Economy', in G. Glaeys (ed.), *Routledge Encyclopaedia Of Nineteenth Century Thought*. London: Routledge.

Gertz, N. and G. Khleifi. 2008. *Palestinian Cinema: Landscape, Trauma and Memory*. Edinburgh: Edinburgh University Press.

Hardt, M and A. Negri. 2001. *Empire*. Cambridge, MA: Harvard University Press.

Herzl, T. 1895 [1960]. *The Complete Diaries of Theodor Herzl*. London: Herzl Press and Thomas Yoselsoff.

———. 1896. *Der Judenstaat*. Leipzig and Vienna: Verlags-Buchhandlung.

Klein, N. 2007. *The Shock Doctrine: The Rise of Disaster Capitalism*. London: Allan Lane and Penguin.

Massad, J. 2006. 'The Weapon of Culture: Cinema in the Palestinian Liberation Struggle', in H. Dabashi (ed.), *Dreams of a Nation: On Palestinian Cinema*. London: Verso.

Naficy, H. 2001. *An Accented Cinema: Exilic and Diasporic Filmmaking*. Princeton, NJ: Princeton University Press.
Segal, H. 2013. 'Anti-Israel Festival', *Yediot Ahronot*, 14 January. Retrieved 26 May 2013 from http://www.ynetnews.com/articles/0,7340,L-4332078,00.html.
Shafik, V. 1998. *Arab Cinema: History and Cultural Identity*. Cairo: American University in Cairo Press.
Taylor, R. 1979. *The Politics of Soviet Cinema 1917–1929*. Cambridge: Cambridge University Press.
Troy, G. 2013. '*The Gatekeepers*: Speaking Spooks' Coup d'Etat', *Jerusalem Post*, 30 April. Retrieved 26 May 2013 from http://www.jpost.com/Opinion/Columnists/The-Gatekeepers-Speaking-spooks-coup-detat-311628.
Warren, B. 1980. *Imperialism: Pioneer of Capitalism*. London: New Left Books and Verso.
Winstanley, A. 2013. 'Is Oscar-nominated 5 Broken Cameras an Israeli or a Palestinian Film?' *Electronic Intifada*, 11 January. Retrieved 28 May 2013 from http://electronicintifada.net/blogs/asa-winstanley/oscar-nominated-5-broken-cameras-israeli-or-palestinian-film.

Filmography

Birth of a Nation. 1915. D.W. Griffith.
The Gatekeepers. 2012. Dror Moreh.
Metropolis. 1927. Fritz Lang.
Modern Times. 1936. Charles Chaplin.
Paradise Now. 2005. Hany Abu-Assad.
The Return to Haifa. 1982, Kasem Hawal.
Route 181. 2003. Michel Khleifi and Eyal Sivan.
The Time that Remains. 2009. Elia Suleiman.
Wedding in Galilee (Urs al-jalil). 1988. Michel Khleifi.
Zindeeq. 2011. Michel Khleifi.
5 Broken Cameras. 2011. Emad Burnat.

CHAPTER 8

The Contemporary Landscape of Video-Activism in Britain

Steve Presence

Oppositional documentary in Britain has been overlooked by scholars of film and media for much of the past twenty-five years. The last book-length study to get anywhere near our current moment, for instance, was Margaret Dickinson's edited collection, *Rogue Reels: Oppositional Film in Britain, 1945–90* (1999). Since then the field has been a quiet one, the single contribution being Petra Bauer and Dan Kidner's *Working Together: Notes on British Film Collectives in the 1970s* (2013). The latter is a valuable book, bringing together many key texts for which there was not space in Dickinson's volume, alongside two new essays and some interviews with those concerned, such as Ann Guedes of Cinema Action or Humphry Trevelyan of the Berwick Street Film Collective. As its subtitle suggests, however, *Working Together* focuses on the so-called 'golden age' (Kidner 2013: 18) of radical film in Britain – a moment that passed more than four decades ago.

In this chapter, I want to start to bring the record up to date by focusing on the contemporary landscape of British video-activism. Dickinson (1999: 83) ends her book by noting the emergence of Undercurrents as one of the groups producing oppositional video in the 1990s. Indeed, Undercurrents went on to become the most established video-activist[1] organization in Britain in that decade (alongside others such as Despite TV and Conscious Cinema), releasing the tenth edition of its newsreel in 1999. Since that time, the development of digital technologies and the internet have resulted in the spectacular expansion of Britain's video-activist culture, such that the contemporary landscape of British video-activism is ostensibly unrecognizable from that of the 1990s. Nevertheless, that landscape not only contains some distinctly identifiable contours but, as I will show, the roots of much of today's video-activist culture lies in the 1990s. Contemporary video-activism cannot, therefore, be understood outside of that context. This chapter thus has two principle aims: the first is to outline the contemporary landscape of video-activism in Britain, identifying the key organizations involved and mapping their relationships with one another across the field as a whole; the second aim is historical, in that I want to explore not only what constitutes Britain's contemporary video-activist culture but show how part of that culture has developed into its current state since 1990.

At present, video-activist culture can be divided into four categories: video-activist NGOs, access organizations, aggregators of oppositional media and radical video-activists. Of course, the boundaries between these categories are fluid – different aspects of the same organization can often be located in more than one category, for instance – yet they remain useful markers with which to navigate the culture as a whole. The chapter begins with an overview of video-activist NGOs, access organizations and oppositional aggregators, before turning to the radical video-activists. Although the latter are likely to be of most interest to readers of a volume with 'Marx' in the title, to focus only on those organizations aligned with the radical left would give a skewed impression of contemporary video-activism: none of the organizations discussed in this chapter operate in isolation from one another and, as we will see, close relationships exist between many access organizations, oppositional aggregators and radical video-activists. Considering each as part of a broader landscape of video-activism is therefore crucial. There are at present five established radical video-activist groups in Britain: Undercurrents, SchMOVIES, visionOntv, Reel News and Camcorder Guerrillas. I will focus my attention on Undercurrents and SchMOVIES here, since these have the closest ties to the video-activist culture of the 1990s (SchMOVIES having developed out of Conscious Cinema), and as such are the most suitable organizations with which to stage both a recovery of the history of British video-activism since that time and begin outlining its contemporary shape today.[2]

Although this history is of course of interest to Marxists and others on the radical left, it is worth stating from the outset that neither Undercurrents nor SchMOVIES (nor any other radical video-activist organization on the left today) necessarily make 'Marxist' films per se – indeed, anarchism is a more suitable ideological label for SchMOVIES, and Undercurrents is probably best described as environmentalist, but both descriptors would likely be rejected by both organizations. That said, while I am not interested in claiming either Undercurrents or SchMOVIES for any particular 'ism', both produce films that would largely resonate with a Marxist audience and this chapter is a work of historical materialism in the sense that I want to explain two radical video-activist organizations in the present by analysing their historical development in light of changing economic and super-structural (technological, social, political) contexts. Marxism remains, after all, the most useful theoretical framework for thinking about the contradictions involved in what is, broadly speaking, anti-capitalist filmmaking in a capitalist context.

Video-Activist NGOs

With their international scope and greater financial resources, video-activist NGOs constitute the largest organizations in the field. Two of the most prominent of these in Britain are One World Media (OWM) and One World TV (OWTV). As their names suggest, the history of these now distinct groups is intertwined. OWM was founded in 1986 as the One World Broadcasting Trust (OWBT), only becoming One World Media in 2009. Set up by a group of media executives from the BBC and the broadcast media regulator at that time, the Independent Broadcasting Authority (IBA),[3] OWBT was established to 'stimulate a greater range of television and radio programmes about the developing world' (One World Media 2012a). Since then it has diversified and expanded, and now funds a variety of video-activist initiatives, albeit ones still oriented predominantly towards first- or minority-world filmmakers covering humanitarian issues in the third or majority world.[4]

OWTV emerged from One World.net, an organization founded in 1994 by two of OWBT's directors, Anuradha Vittachi and Peter Armstrong.[5] One World.net was originally developed within OWBT as the world's first online 'civil society portal' (One World Group 2012), an online hub for the sort of media coverage OWM supports. In 1995 One World.net separated from OWBT to become the independent organization One World U.K., which is now part of One World Group, a global conglomerate primarily located in Britain and the UNITED STATES (but with bases around the world), which focuses on media for social, economic and political change. Part of One World Group, OWTV was set up by Armstrong in 2001 as an international video-activist portal to showcase 'brief, raw, attention-grabbing, [and] up-to-date' documentary by both amateur and professional filmmakers (Plunkett 2002).

With their considerable resources and focus on using video for social change, video-activist NGOs like OWM and OWTV constitute a significant presence in British video-activism. However, with their existence dependent on the continued financial support of the government – which is the principle funder of both, in the form of the Department for International Development (DfID) – video-activist NGOs rarely stage the kind of political critique found in the work of the radical video-activists or hosted by oppositional aggregators. Their emphasis tends to be on 'objectivity' and human rights rather than anti-capitalism or class struggle, and they are often closely aligned with the political establishment. OWM's awards ceremony in 2011 featured Conservative MP and former oil trader turned minister of state for DfID, Alan Duncan, as the keynote speaker (One World Media 2012b), for example.

While OWM and OWTV share this close relationship to government, the differences between them are also indicative of the blurred boundaries between different sectors of the video-activist landscape, with OWTV arguably functioning as an aggregator as much as a video-activist NGO. Despite their differences, however, the intimate relationship with mainstream politics and big business – characteristic of video-activist NGOs – is the defining feature of both. Understanding the role of video-activist NGOs in the video-activist landscape overall, it is helpful to draw comparison with their counterparts in the field of oppositional feature documentary, the liberal-humanist strand of which shares this symbiotic relationship with the political and business establishment. As well as demonstrating the interwoven nature of the video-activist and feature documentary communities, these parallels help explain the largely reformist, conciliatory role of video-activist NGOs in the former. Since the mid-2000s, the liberal-humanist strand of oppositional feature documentary has become a distinct commercial sector within the film industry, complete with dedicated production and distribution companies, such as Dartmouth Films and Dogwoof, and funding organizations such as the Channel 4 BRIT-DOC Foundation.

Video-activist NGOs and the companies and filmmakers behind documentaries such as *Black Gold* (Nick and Marc Francis 2006) or *The End of the Line* (Rupert Murray 2009) share broadly the same ideological orientation. Appealing to tolerance and conflict-free notions of 'universal' human characteristics, liberal-humanism 'enshrines the autonomous and rational individual as the central unit of society' (Carroll 1993: 124) and disavows the social and ideological structures those individuals inhabit. It is this ideology that allows video-activist NGOs like OWTV to count Vodafone – one of the principle corporations involved in tax evasion in the U.K. – among its corporate partners and funding organizations such as BRITDOC to broker partnerships between documentary filmmakers and Walmart – 'one of the most ruthless employers in the world' (Corporate Watch 2004). Thus, while the video-activism and feature documentaries these organizations produce can be influential tools with which to draw attention to pressing social and political problems, their liberal-humanist inability to grasp the social and economic structures underpinning them means they shy away from challenging the fundamental inequalities in control and ownership of resources that give rise to many of those problems in the first place. As a result, they frequently suggest solutions that are fundamentally compatible with the status quo, such as political lobbying or ethical consumerism.

Access Organizations

Because they focus on expanding access to production rather than the content of what is produced, access organizations also tend to produce less oppositional video-activism. However, equipping disadvantaged or marginalized groups with the skills and experience to represent themselves is a fundamentally radical act. One often finds, therefore, that access organizations not only aspire to social goals amenable to the radical left but that they also have close working relationships with other, more explicitly oppositional video-activist organizations. Again then, we can see how the categories dividing video-activist culture are porous. Spill Media, for instance, is a social enterprise production company based in Swansea that combines more lucrative marketing and promotional work with community training and outreach initiatives in order to fulfil its 'social aims': to 'increase people's confidence and self-worth, reduce isolation and help people develop creatively' (Spill Media 2012a). These 'social aims' have resulted in its collaboration with Undercurrents on Swansea Telly, for instance, a 'digital inclusion project' teaching 'all aspects of media production' to older people, the recently unemployed and social housing tenants (Spill Media 2012b).

Other access organizations, such as WORLDbytes: School of Citizen TV (based in London), Hi8us (in London and the Midlands) or the Oxford-based InsightShare, produce more explicitly political work closer to the oppositional values of radical video-activists. WORLDbytes, for instance, is an 'online Citizen TV channel' whose slogan ('Don't shout at the telly – change the message on it!' [WORLDbytes 2010]) is comparable to the better-known Indymedia phrase, 'don't hate the media, be the media' (cited in Fountain 2007: 40). Insightshare, a 'participatory video' organization that works predominantly in 'developing' countries, also produces more overtly political films, often around themes of climate change and sustainability (InsightShare 2012).

Closer analysis of the historical trajectories of these organizations also reveals both the extent to which contemporary video-activist culture is built on relationships formed in the 1990s, and how much the organizations involved overlap. The founders of InsightShare, Nick and Chris Lunch, were in close touch with Undercurrents when it was based in Oxford, for instance, and regularly attended video-activist gatherings at The Lacket, a series of weekends held throughout the 1990s at the family home of Zoe Young, a video-activist with the Brighton-based organization, Conscious Cinema. These weekends were a significant contribution to oppositional film culture in the 1990s, providing opportunities for coordination, networking, critique and so on, and the list of filmmakers who attended them reads like a roll call of video-activist filmmakers at this time (Young 2011: 5). More recently, in June 2012, InsightShare, along with Mick Fuzz and other participants from the Transmission network (see below), many of whom also worked closely with Undercurrents and Conscious Cinema in the 1990s, were among twelve organizations from around the world to attend the 'video4change Retreat and Sprint', a gathering co-hosted by EngageMedia, a video-activist collective based in Australia and Indonesia (but with connections to British video-activist culture again via Undercurrents),[6] and WITNESS, the international video-activist NGO based in the United States (Cinco 2013). Although there is not space here to give these histories the attention they deserve, unearthing them is important. Not only do they demonstrate the existence of a lively, internationalist video-activist culture in Britain since the 1990s, but they make clear the genealogical links that exist between what appears to be today's unfathomably fast-moving digital video-activist landscape and previous radical film cultures.

Oppositional Aggregators

With vast numbers of individuals and groups producing video-activism in the digital era, oppositional media aggregators form a key part of the contemporary video-activist landscape. Dedicated to collecting and ordering video-activism online, these sites are important sources of a whole range of oppositional media, in which video is often featured alongside other sections devoted to text, photography, radio, events and so on. As the quantity of online content increases, aggregation is becoming an ever more crucial part of oppositional media organization. This is one of the reasons for the decline of Indymedia, the international network of oppositional media organizations established to provide independent coverage of the anti-summit protest in Seattle in 1999. Developed prior to the kinds of social networking we see online today, most Indymedia Centres (IMCs) are based on the principle of open publishing rather than aggregation. According to activists at Indymedia London (which closed down after thirteen years in October 2012):

> Since that time the internet and the way people use it has changed dramatically. [Today] self-publishing is the norm … and the mass adoption of Facebook, Twitter, Flickr, YouTube and third party curation and sharing tools has created new complex communities of interest [empowering] the production, organisation and distribution of content as never before. The main raison d'être for Indymedia's existence is no longer there. (IMC London 2013)

So, although many regional Indymedia centres remain active, aggregators such as BeTheMedia are increasingly common. Launched in 2011 by activists who split from Indymedia U.K. on the issue of aggregation (SchNEWS 2011), BeTheMedia aggregates video and other content from a range of sources, including several regional IMCs, oppositional radio and political and environmental organizations, and has become a prominent aggregator of oppositional media in Britain.

As the quote above suggests, YouTube and other corporate social media also provide platforms capable of aggregating oppositional video, and many video-activist organizations make extensive use of these platforms. Indeed, as well as providing useful platforms for video-activists, sites such as YouTube have also enabled left-wing political parties and organizations to become oppositional media aggregators. The Socialist Workers Party (SWP) and Socialist Party (SP) both have designated YouTube channels hosting videos relevant to their work, for example, as do some branches of the Anarchist Federation and Solidarity Federation. Others, such as Counterfire, The Commune and the British and Irish region of the Industrial Workers of the World (IWW), embed YouTube videos on their own sites under designated video tabs. However, the use of corporate platforms for video-activism is hardly ideal. Aside from the contradictions involved in using capitalist media organizations to host anti-capitalist content, with one hundred hours of video uploaded to YouTube every minute, finding ways to make video-activism stand out from the range of other content on the site is difficult (YouTube 2013).[7] Video-activists and other organizations interested in oppositional media aggregation thus tend to use YouTube and similar platforms as a means of advertising their own site, or as an easy means of hosting videos which can then be embedded elsewhere. However, there have also been attempts to develop alternative aggregators, which, like YouTube, aggregate video exclusively but which are more suited to the political interests of video-activism.

The Transmission network, an international group of video- and media-activists,[8] is one such initiative, whose stated aim is to develop 'online video distribution tool[s] for social justice and media democracy' (Transmission 2012). Another is the Miro Community project, a template video-aggregation site that emerged from the U.S.-based Participatory Culture Foundation in 2010, and which allows its users to collect video from elsewhere on the web and curate it to suit their interests. This has seen some success, with the software currently used to power each of visionOntv's five channels, access projects like Swansea Telly and other local video-activist initiatives such as the Merseyside Street Reporters Network (which visionOntv helped establish) and the Bristol Community Channel (set up by iContact in 2011, another long-standing video-activist organization with links to Undercurrents).

Aggregation is clearly a key part of the contemporary video-activist landscape, with the need to develop filtration and distribution tools increasing in-step with the amount of content online. However, this is an under-researched area, and more work is needed if this sector of video-activist culture is to be understood. Who are the audiences these aggregators are reaching, for example? What are their sizes and demographics? Recent years have also seen an increase in organizations dedicated to exhibiting oppositional film, with organizations like the Bristol Radical Film Festival or the Manchester Film Coop, for example. If, as my experience with the former has shown, public screenings are a vital part of engendering the political engagement that oppositional film aims for, perhaps we should be exploring how aggregation and distribution strategies can be coordinated with those working in exhibition. These will remain open questions until such research takes place.

Undercurrents

Undercurrents' widespread connections across the contemporary video-activist landscape are indicative of its established place in Britain's oppositional film culture. Founded during the anti-roads protests in the early 1990s, Undercurrents' newsreel capitalized on the convergence of this vibrant form of activism with the availability of low-cost camcorders and the refusal of the mainstream media to document it accurately, if at all (Harding 1998: 83). As the direct-action movement of the 1990s spread, Undercurrents established a network of video-activists across the country (and further afield) whose work, once edited together into the newsreel, was distributed on VHS, via Royal Mail, to its network of subscribers. In this way, Undercurrents created the first successful nationwide oppositional newsreel in Britain.[9] Dubbed 'the news you don't see on the news' (ibid.: 88), Undercurrents' videos combined politically committed reporting with irreverent satire of the police, politicians and the mainstream media, and gained widespread recognition and acclaim as a result.[10]

Undercurrents has adapted and developed a great deal as it has sought to survive the major technological and sociopolitical changes that have taken place since that time. These have included personnel and geographic changes as well as structural ones. Paul O'Connor is the only founding member left at Undercurrents, for example, which now consists of only two other full-time members,[11] and after to moving from London to Oxford in 1995, Undercurrents is now based in Swansea, where it moved in 2000. Since moving to Swansea the structure of the organization has also shifted from a not-for-profit company to a registered charity, it being a lot easier to get funding for charitable organizations (O'Connor 2011: 7). Perhaps the most significant change at Undercurrents, however, has been the development of a bilateral business model in which its radical projects are subsidized by commissions for more commercial activities and for its work as an access organization. Again, not only is this development another instance of the blurred boundaries between radical groups and other parts of contemporary video-activist culture, but it also demonstrates the practical realities of oppositional filmmaking in a capitalist context: with paying audiences for radical video small and funding opportunities limited, this is one business model that allows for some measure of sustainability.

Access work constitutes a key part of Undercurrents' financial stability, and has seen the organization develop 'a host of community media projects' since the mid-2000s (O'Connor 2011). As well as the Swansea Telly project mentioned above, others include projects like the 'Broad Horizons' initiative for female filmmakers (which released a DVD in 2006) and educational programmes for disadvantaged young people. As with other access organizations, the nature of this work – in which the focus is on imparting skills rather than producing oppositional content – often results in much less overtly political films than those Undercurrents produced in the 1990s. Undercurrents' commissioned films also adopt a less outspoken approach to political issues. In 2006, for instance, Undercurrents was commissioned by the Community Channel to produce *Living in the Future: Ecovillage Pioneers* (Undercurrents 2006), an online series about attempts to develop a low-impact 'ecovillage' in the Welsh countryside. As with many of Undercurrents' more commercial activities – including *A-Z of Bushcraft* (Undercurrents 2009) or *On the Push: A Surfer's Guide to Climate Change* (Undercurrents 2009) – the films' themes are broadly aligned with Undercurrents' original environmentalist ethos. However, the oppositional stance of the newsreel has been discarded in favour of a more subtle approach designed to appeal to a wider audience base. *Living in the Future* begins with a brief history of the 1750 Enclosures Act and the displacement of working people from common land, for instance, but any explicitly political perspective is quickly effaced in favour of the practical aspects of low-impact living and the efforts of the group to obtain planning permission.

This is understandable given that these projects are intended to provide Undercurrents with the income it needs to survive. Indeed, making money from these kinds of films is not an easy task in the era of online video, and reaching a paying audience has required Undercurrents to place much of its work online for free, and then experiment with various participative pricing initiatives in which audiences decide for themselves what to pay for the work. Despite such a potentially risky strategy, according to O'Connor this is proving financially sustainable:

> By putting the series online for free we're basically saying: 'if you like this series, buy the DVD'. And that keeps us in the frame. Like the Bushcraft series. That sold a thousand videos. And we put it out there saying: 'if you like what you see on this show, pay what you like for the DVD'. So you think 'well, okay, that's kept us going to make the next one'. (2011: 5)

While some might argue that the absence of overt political arguments in these videos is inadequate, the financial stability provided by these projects is what has enabled Undercurrents to pursue other, more explicitly oppositional projects. Indeed, Undercurrents has been producing radical video-activism alongside its more commercial work since the end of the newsreel in 1999, resulting in more than a decade of oppositional filmmaking that would not exist were it not for this strategic financial approach.

Undercurrents' first oppositional project after the final edition of the newsreel in April 1999 was a collaboration with Bristol's iContact Video. Released in July that year, *J18: The Story the Media Ignored* (Undercurrents 1999) is a celebration of the 18 June Carnival Against Capitalism in London and the efforts of oppositional media activists to combat the misrepresentation of the protest in the mainstream media. Beginning with the satirical, Hollywood-style trailer made to publicize the event, *J18* maintains the humorous, tongue-in-cheek tone of the newsreel. Documenting the protest and those involved in it – from Samba musicians and Meat is Murder campaigners to masked black bloc activists and nervous-looking bankers – the film also makes its own position on the topic clear. Along with intertitles such as '*Cap'italism n. A system by which the few profit from the exploitation of the many*', the film includes condemnatory footage of armed riot police attacking crowds of peaceful, unarmed protestors, and celebratory scenes of property destruction, with upbeat folk music playing over footage of a badly damaged McDonald's outlet.

J18 is also indicative of the shifting technological context in which it was made, however, and which saw Undercurrents enter a period of uncertainty. A thirty-minute video released on VHS, *J18* also includes footage of the event being streamed live on a computer screen, capturing one of the first times the internet was used to broadcast video-activism online. As O'Connor explains:

> Indymedia was out there and things were going online and you were thinking 'great, we're going to have videos on the web'. [But] video on the web didn't take off for another four, five years. YouTube was 2005. So we were in this doldrums for a couple of years not really knowing what our distribution model was. (2011: 5)

One of Undercurrents' first responses to this context was to attempt an online TV studio, Pirate TV. Little evidence remains of this ambitious and experimental project, a two-hour weekly webcast of an eclectic mix of video-activism and electronic music produced in association with the record label, Ninja Tune. Despite running for nearly a year, Pirate TV was eventually abandoned because of low audience numbers. Streaming online was still an innovative and ambitious use of the internet at that time and, although it was a valuable learning experience for those involved, its most immediate lesson was that web video was not yet viable. Thus the first years of the 2000s saw Undercurrents move offline and begin distributing video-activism on CD-ROM. Ruff Cutz, as this next project was called, ran for the two or three years until web video became a more practical possibility.[12] Indeed, the low cost and highly reproducible nature of CD-ROM saw it become the format of choice for oppositional media activists in Britain and around the world (Campbell 2011: 3; Lovink and Schneider 2003: 1). Whilst experimenting with online video and CD-ROM, however, Undercurrents also continued with VHS productions, releasing *Undercurrents 10¾* (Undercurrents 2002) in another collaboration with iContact.

The title of this video is indicative of Undercurrents' uncertainty at a time in which, as well as being a period of technological change, the political context was also rapidly developing. In particular, by the end of the 1990s, many so-called 'single issue'[13] campaigns from earlier in the decade had coalesced into the international anti(alter)-globalization movement, in which capitalism and its key global institutions (especially the International Monetary Fund [IMF], World Bank and World Trade Organization [WTO]), were explicitly targeted. Indeed, this shift was one of the primary reasons for the decline of Undercurrents' original newsreel. According to O'Connor:

in the early 1990s with the roads protests it was all kinds of local. But by the end of that decade it was a worldwide movement. So people were going off to summits, Prague [September 2000], Genoa [July 2001] and all that ... I think we realised that we just couldn't sustain it ... So we thought 'that's it, we're not doing anymore videos until we've worked out what we're doing, how we're going to survive, all that kind of thing. (2011: 6)

However, Undercurrents had continued producing films throughout this period, including a collaborative[14] work on the anti-summit protest in the Czech Republic: *Revolting in Prague: IMF Protests 2000* (various 2000), and a film about the shifting technological context of the time and its ramifications for oppositional media: *Globalisation and the Media* (Undercurrents 2002).

With no alternative distribution outlet, Undercurrents and iContact decided to release these longer films (twenty-six and twenty-one minutes respectively) along with two other shorter films as another compilation. Not

Figure 8.1. *Globalisation and the Media* (2002). Screen capture from YouTube.

wanting to resurrect the original newsreel, they decided to release the tape as *10¾* rather than *Undercurrents 11* (O'Connor 2011: 5-6).

Undercurrents also attempted two other newsreel projects in the first half of the 2000s. The first was based on a project by the U.S.-based satellite TV channel, Free Speech TV, which broadcast a weekly compilation of video-activism as the *Indymedia Newsreal*.[15] Inspired by the U.S. project but wary of the burnout that contributed to the decline of its first newsreel, in 2002 Undercurrents launched the *Indymedia European Newsreel* (Undercurrents 2002) by hosting a European video-activist gathering, at which it was agreed that responsibility for editing the newsreel would be passed from group to group (Undercurrents 2012). Despite these efforts and a £1000 donation from Free Speech TV, only one issue was produced (under Undercurrents' aegis). According to the ex-Undercurrents video-activist Hamish Campbell (now of visionOntv), subsequent attempts suffered from low production values and ideological infighting and never materialized (2011: 3). Two years later, Undercurrents again attempted newsreel production, this time with the *Undercurrents News Network (UNN)* (Undercurrents 2004). However, although it was intended to be distributed regularly on DVD, only one issue was released before the project was abandoned. With Undercurrents undergoing personnel changes at the time and only O'Connor and Zoe Broughton able to work on the project, *UNN* took three months to produce. At a time when web video was looking increasingly viable, the potential lifespan of a regular DVD newsreel must have seemed short indeed, and another issue was not attempted.

As this brief history shows, Undercurrents' contemporary formation cannot be understood outside of the changing socioeconomic, political and technological contexts in which it was operating. From the roads protests of the 1990s to the anti-capitalist movement at the turn of the century and the urgent environmental crises we face today, Undercurrents has consistently produced radical video-activism across a variety of audio-visual media, from VHS and CD-ROM to early web video in all its guises. Without the bilateral business model Undercurrents developed to subsidize its more radical endeavours, the organization would not have survived to make them. Today, Undercurrents continues operating according to this model, producing commissions and running access activities to subsidize its more radical work, much of which has been produced in collaboration with visionOntv, the radical aggregator it helped develop in 2010.

SchMOVIES

Although SchMOVIES is a more recent addition to video-activist culture than Undercurrents, its history is also embedded in the video-activism of the 1990s. As with Undercurrents, then, to understand SchMOVIES' place in contemporary British video-activism one must first understand the video-activist culture of the 1990s from which the organization developed. The video-activist 'unit' of the Brighton-based weekly radical newsletter, SchNEWS (Light 2008), SchMOVIES was set up in 2004 when activist and SchNEWS journalist Paul Light stepped into the gap left by Conscious Cinema in the preceding decade. Since then SchMOVIES has produced two feature documentaries and six DVD compilations of 'over two hundred short direct-action/campaign films' (Light: 2008), ranking it among the most prolific video-activist and oppositional filmmaking organizations in Britain. Unlike other contemporary radical video-activists groups, however, SchMOVIES is run single-handedly by Light from the studios of his commercial film production company, Bite Size Movies (BSM). So, although much of its video-activist work appears online soon after it is produced, SchMOVIES tends to release only one DVD compilation of video activism per year.[16] This rate of production means it requires few resources to run, enabling Light to contribute the income from SchMOVIES to the publication of SchNEWS. Uniquely among contemporary video-activist groups, then, SchMOVIES is a video-activist subsidiary of another radical media project that it exists to support.

Of course, SchMOVIES can operate in this way because it can draw on the infrastructure of BSM, the commercial activities of which subsidize SchMOVIES' video-activism. Like the relationship between Undercurrents' commercial activities and its more radical video-activist work, BSM's films also lack the outspoken radicalism of SchMOVIES, albeit without losing focus on issues relevant to the political left. For example, BSM describes itself as a 'community and campaign-based' production company, and has produced a number of short films promoting community allotments or recycling projects (Bite Size Movies 2012a). In 2009, it produced a series on 'green issues and services in the Sussex area' (Bite Size Movies 2012b), while other recent projects include films for community engagement programmes and charitable groups focusing on drug and alcohol rehabilitation, family intervention support and community health and wellbeing. BSM also operates as an access organization, running a number of filmmaking courses throughout the year as well as the annual Court Farm Kids Course, a weekend workshop at a local community centre teaching film skills to travellers' children and their friends and families. In this respect, the relationship between BSM and SchMOVIES operates much like the commercial and oppositional sides of Undercurrents. However, there are also some key differences between SchMOVIES and Undercurrents, which stem from their relationship in the 1990s and Light's alignment with SchNEWS and Conscious Cinema rather than Undercurrents.

Conscious Cinema was founded in Brighton in 1994 – the same year as Undercurrents – by Dylan Howitt, Johnny Cocking and Gibby Zobel. This marks the beginning of what were two incarnations of the collective.[17] In this first period, from 1994 to 1997, Conscious Cinema functioned similarly to Undercurrents, producing a video-activist newsreel for the direct-action community on subjects ranging from anti-roads protests to Reclaim the Streets actions, struggles against privatization, and so on.[18] Whereas Undercurrents emerged from the anti-roads movement, however, Conscious Cinema was initially a response to the Criminal Justice Bill (CJB). With the anti-roads protests in full swing, the CJB's criminalization of many formerly civil offences associated with activism was widely regarded as an attack on citizens' right to protest. It criminalized a whole range of alternative ways of living, for instance, but especially targeted travellers, free parties and squatting. It also cut back unemployment benefits, clamped down on trespass and unauthorized camping, and dramatically increased police powers, allowing in particular for unsupervised stop and search and for inferences to be drawn from what had previously been a right to silence. With its road-building programme being met with determined and resourceful resistance, the CJB was a powerful weapon for the government and provoked an urgent response from the communities it attacked. In Brighton, this emerged in the form of the Justice? campaign when activists opposed to the bill aptly squatted an abandoned court house, staging a variety of events and meetings there to draw attention to the bill. Conscious Cinema and SchNEWS were two of the oppositional media projects that developed from this campaign.

Originally from Poole, Light's political orientation was forged in the context of the Poll Tax, the anti-roads protests and the CJB. It was the latter that really 'galvanized' his politics (Light 2012: 1), however, and his participation in this struggle saw Light to move to Brighton to join the Justice? campaign. As well as organizing initiatives like the squatters' estate agents, SchLETS (SchNEWS 1996), Light began writing for SchNEWS and working with Conscious Cinema; the latter's approach to video-activism provided the model Light would later adopt for SchMOVIES. In order to mark the newsletter's tenth anniversary in 2004, SchNEWS organized a tour of the U.K.'s direct-action scene as well as the publication of a book (SchNEWS 2004a) and a film commemorating the achievements and struggles of the previous decade. Having learned the basics of filmmaking working with Conscious Cinema in the 1990s, Light was responsible for the film (which became the feature documentary, *SchNEWS at Ten: The Movie* [SchMOVIES, 2005]).

As well as filming on the tour itself and recording the numerous actions that took place during it, Light also issued a public request for footage from the last ten years of direct-action protest (see SchNEWS 2004b). Consequently, he accumulated enough footage to begin releasing short films as well as putting together material for the feature, and SchMOVIES was born. As he says:

Figure 8.2. *SchNEWS at Ten* (2005). Screen capture from *SchNEWS at Ten* (DVD, SchNEWS, 2005).

I was filming on the [SchNEWS at Ten] tour and out of that came lots of actions via the places we were going – so I was filming them, too. And when we got back I thought, 'there's loads of little films here, not just those for the tour but lots of individual ones as well. Why aren't we putting these out?' So that's how it started really, I just ended up travelling round with a camera and filming and putting the films together, [but] we nicked the blueprint from Conscious Cinema – short-ish, direct-action, campaign-based films.
(Light 2012: 2–3)

SchMOVIES is thus the direct descendant of Conscious Cinema. Historically, then, the relationship between Undercurrents' and SchMOVIES is a close one, Undercurrents and Conscious Cinema being two of the most significant video-activist collectives in Britain in the 1990s.[19]

However, the relationship between the two organizations was, at first, somewhat strained. In fact, with Undercurrents perceived as 'the McDonalds of activist video' at that time, Young recalls that 'part of the reason for Conscious Cinema being Conscious Cinema was to have something that wasn't Undercurrents' (2011: 2). Indeed, Undercurrents were heavily criticized by sections of the direct-action movement in the latter half of the 1990s for practices that were deemed at odds with the values of that movement. In particular, these criticisms focused on those aspects of Undercurrents' practice that were judged compromisingly close to the mainstream media, such as its hierarchical operating structure and its policy of selling activists' footage to television news channels.[20] By contrast, Conscious Cinema was much more closely aligned with the anarchist-oriented culture of the 1990s direct-action movement, described by George McKay as 'DiY culture' (1998).

Typical of this culture was an absolute rejection of the commercial values and practices associated with capitalism. For example, Conscious Cinema did not charge for its videos but copied them onto second hand tapes bootlegged from London production houses and distributed them for free instead (Conscious Kev cited in SchNEWS 2004a: 43). Today, although Light sells DVDs of SchMOVIES' work, the proceeds from these go towards the publication of the SchNEWS, and BSM and SchMOVIES are kept strictly separate so as to underscore the fact that SchMOVIES is, like Conscious Cinema before it and SchNEWS[21] today, a definitively unpaid, voluntary pursuit. Indeed, Light's desire to continue to run SchMOVIES according to this ethos is what gave rise to BSM in the first place, which Light describes as:

> kind of an offshoot really, because I was starting to get work from other sources. And I was thinking 'this isn't a SchMOVIE, they want to pay me money and I don't do SchMOVIES for money'. It's as simple as that. I don't do that for money and I have a clear divide between SchNEWS and SchMOVIES and my work, my other work. So I could get a commission for a film from an NGO or something like that – that would be under Bite Size Movies, that's my job. SchMOVIES is video-activism which is unpaid, but obviously it's what I do, it's my passion and I think it's a good thing to do. But the two are distinct. (2012: 4)

So, although his professional work is largely what enables SchMOVIES to continue as a video-activist organization today, the desire to isolate the profit motive from activities motivated by passion and political conviction derives from the anarchist-oriented, DiY approach to media activism that Light inherited from SchNEWS and Conscious Cinema.

Another trait of the DiY approach is a belief in the centrality of action over how that action is organized. Epitomized in SchNEWS' tagline, 'a single act of defiance is worth more than a thousand words' – and adapted for *SchNEWS at Ten: The Movie* to read 'a single act of defiance is worth a thousand feet of film' – the primacy of action, of getting the films made, also characterizes SchMOVIES' mode of production. So, although Light draws on footage from other video-activists, the postproduction and distribution of that material is largely his responsibility. Unimpeded by the organizational labour of other groups, Light cites this independence as a key factor in enabling him to sustain his video-activist work. Indeed, with the support of BSM's infrastructure, Light is able to fund SchMOVIES primarily from a series of monthly public screenings held at Brighton's social centre, the Cowley Club, which also emphasizes that it is 'run entirely by volunteers – no one gets paid, and no one is making any profit' (Cowley Club 2012). An emphasis on organizing public screenings as a means of stimulating political engagement is another indicator of SchMOVIES' alignment with direct-action culture and its emphasis on action. Conscious Cinema's aim in the 1990s, for instance, was that:

the videos would be shown in community settings – getting away from people watching things by themselves at home – because often you feel unable to do anything as an individual. We wanted people to watch 'em in group settings so they could discuss what they had seen and work together to take action. (Conscious Kev cited in SchNEWS 2004: 43)

Likewise, Light recognizes the political importance of holding screenings: 'it's that screening angle that I'm really into, there's not enough of that. You need the events to galvanize people and get people talking about stuff' (2012: 3).

Conclusion

Exploring the respective historical trajectories of Undercurrents and SchMOVIES demonstrates the extent to which their current practices and positions in the contemporary video-activist landscape are bound up with the combination of socioeconomic, technological and political forces in which they developed. Marxism offers the most useful set of theoretical tools with which to explore this development, and most Marxists would be broadly sympathetic to the work that Undercurrents and SchMOVIES produce. Yet a Marxist perspective on these organizations also illustrates the extent to which these are *not* Marxist organizations. This is strikingly evident from the almost total lack of any reference to class in both Undercurrents' and SchMOVIES' work. Again, this is indicative of the lack of class politics in the 1990s direct action scene more generally – class is also conspicuously absent from the supposedly anarchist critiques of Undercurrents during the 1990s. Exploring these critiques and the reasons for the absent class paradigm in this section of the radical left is beyond the scope of this chapter, but serves to illustrate again how these video-activist organizations are products of the particular set of historical and material conditions in which they developed.

Of course, Undercurrents and SchMOVIES are just two organizations in a contemporary video-activist landscape that is vastly different from the period in which they were established. Yet despite the transformation of that culture and the ever-expanding mass of content available online today, the structure of the contemporary video-activist landscape remains distinctly identifiable.

As we have seen, although the distinctions between video-activist NGOs, access organizations, oppositional aggregators and radical video-activists are porous – with numerous connections existing across the field as a whole and different groups combining different practices in distinct ways – the categories themselves remain useful markers with which to begin mapping the field and understanding the role of the more radical groups within it. Furthermore, more recent additions to that landscape, such as Reel News (2006–), are much more explicitly class conscious, and operate very different business models to fund their work. Reel News is funded exclusively by donations and sales of and subscriptions to its newsreel, while Camcorder Guerrillas focuses on securing funding for its work, which is then organized and carried by consensus. Yet these and other contemporary video-activist organizations also have roots in the 1990s and, like Undercurrents and SchMOVIES, cannot be understood in abstraction from it. For example, Reel News was also shaped in the context of the anti-globalization movement and its founder, Shaun Dey, cites Undercurrents and Conscious Cinema as 'trailblazers' of contemporary video-activism (Dey 2011: 10). In fact, far from the digital era marking a break with previous histories of radical British filmmaking, one could trace these genealogical links further back. Reel News' emphasis on class struggle has clear affinity with Cinema Action's approach (1968–86), for example, while Camcorder Guerrillas' close relationship with the communities in which it works echoes that of Amber (1969–). visionOntv's efforts to foster 'the widest possible distribution of video for social change' (visionOntv, 2012) also resonates with previous attempts, such as those by The Other Cinema (1970–77) or the feminist group Circles (1979–92).

Moreover, video-activism is just one part of the thriving contemporary culture of oppositional documentary in Britain. While companies such as BRITDOC and Dogwoof cater for the more liberal strand of oppositional documentary (unless handling the work of oppositional auteurs such as Ken Loach or John Pilger), swathes of more radical feature work also exists outside of the mainstream distribution and exhibition circuits. *Secret City* (Michael Chanan and Lee Salter 2012), *Who Polices the Police?* (Ken Fero 2012) and *Riots Reframed* (Fahim Alam 2013) are just three recent examples. The artists' film and video community also includes filmmakers producing oppositional work, such as David Panos, Luke Fowler and the Otolith Group. As well as the films and filmmakers, we have also seen a groundswell in groups and organizations dedicated to showcasing politically radical film, spread across the country in cities from Bristol, Brighton and Leeds to Glasgow, Liverpool, Manchester and London. So, although I have barely scratched the surface here, Britain's radical film culture is clearly alive and well, as are oppositional film cultures elsewhere. I hope this chapter, and the volume of which it is a part, contributes to the renewed study of radical film around the world. More than any others, these are the films that will contribute to the radical political, economic and environmental changes we so badly need.

Notes

1. 'Video-activism' is an ambiguous category, of course. Although in the 1990s 'video' was associated with magnetic tapes and VHS, today it is frequently used to describe moving images online. Here too video refers both to analogue and digital formats, much as we continue to talk about films even when not printed on celluloid. Video-activism deserves more discussion than there is space for here. Suffice to say that, in this chapter at least, it refers to short films, typically in the form of radical newsreel, but which also draw on traditions such as agitprop to access television and remix.
2. Of the others, visionOntv is the youngest. Set up in 2010 by two ex-Undercurrents members, Hamish Campbell and Richard Hering, visionOntv is a London-based aggregator dedicated to providing a platform for radical video-activism. Reel News, also based in London, was established in 2006, and releases a bi-monthly newsreel for the radical left. Camcorder Guerrillas, meanwhile, is based in Glasgow and emerged from an Indymedia Scotland initiative in 2003. Since then it has produced a range of high-quality short films on a variety of topics, from climate change and the Zapatistas to the Faslane Peace Camp. Of course, in addition to these more established organizations there are also countless video-activists producing and distributing radical video-activism across the country. However, the reality is that much of this work, lacking funding or support, is sporadic, disorganized or poorly made ('quality' is subjective, of course, and lower production values can be an important part of the aesthetic identity of oppositional film. However, much video-activism also suffers from a lack of production skills, and this should be acknowledged where relevant). As a result, it tends to be swallowed in the sea of other moving images online (unless aggregated by visionOntv or one of the other organizations discussed below).
3. The IBA was succeeded by the Independent Television Commission (ITC) in 1991 and Ofcom in 2003.
4. OWM also looms large on the feature documentary industry, hosting sessions at

Sheffield International Documentary Film Festival and listing Channel 4's BRIT-DOC Foundation as one of its many partners.
5. Peter Armstrong is the father of the noted oppositional feature filmmaker, Franny Armstrong.
6. Anna Helm of EngageMedia worked with Undercurrents in the late 1990s and during that time got to know Fuzz, Young and others in Britain's video-activist culture (Young 2011: 6).
7. For a discussion of YouTube's failings with regards to political film, see Juhasz (2008).
8. The Transmission network includes Mick Fuzz and Clearer Channel, the organization he runs; EngageMedia; Zoe Young; visionOntv; *Mute,* the London-based magazine of radical culture and politics; and others.
9. Of course, earlier precedents exist, beginning with those attempted by the workers' film movements in the 1920s and 1930s (Hogenkamp 1986), but Undercurrents' was the first newsreel to achieve anything like this level of success.
10. Indeed, the little academic attention British video-activism since 1990 has received has focused almost exclusively on Undercurrents' newsreel period. Harding (1998) is one of the most useful resources; see also Heritage (2008), Atton and Hamilton (2008: 87–89), Atton (2003: 20; 2004: 42–43; 2005: 22–23) and McIver (1997).
11. Of the other three founders (Thomas Harding, Jamie Hartzell and Zoe Broughton) only Broughton still works as an independent filmmaker. Hartzell works in property management, letting properties to ethical businesses. Harding married Deborah Cackler, who also worked in distribution for Undercurrents in the 1990s, and they emigrated to the United States in the mid-2000s, where they run their own business.
12. Although not cited as part of the Ruff Cutz series, Undercurrents also released *Informed Dissent,* their interview with Noam Chomsky, on CD-ROM in 2002.
13. Characterizing campaigns as 'single issue' can be misleading. Not only does it shroud the fact that issue specificity does not necessarily exclude awareness of the wider context in which struggles take place, but many single issue campaigns cover a plethora of concerns. As George McKay has argued, 'the "single issue" of No More Roads includes topics like rural landscape, housing, the challenge to government and big business, the environment, public health, personal political strategy, and social reformation – not bad for a single issue' (1998: 38).
14. *Revolting in Prague* was the product of a variety of video-activists working at this time, including iContact, Mick Fuzz, Zoe Young, Anna Helme and Hamish Campbell (credited as Pirate TV).
15. *Indymedia Newsreal* is an ongoing project in the United States, where it continues to be broadcast by Free Speech TV every Thursday.
16. These are *SchMOVIES DVD Collection* (SchMOVIES, 2005), *V For Video-activist* (SchMOVIES, 2006), *Take Three* (SchMOVIES, 2007), *Uncertified* (SchMOVIES,

17. 2008) and *Raiders of the Lost Archive, Vol. 1* and *2* (SchMOVIES, 2008–2011). After a lull in recent years, in which Light has begun a family, a new SchMOVIES DVD is reportedly coming soon.
17. In the second period, from 1999 until 2003, Conscious Cinema was resurrected by Howitt and Zoe Young (present during the first stage of the group but not as active as she was in the second), but focused predominantly on feature documentary films, such as *Suits and Savages: Why the World Bank Won't Save the World* (Conscious Cinema, 2000) and *Not This Time: The Story of the Simon Jones Memorial Campaign* (Conscious Cinema, 2002).
18. Few original tapes from this initial period remain, however, and although a 'best of' was released in 1997 as *The Campfire Tapes: Tales From the Frontline, '94–97* (Conscious Cinema, 1997), I have not been able to locate a copy.
19. Indeed, Undercurrents and SchMOVIES remain close today: the former accompanied SchNEWS on its 2004 tour, for instance, promoting the newly released *UNN*, and Light and O'Connor have plans for a collaborative project in the future (Light 20012: 1).
20. Many of the various (and sometimes unjustified) criticisms of Undercurrents at this time can be found in the environmental activists' journal, *Do or Die* (Do or Die 1997).
21. SchNEWS is also unambiguous about its approach to funding: 'SchNEWS is run on a voluntary basis – no one gets paid … we reckon to be spending around £24,000 a year [and] rely entirely on subscriptions, benefit gigs and our readers' generosity to keep us afloat' (SchNEWS 2012).

Reference List

Atton, C. 2003. 'Organisation and Production in Alternative Media', in S. Cottle (ed.), *Media Organisation and Production*. London: Sage, pp. 41–55.
———. 2004. *An Alternative Internet*. Edinburgh: Edinburgh University Press.
———. 2005. 'Ethical Issues in Alternative Journalism', in R. Keeble (ed.), *Communication Ethics Today*. Leicester: Troubadour, pp. 15–27.
Atton, C. and J.F. Hamilton. 2008. *Alternative Journalism*. London: Sage.
Bauer, P. and D. Kidner (eds). 2013. *Working Together: Notes on British Film Collectives in the 1970s*. Southend-on-Sea: Focal Point Gallery.
Bite Size Movies. 2012a. 'About Bite Size Movies', *Bite Size Movies*. Retrieved 6 September 2012 from http://www.bitesizemovies.org.uk.
———. 2012b. 'The Positive News Film Project: Filmography 2009 to Present Day', *Bite Size Movies*. Retrieved 1 July 2012 from http://www.bitesizemovies.org.uk/the-positive-news-film-project.
Campbell, H. 2011. Unpublished interview with the author.

Carroll, J. 1993. *Humanism: The Wreck of Western Culture*. London: Fontana.
Cinco, C. 2013. 'Video4change Retreat and Sprint Highlights', *EngageMedia*. Retrieved 1 July 2013 from https://www.engagemedia.org/blog/gathering-video4change.
Corporate Watch. 2004. 'ASDA/Wal-Mart: A Corporate Profile', *Corporate Watch*. Retrieved 29 March 2012 from http://www.corporatewatch.org.uk/?lid=800.
Cowley Club. 2012. 'Intro', *Cowley Club*. Retrieved 1 July 2013 from http://www.cowleyclub.org.uk/?Intro.
Dey, S. 2011. Unpublished interview with the author.
Dickinson, M., ed. 1999. *Rogue Reels: Oppositional Film in Britain, 1945–90*. London: BFI.
Do or Die. 1998. 'Lights, Camera... Activism!: Video Media and Direct Action', *Do or Die* 7. Retrieved 3 August 2012 from http://www.eco-action.org/dod/no7/5-8.html.
Fountain, A. 2007. 'Alternative Film, Video and Television, 1965–2005', in K. Coyer, T. Dowmunt and F. Fountain (eds), *The Alternative Media Handbook*. London: Routledge, pp. 29–46.
Harding, T. 1998. '*Viva Camcordistas!* Video-activism and the Protest Movement', in G. McKay (ed.), *DiY Culture: Party & Protest in Nineties Britain*. London: Verso, pp. 79–99.
Heritage, R. 2008. 'Video-Activist Citizenship and the Undercurrents Media Project: A British Case-Study in Alternative Media', in M. Pajnik and J.D.H. Downing (eds), *Alternative Media and the Politics of Resistance: Perspectives and Challenges*. Ljublana: Peace Institute, pp. 139–61.
Hogenkamp, B. 1986. *Deadly Parallels: Film and the Left in Britain, 1929–39*. London: Lawrence and Wishart.
IMC London. 2013. 'Time to Move On: London IMC Signing Off', *Indymedia London*. Retrieved 1 July 2013 from http://london.indymedia.org/articles/13128.
InsightShare. 2012. 'Story So Far', *InsightShare*. Retrieved 31 August 2012 from http://www.insightshare.org/about-us/story.
Light, P. 2008. 'SchMOVIES', *Facebook*. Retrieved 29 August 2012 from https://www.facebook.com/groups/152884905628/members.
———. 2012. Unpublished interview with the author.
Lovink G. and F. Schneider. 2003. 'A Virtual World is Possible: From Tactical Media to Digital Multitudes', *Universitat Oberta de Catalunya*. Retrieved 21 September 2012 from http://www.uoc.edu/portal/en/index.html.
Juhasz, A. 2008. '"Documentary on YouTube": The Failure of the Direct Cinema of the Slogan', in T. Austin and W. de Jong (eds), *Rethinking Documentary: New Perspectives, New Practices*. Maidenhead: Open University Press, pp. 299–311.
McIver, G. 1997. *Media and the Spectacular Society*. University of Westminster Hypermedia Research Centre. Retrieved 1 August 2012 from http://www.hrc.wmin.ac.uk/hrc/theory/mediaspectacular/t.1.3%5B7%5D.html.
McKay, G. 1998. 'DiY Culture: Notes Towards an Intro', in G. MacKay (ed.), *DiY Culture: Party & Protest in Nineties Britain*. London: Verso, pp. 1–53.
O'Connor, P. 2011. Unpublished interview with author.

One World Group. 2012. 'About', *One World Group*. Retrieved 3 September 2012 from http://www.oneworldgroup.org/about.
One World Media. 2012a. 'History and Achievements', *One World Media*. Retrieved 3 September 2012 from http://oneworldmedia.org.uk/trust1/about/history.
———. 2012b. 'Awards 2011', *One World Media*. Retrieved 3 September 2012 from http://oneworldmedia.org.uk/awards/previous_awards/2011.
One World. 2013. 'One World Founders Hand Over the Keys'. Retrieved 20 June 2013 from http://oneworld.org/2013/03/21/oneworld-founders-hand-over-the-keys.
Plunkett, J. 2002. 'Reality Bytes', *The Guardian*, 29 July. Retrieved 3 September 2012 http://www.guardian.co.uk/media/2002/jul/29/mondaymediasection7.
SchNEWS. 1996. 'Squatters' Estate Agency', *SchNEWS*. Retrieved 5 September 2012 from http://www.schnews.org.uk/archive/round-squatters-estate-agency.htm.
———. 2004a. *SchNEWS At Ten: A Decade of Party and Protest*. London: Calverts Press.
———. 2004b. 'SchNEWS At Ten', *SchNEWS*, 26 March. Retrieved 5 September 2012 from http://www.schnews.org.uk/archive/news447.htm#seven.
———. 2011. 'From the Rubble of Double Trouble', *SchNEWS*, 6 May. Retrieved 20 July 2012 from http://www.schnews.org.uk/archive/news7706.php.
———. 2012. 'About Us', *SchNEWS*. Retrieved 29 August 2012 from http://www.schnews.org.uk/about_us.
Spill Media. 2012a. 'Social Aims', *Spill Media*. Retrieved 31 August 2012 from http://www.spillmedia.co.uk/social-aims.html.
———. 2012b. 'Spill Media Embark on New Swansea Telly Project!', *Spill Media News*. Retrieved 21 June 2012 from http://spillmedianews.blogspot.co.uk/search?q=swansea+telly.
Transmission. 2012. 'About', *Transmission*. Retrieved 27 September 2012 from http://transmission.cc/about.
Worldbytes. 2012. 'Who We Are', *Worldbytes*. Retrieved 31 August 2012 from http://www.worldbytes.org/who-we-are.
Undercurrents. 2010. 'A Brief History of Undercurrents', *Undercurrents*. Retrieved 11 October 2010 from http://www.undercurrents.org/history/index.htm.
Young, Z. 2011. Unpublished interview with the author.
YouTube. 2013. 'Press Room', *YouTube*. Retrieved 1 July 2013 from http://www.youtube.com/yt/press.

Filmography

A-Z of Bushcraft. 2009. Undercurrents.
Black Gold. 2006. Nick and Marc Francis.
The End of the Line. 2009. Rupert Murray.
Globalisation and the Media. 2002. Undercurrents.

Indymedia European Newsreel. 2002. Undercurrents.
J18: The Story the Media Ignored. 1999. Undercurrents.
Living in the Future: Ecovillage Pioneers. 2006. Undercurrents.
On the Push: A Surfer's Guide to Climate Change. 2009. Undercurrents.
Revolting in Prague: IMF Protests 2000. 2000. Various.
Riots Reframed. 2013. Fahim Alam.
SchNEWS at Ten: The Movie. 2005. SchNEWS
Secret City. 2012. Michael Chanan and Lee Salter.
Undercurrents 10 ¾. 2002. Undercurrents.
Undercurrents News Network (UNN). 2004. Undercurrents.
Who Polices the Police?. 2012. Ken Fero.

CHAPTER 9
Marxist Resistance at Bicycle Speed
Screening the Critical Mass Movement

Lars Kristensen

Activism today is no longer a case of putting bodies on the line; increasingly, it requires and involves bodies-with-cameras.
—Constance Penley and Andrew Ross, quoted in Patricia R. Zimmerman, *States of Emergency*

Since the early 1990s, the Critical Mass movement has been associated with groups of bicyclists riding through inner cities in numerous countries. On every last Friday of the month, people on bicycles gather at a certain spot to collectively ride through the city, thus actively disrupting the traffic flow of motor vehicles. Not accurately described as a bicycle advocacy organization, Critical Mass is instead labelled a celebration of the bicycle (Blickstein and Hanson 2001: 352). In the words of Chris Carlsson, the editor of *Critical Mass: Bicycling's Defiant Celebration*: 'Critical Mass bicycle rides are no protest movement as we commonly imagine. Instead riders have gathered to celebrate their choice to bicycle, and in so doing have opened up a new kind of social and political space unprecedented in this era of atomization and commodification' (Carlsson 2002: 5–6).

These mass rides make visible, in a traditional minoritarian fashion, how the urban environment is constructed according to the circulation of capital and how private cars get preference over other forms of velocity. According to Tim Creswell, 'free and equal mobility is a deception' within urban transportation (quoted in Vivanco 2013: 14). Thus, Critical Mass rides highlight how the urban environment is hierarchical and thereby press for changes in how we move, for leisure or work, within the city. The campaigning aim of Critical Mass is to improve conditions for urban bicyclists. A key part in the rise of the movement has been its visual representation of mass bicycle rides, from its first appearance in Ted White's film, *The Return of the Scorcher* (1992), to an ever increasing amount of clips posted online, shot and produced by anonymous riders and spectators.

This chapter will examine both the Critical Mass movement and films related to this form of activism. It will consider the relationship between bike activism and Marxist activism and ideology, and ask the question whether the moving images of the Critical Mass movement are a form of activism or merely representations of activism. In order to explore these points, the chapter considers, firstly, the activism of rider and the activism of bicycles as eco-machines; secondly, it looks at the moving images themselves and the viewing practices that these images entail.

The Critical Mass Rider

Individuality has always been associated with the bicycle rider. All bicycle historians point to the benefit of being mobile and autonomous as the single vital component in the development of the bicycle (Boal 2002; Herlihy 2004). It was the craving for singularity that was the attraction of the bicycle; a singularity seen clearly in the way women used the bicycle to liberate themselves from the patriarchal structures of society. Once on your bicycle, you were autonomous (Herlihy 2004: 266). But it seems that this is reversed when riders ride together, forming a collective identity.

Mass bicycle rides began in 1992 in San Francisco. Under the name 'Community Clout', a group of bicyclists gathered to ride together through the city. These riders were like-minded people, who liked to socialize while riding their bicycles. This phenomenon was spontaneous and playful, but also driven by a desire to perform at a collective and political level. What bicycle riders discovered was that when they ride in large groups, automobiles – cars, trucks and busses – had to yield to the group of riders, a reversal of the status quo. In particular, in U.S. inner cities, bicycle riders must give way to motorized vehicles, and motorists often look upon these riders as freaks or outcasts, unfit for modern urban traffic. For brief moments, mass bicycle rides change this structure. However, reversing the traffic hierarchy can only happen through collective effort and it was only through the collective rides that the movement discovered its political dimensions. As Zack Furness states: '[W]hen a cyclist takes that same ride with a group of likeminded individuals – whether the ride is a celebration, or a protest against the oil industry – they transform the meaning and function of the bicycle inasmuch as they are able to communicate that message to one another, and hopefully, to people in the general public' (Furness 2005: 403).

Ascertaining its political dynamics, the movement quickly grew and changed its name to Critical Mass. It was this dynamic, the taking over the direction of traffic, that the San Francisco riders seized upon. The riders acted on the assumption that if enough people ride bicycles together, such action would force a new direction of society and create a new flow. And, indeed, the movement has changed the direction of traffic in the sense that city planners are today taking the plight of bicyclists seriously. The view of urban bicycle riders has changed from freaks on wheels to daily commuters travelling from average suburban homes to average inner city jobs. Bicycle enthusiasm is nowadays less about embracing counter-culturists and alternative living, and more about making actual and sustainable change in how people get around. According to Luis A. Vivanco, the buzzword from city administrations is 'liveability', which aims at limiting noise and pollution from congested roads and promoting alternatives that are 'cost-effective and environmental-friendly' (Vivanco 2013: xix). Middle- and upper-class professionals are at the high end of the priority list of city planners, and creating bicycle culture helps attract them. While this certainly makes the Critical Mass movement and its lobbying potential a one-issue type of protest, the riders might, however, see it differently. More likely they perceive themselves as part of a 'nowtopia', as described by Chris Carlsson (2008), where one's labour is divided between bread jobs and meaningful activism. There is a clear distinction between labour and protest, between activist performing and performing work. Such attitude, which has kindled since the fall of communism in Eastern Europe, is, however, rejected by hardened Marxists, arguing that the effect of protest will be erased by the effect of work. However, Marxism has historically been unkind to such one-issue movements as Critical Mass, as well as to feminism, because these cultural rights issue are not based on class struggle. James O'Connor observed that 'ecology and nature; the politics of the body, feminism, and the family; and urban movements and related topics are usually discussed in post-Marxist [rather than Marxist] terms' (O'Connor 1988: 12). O'Connor argues that this should not be the case, since these issues are part of a capitalist production system and part of the overall condition that capitalist production feeds on. Ecology, feminism or urban bicycle protest can thus be seen as activism that aims at disrupting the feeding mechanism, despite their post-Marxist tactics of being beyond class struggle. This is likely to be a feeling shared among Critical Mass riders; that class belonging is a nonissue. The dictum seems to be that 'as long as you are riding a bicycle, you are one of us', which excludes nobody expect those who cannot ride bicycles.

If this activist position of the bicycle rider is correct, then it also fixes the rider to a certain historical account of bicycle activism. For example, Zack Furness sees the Critical Mass rider as part of a continuation of the late-nineteenth century feminist bicycle riders' movement and Dutch Situationists of the 1970s (Furness 2005). As these classical examples show, Critical Mass riders seek to obstruct the speed and progression of inner cities, which, according to the riders, have led to an inhospitable society and ecological devastation. Thus, the activism of a Critical Mass rider is best summed up as a movement that is hostile towards speed and acceleration of urban traffic, and it is here that the movement gains its revolutionary characteristics. As Paul Virilio writes in the first pages of *Speed and Politics* (1986: 3): 'The revolution contingent attains its ideal form not in the place of production, but in the street, where for a moment it stops being a cog in the technical machine and itself becomes a motor (machine of attack), in other words a "producer of speed"'. It should be noted that the eco-machine is not the same as Virilio's technical machine. In fact, the eco-machine is something opposite, which I will deal with next. For now it worth noting how the Critical Mass riders become, on the last Friday of each month, the 'producer of speed' and the motor that drives forward revolutionary changes. The bike activists bite into this concept and feed on the beliefs that by slowing down traffic, and thereby modernity and progress, the riders force a change in the socioeconomic structures that underpin capitalist society. However, if this accounts for the Marxist traits of the Critical Mass rides, then it still does not address the machine, the bicycle, on which the change is attained.

The Eco-Machine

The bicycle is the answer to all evils, as a bicycle activist tells anthropologist Luis Vivanco: 'If I were running for office, here is what my campaign platform would be. Less crime. Better school performance. Reduced greenhouse gases.

Better looking communities. Friendlier neighborhoods. A more prosperous business district. And you know how I would be able to achieve these things? Bicycles.' (Vivanco 2013: 6).

While we can detect a certain naivety, it is not uncommon for a one-issue movement to apply a single solution to a host of problems; a kind of utopian thinking, which touches ground with Romanticism and the ideal of a precapitalist world (Löwy, 2002: 122). On this account, the ecosocialists are struggling with classical Marxism. On the one hand, they reject capitalist, progressive consumer-driven production on the grounds that it exploits humans and nature, which leads to an uneven society, but, one the other, they must reject Marx's and Engel's 'uncritical attitude towards those aspects of industrial civilization that have contributed to its destructive relationship to the environment' (Löwy 2002: 123). One of the leading ecosocialists is Michael Löwy, and in his opinion this ideological clash leads to: 'the great challenge for a renewal of Marxist thought at the threshold of the twenty-first century. It requires that Marxists undertake a deep critical revision of their traditional conception of "productive forces," and that they break radically with the ideology of linear progress and with the technological and economic paradigm of modern industrial civilization' (Löwy 2005: 16). Instead, we need to take a 'detour' through history in order to arrive at an ecosocialist future (Löwy 2002: 122). That said, the 'greens' and the 'reds' endure a difficult relationship, since as long as technical progress and growth does not exploit nature or humans, it will pass for the environmentalist. In the argumentation above from the bicycle activist, there should be no doubt about the seriousness of the utterance – the bicycle activists see their vehicles as the solution to all ills of society. Thus, in short, green values collide with Marxist perspectives, since green values are utopian, and maybe rightly so, but not correctly based on class struggle. As the founding member of the journal *Capitalism Nature Socialism*, James O'Connor, noticed in the late 1980s, 'the struggles of "new social movements" over conditions of production are generally regarded in the self-defined post-Marxist universe as non-class issues or multi-class issues' (O'Connor 1988: 37). This resembles the Critical Mass ethos of being a heterogeneous movement. For ecosocialists, the beyond-class struggle springs from the universal nature of environmental concerns; nature affects us all and this moves the struggle of reaching a global ecological balance beyond nation, identity and class. However, capital exports pollution to countries with low emission restrictions, which is in the global south, i.e. the countries with the lowest costs and with the lowest salaries (Löwy 2005: 22). Environmental problems 'are bigger problems from the standpoint of the poor, including the working poor, than for the salariat and the well-to-do' (O'Connor 1988: 37). O'Connor's point is that once ecosocialism accepts its class struggle perspective, green value cannot be classless or beyond class concepts: the 'issues pertaining to production conditions are class issues, even though they are also *more* than class issues' (O'Connor 1988: 37). Ecosocialism is precisely about class and exploitation – who gets polluted, who can afford to pollute and who are too poor to refuse the pollution of others.

The theoretical foundation of ecosocialism is located in drawing attention to the *conditions* of production, as well as the capitalist production in itself. For the ecological Marxist, the point of departure is the condition in which capitalist production takes place. In other words, the condition of capitalism extracts natural resource and human labour, and relies on transportation and communication. The key issue is: 'The contradiction between capitalist production relations and productive forces and conditions of production. Neither human laborpower nor external nature nor infrastructures including their space/time dimensions are produced capitalistically, although capital treats these conditions of production as if they are commodities or commodity capital' (O'Connor 1988a: 23). The fact that labour power and nature are not produced capitalistically, but treated as if they were so by capitalism, means that societies, communities or the masses must intervene in order to regulate capital, the condition of production. The ecosocialist must actively intervene in the dispute between capital and nature. Left on its own, capital would self-destruct in a cataclysm of irreversible progress or, as O'Connor (1988: 25) states, 'by impairing or destroying rather than reproducing its own conditions'. The condition of capitalist production is defined in terms of both its social and material dimensions, placing it outside commodities and capitalist consumption. Technical progress and economic growth is not the evil here, and this opens up for a pragmatic view of the machine in ecosocialism. It is in this regard that I want to look at the bicycle as an ecomachine that is beyond the extraction of the worker's blood, sweat and tyres.

Ecosocialism has a progressive view on machines and technology. It rejects the relativism of living species, that all species are equal, which is found in circles termed 'extreme', 'fundamentalist' or 'deep-ecology' (Löwy, 2005: 17).

It seeks to move away from an ascetic Marxism, which, as Sean Sayers (2011: 164) notes, relies on a romantic relationship with nature. In the ecosocialist's opinion, technology, and thereby the machine, should help restore the environment. These machines: 'may or may not be functional for capital as a whole, individual capitals, in the short-or-long-run. The results would depend on other crisis prevention and resolution measures, their exact conjuncture, and the way in which they articulate with the crisis of nature broadly defined' (O'Connor 1988: 32). Whether or not this technology can serve capitalism is the tricky question that the ecosocialist must face, which resembles Marx's own concerns at the machine and its worker.

In *Grundrisse,* we find Marx's frequently quoted reflection on the machine, where he argues that the machine 'is itself the virtuoso, with a soul of its own [and] the worker's activity [when working at the machine] reduced to a mere abstraction of activity' (Marx 1971: 133). The machine accumulates capital through the negation of necessary human labour, but also forces a human to adjust to its speed; it forces man to become machine. The tool, on the other hand, is the appendix of man, as it is handheld and without a speed of its own; the activity of the worker animates the tool, which depends on the 'dexterity' of the worker's action (Marx 1971: 133). In other words, the tool is soulless and lacks the ability to dictate the speed of its user. We should not see Marx's injection of soul into the machine as a dystopian prediction of the world domination of the machine, but rather as an image of how we should interact with the machine (Kemple 1995: 27). As in ecosocialism, the bike activist's relationship with eco-machines is dual. On the one hand, the machines, and in particular cars, are seen as the cause of all problems, but on the other, machines might help clean the environment. If the eco-machine is reconsidered as a tool, though, it can be useful in eco-restoration, liberating humankind from enslavement. I will argue that the bicycles in the Critical Mass films are within the tool paradigm, which is supported by Ivan Illich's conceptualization where the bicycle is seen as a tool of conviviality, as an extension of man rather than man as a virtuoso machine (see Illich 1973). However, while the tools liberate the worker and the machine fixes capital to the machine (Marx 1971: 138), the bicycle has historically been viewed as a tool that affords liberty and independence as escape from social structures.

One way of detecting the tool connection, the leisure paradigm or 'free rider' perspective is to look at the context of the Critical Mass movement, which can be seen as the culmination of the popularity of the mountain bike. Every bicycle boom has its own specific context, where several 'events' and inventions concur (Vivanco 2013: 40–41), and in the Critical Mass movement one of these was the mass production of mountain bikes, which popularized the ability to go 'off road' in the pursuit of leisure (Rosen 2002: 3; Herlihy 2004: 9).[1] Developed in the early 1970s by hippies, the mountain bike broke with the concept of the 'Rover safety bicycle', the model that had been quintessential in making bicycles mainstream during the boom of the 1890s. Where the safety bicycle took the machine away from the ethnic- and class-segregated wheelsmen clubs and into the hands of, foremost, women, and later workers, the mountain bike removed the ordinariness of bicycling and infused it with thrills, excitement and danger, the complete opposite of safety – just as on the highwheeler a century earlier, the rider 'demonstrated qualities of control and mastery over one's body and machine, endowing the rider with social distinction as progressive and modern' (Vivanco 2013: 40). Mountain bikers, according to Paul Rosen, 'situate themselves … within the often-contradictory discourse of new environmental social movement and "wildness" … on the one hand and with urban land and transportation on the other' (Rosen 2002: 148). It is this contradiction that fits the concept of the eco-machine; eco-friendly, but without the negative productivism associated with classical Marxism.

The point is that when the bicycle switches from being conceptualized as a machine of transportation to being associated with wilderness, nature and escapism, the identity of the rider changes accordingly. Thus, Critical Mass riders are best categorized as 'free-riders' using the bicycle as a tool for activism. However, when these free-riders become a collective they reach eco-machine proportions. It is only here that they become producers of bicycle speed.

The Critical Mass Films

There are numerous moving images that can be attached to Critical Mass, and many of them bear a similarity to the early leftist filmmaking of the 1920s and 1930s, in which screened 'protest and marches' were the main theme (Thompson and Bordwell 2010: 281). That said, the framework presented here does not limit itself to include only those films that have 'documentary value', i.e. such films that feature talking heads or have a certain length of narration, since this would exclude a whole set of moving images of Critical Mass activism, which equally are meant to capture the rides, but without the established form of documentary cinema. Rather than focusing on a few established documentaries, this section hopes to indicate the diversity of moving images available; all of which aim at capturing the uniqueness of Critical Mass both in form and content.

Firstly, the space in which these films take place has to be addressed. It has been reported that Critical Mass events have been held in more than three hundred cities around the world (Madden 2003), but there are no exact figures for the spread of mass bicycle rides. What is clear, though, is that its claim to be a global phenomenon is somewhat suspicious, since it is chiefly post-industrial Western cities that attract the huge numbers of riders. Listing cities where major Critical Mass rides (more than one thousand riders) have taken place, Susan Blickstein and Susan Hanson write 'that one hundred cities globally currently have or have had Critical Mass rides, including Chicago, New York, Seattle, Tucson, Sydney, Paris, London, Barcelona, Portland (Oregon), Johannesburg, Dublin, Zurich, Tokyo, Taipei and Hobart (Tasmania)' (Blickstein and Hanson 2001: 352). Critical Mass rides have also been organized in other cities, like Mumbai, Cairo and Rio de Janeiro, but on a more modest scale. For example, in Cairo, no more than fifty bicyclists would participate, and events would be attached to organizations or clubs, such as the society of cardiologists or the Dutch embassy in Cairo. Evident from Blickstein and Hanson's list is that bicycle cities, such as Amsterdam or Copenhagen, are not typical Critical Mass sites,[2] which suggests that the activism of Critical Mass works best in car-dominated societies where bicycling is seen as abnormal and traffic is regulated for motorized vehicles.[3] By default in city narratives, the films engage with urban features like the architecture and historicism of each particular city, such as famous monuments, squares and bridges, each signifying where the event takes place. As one U.S. Critical Mass rider says, '[Critical Mass] is local but it is a different kind of local. It is everywhere, *locally*' (Culley 2002: 13). The city iconography is central to this everywhere-ness of the films.

The person filming can be a professional filmmaker or an ordinary participant of the ride. Where the former seeks to describe and contextualize Critical Mass, the latter aims to give an inside view of an actual ride or several rides. The films can also be from the point of view of a spectator of the ride, a news media source or an individual blogger, for whom the moving images function as evidence in a media discourse; they could also be just tourist shots of a particular city. The distribution of the moving images varies, just as the people shooting the event, but chiefly the films are spread through digital video-sharing channels or through designated video blogs, as well as through more specialized bicycle film festivals, which have screened well-known documentaries on Critical Mass. Self-retail of DVDs is also an option used to reach audiences. In particular, professional filmmakers are using this channel of distribution, since it maintains a source of formal income for the filmmaker while also making contact with specific viewers. Ted White, for example, has made two films, *The Return of the Scorcher* and *We Are Traffic!* (1999), claimed to be the official films of the movement, which he sells through his website.

This leads us to the content of the films, which can be themed from time to time, such as Halloween rides, nude rides or Earth Day rides. The majority of films, though, are just moving images of bicyclists riding through cities. Where a film attains more 'value' than others, for example by being screened at a film festival or being released through commercial channels, it is likely be on a specific topic, such as in the case of *Still We Ride* (Andrew Lynn, Elizabeth Press, Chris Ryan 2004). The film describes for the New York Police Department's clampdown on bicyclists in the days before a Republican convention, leading to the illegal mass arrest of Critical Mass riders and the impoundment of their bicycles. In *Still We Ride,* infringement of civil liberties, abuse of power, police manufactured evidence, surveillance and mass media blindness are at the core of the film's message of injustice towards not only bicyclists in general but Critical Mass in particular.

While Ted White's two films and *Still We Ride* are exceptions, the vast majority of the films are anonymously authored films posted online. In these films the story is mostly linear – the bicyclists riding from point A to point B, although it might not be explicit where A and B are located. There can be stories embedded in the narrative, such as focusing on one rider through the ride, an accident happening en route or a violation against minority rights. Many films will adhere to a narrative structure, starting with a departure point where riders gather, then following the ride through edited cuts, but ending with riders reaching their intended destination. Achieving the ride's goal can be emphasized through a celebration, with every bicyclist lifting their means of transport in the air in triumph, or through an informal dispersal of the riders. However, unedited stories are also posted, where we as spectators see only riders pass-

Figure 9.1. Critical Mass Houston, United States. From YouTube, 'Houston Critical Mass – July 2013', uploaded by Abrahán Garza.

ing a static camera, thus not indicating a beginning and an end of the ride, but emphasizing the number of riders.

This technique underscores the size of the particular event – the more riders, the longer the film, and the longer the film, the greater the spectator's impression of the event. Different films connote different aspects of bicycle activism, but equal for them all, the more people joining, the more velocity of the movement. Critical Mass riders, in such movements, or moments, become the proletarians, who in the words of Marx and Engels, 'have nothing to lose but their chains. They have a world to win'. Just as Sergei Eisenstein's film *Battleship Potemkin* (1925) travelled the world physically in various editions and cuts, these moving images of Critical Mass rides has a chance to form mass movement of united bicyclists.

This leaves us with the style of filmmaking, in other words, the camera, editing and sound. Again, the variation is huge. The camera can be immobile, as with static tripod shooting as noted above. Other films use fixed cameras, but, rather than being at the roadside, these are fixed to the bicycle, forming long tracking shots of the ride.

Fixing the camera either onto the bicycle or the rider, e.g. onto the helmet, centres the narrative around one particular individual, thus framing the ride within this rider's realm, capturing other co-activist riders – but not the film-

Figure 9.2. Critical Mass Hamburg, Germany. From YouTube, 'critical mass hamburg 24.06.2011', uploaded by Martin John.

ing the self (the 'selfie'). In films where the camera is handheld and therefore allows for images of the self, a more holistic event is created, as the camera can spin 360 degrees or change hands from one rider to another, creating multiple centres. While one-camera films are in the majority, more elaborate multi-camera films are available as well. In these, several riders film the event, or two cameras are fixed to one particular bicycle, e.g. one camera shooting backwards, the other forwards, and the footage is then edited into a single film.

In these films, the editing is linear and done with attempts of creating continuity in the films; however, when the editing is more loosely built, we get jump cuts, fast rhythmic editing or montage sequences, or even still images that almost deny the movement of the riders. In more elaborated film, the image has been colour toned or is in black and white. Lastly, the sound varies as well, but the sound, or the soundtrack, is also likely to be a key element dictating the filmmaking style, such as camera, editing and theme. This is because often prefabricated music is played with the moving images, so that the film, and thereby the ride, is cut according to the length of the piece of music, which can be from various genres. Different from traditional non-diegetic musical composition intended to mirror the emotions on screen, the music in these films is more in the direction of general popular taste, or, in other words,

Figure 9.3. Critical Mass Cluj-Napoca (Kolozsvár), Romania. From Vimeo, 'Critical Mass March 2013 Cluj-Napoca/Kolozsvár', uploaded by Torok Tihamer.

the filmmakers' favourite tracks. That said, no less than a musical score of an epic science fiction film, the soundtrack is meant to create an affinity with the audience. When prefab music is not used, the soundtrack consists of camcorder sounds, mixing bicycle sounds with conversations and surrounding street sounds, if the films do not have a voiceover narrative. A signature of Critical Mass rides is, though, the sound of bicycle bells and whistles, creating a cacophony of noise that is meant to attract the city dwellers' attention.

If this sketchy outline of the films merely hints at the diversity presence, then it is wholly deliberate, because whether or not these films are deliberate activist films, they represent activism by screening Critical Mass events. I hold that since they screen Critical Mass events, they are per definition activist text. However, they are also marked by form and viewing context, which makes them closer to cinema of attraction than to traditional narrative cinema. In other words, they have what Joost Broeren (2009: 159–60) terms 'physical display'; that is films that centre on the display of physicality – a stunt, a trick or, in this case, a Critical Mass ride. My aim is not to 'read' these films as activist texts or to create an hierarchy among the texts according to which they are more or less activist, but to examine the intention of the filmmakers – the producers of the moving images. Already we have seen that the rider takes the position of the activist using the bicycle; thus, at leisure speed, the rider slows the flow of traffic, highlighting a more sustainable alternative to city transportation. But if there is a causal link between the activism of the rider and the bicycle as means of leisure, can there be the same link between the films portraying activism and the audiences who view the films? To answer this question, we will need to look at authorial intent, as well as the audience's reaction, because intention does not matter, if the film leaves the audience indifferent.

Filmmaker's Intent and Viewing Practice

The art historian EH Gombrich has argued for a constructivist approach when interpreting artwork, i.e. that the intention of the artist should guide the reading of the work (Gaut 2010: 166). Talking about appreciating artworks in a museum, he writes:

> *For most of the paintings and statues which are now lined up along the walls of our museums and galleries were not meant to be displayed as Art. They were made for a definite occasion and a definite purpose which were in the artist's mind when he made it. Those ideas, on the other hand, that we outsiders usually worry about, ideas about beauty and expression, are rarely mentioned by the artists. (Gombrich 2006: 28)*

First we notice the displacement of the artwork, which suggests that considering artwork out of its 'rightful' context should prompt us to read into the piece the ideas and concepts that the artist intended for it. In pronouncing 'the death of the author', Roland Barthes would of course reject such authorial intention in a text, but intent in an artwork resembles intent in activist texts, i.e. its meaning is to change the perception of the viewer. Secondly, and following from the first assertion, artists intend for expression in their work, an expression that we as viewers 'must' consider when interpreting the artwork. Likewise, viewing the Critical Mass films, we 'must' consider the intention of the filmmaker and the context in which they were meant to be screen. Once the intention of a Critical Mass film has been examined, it becomes easier to decide whether the activism presented in the films is passed on to the viewers.

The concept of activism in the moving images of bicycles is centred on advocating minority rights. In this sense bicycle activism is similar to other forms of minorities in pursuit of political recognition, such as gay rights or institutionalized racism. Representation of these minorities through moving images has been vital for their recognition, socially as well as politically. In the post-Marxist critique, the right to political recognition (often gained through media representation) is accepted without alternation of the apparatus that presents the message. Critical Mass, whether at an actual rally or in a representation of that rally on screen, is about drawing attention to the violation of a bicycling minority. However, the bicycle activist also strongly believes that the act of riding a bicycle produces more utilitarian happiness and pleasure, not only through individual happiness but also through sustainable living and gentrification of city neighbourhoods (Vivanco 2013: xix). There are strong sentiments that bicycle politics will increase people's happiness. More pleasure and less pain comes from riding a bicycle, which is what Critical Mass rides advocate when celebrating bicycling; but is that the same for the films? If the Critical Mass filmmaker 'passes on' the pleasure of the bicycle through filmmaking, the intention is to produce pleasure and reduce pain.[4]

In Critical Mass films, rarely do we actually know who the 'producer' is, and often the film seems to have no obvious 'message' – it is just bicyclists riding by the camera. And finally, who is the intended receiver of the film's activist message – friends from the rally, other activists, city commuters or ardent motorists? Even if the intentionalism of the filmmaker is explicitly bicycle activism ('biketivism') and the message of the film is that bicycling is good for a sustainable future, there is no guarantee that the viewer will act on the message. Since the viewing practices of Critical Mass films take place online, there no direct communication between audiences. This might be resolved through bicycle film festivals, which cater specifically to this community and already committed audiences. But, unless you are part of the images there is no inherent communitarian 'sharedness' pervading from screen to the viewer.

This is largely because of the limitations of the Internet and online viewing. The Internet 'has colonized and transformed everything in its path' (McChesney 2013: 3) to a degree where media content industries form an oligopoly of a few conglomerate companies. In this way the Internet is similar to mainstream Hollywood, which also feeds on the illusion of free market economics (Miller 2005: 182–93). Media empires acquire market shares that impede plurality and the views of minorities, since corporate business by definition would rather play safe than experiment in innovation. A key idea associated with the Internet – that everyone can be both producer and consumer, or the 'prosumer', and often both at the same time, in a marketplace where supply and demand of the moving image are perfectly balanced – conceals the economics that also limit the system (Zimmermann 2000: xv). The word 'prosumer' makes Toby Miller see red, rejecting it as a new phenomenology of labour. 'It is', writes Miller (2009: 435), 'reoccupying and resignifying the space of corporate-driven divisions of labor in ways that cybertarians have simply ignored'. But how does this corporate enterprise work in practice with Critical Mass films on the Internet?

Danny Birchall lists four distinct features of online documentaries (Birchall 2008: 278–83), and all four features are evident in the Critical Mass films online: Firstly, Birchall notes the way the Internet connects people with common interests across geographical borders, which is applicable to Critical Mass riders around the world, who can assess each other's films and form communities in a way that was previously impossible due to physical distances. This is one of the reasons why Critical Mass has had the impact is has, being near global in its reach. However, the anonymity of the Internet and/or the remoteness that it thrives on remain a barrier between audiences. This is what the bicycle film festival avoids: actually manifesting a sharedness among viewers. Secondly, the Internet is ideal for political campaigning with moving images; films 'that seek to change people's mind or reinforce a viewpoint' (Birchall 2008: 278). In Birchall's account, there is little emphasis on changing viewers more broadly according to Marxist principles; rather, the argument reaches back at analogue film distribution and reaching the viewers physically at cine-clubs and provincial screens. This political and campaigning feature of online moving images shares similarities with PR agency strategies and corporate branding. Thus, the Critical Mass films add to the cine-scape of political campaigning by portraying activists on bicycles. We can safely claim that Critical Mass films are part of a larger campaign of promoting urban bicyclism.

Thirdly, Birchall identifies 'dirty reality' as a practice in online documentaries, a category where shocking images that were usually embedded within a moral or political context are now posted online as 'the unedited reality'. On the Internet, this posting of raw violence can also be observed within Critical

Mass films. The most popular clips, i.e. those which are viewed most, are in fact of Critical Mass rides where accidents occur during the filming, such as a car ramming through a Critical Mass ride or a policeman knocking down Critical Mass riders. These collisions, or dromological accidents, following Paul Virilio, with other vehicles or state authorities are also visual evidence used in court cases. Critical Mass' political campaign of making visual evidence is central to progressively push for a more humane, common bicycle culture. Finally, Birchall's list ends with the segment of 'the lives of others', where self-posting, or self-publishing, is open for others to see. As mentioned, the selfie is a standard image in the Critical Mass film, where the filmmaking self is recorded as a Critical Mass activist. Posting yourself for others to see is explicitly the intention of the filmmaker, arguing that 'I am doing it, and so should you (the viewer)'.

Whether audiences do this or not is the object of Alexandra Juhasz' examination of queer culture online (Juhasz 2008: 299–312). What she discovers is that although valuable material is accessed through online video site, the viewing practice fails to create communities of activism. Documentaries begin in the world and end in the room, and it is the latter that Juhasz is concerned with. Where the moving images explode in numbers online, they implode in other features, namely theoretical, political and historical awareness and discussion (Juhasz 2008: 310). This creates a contradiction: on the one hand, we can detect how the online Critical Mass film reaches its limits in promoting its campaign message – it simply leaves viewers removed from the specificity and motivating clarity of cause and community. However, on the other hand, and more in line with Birchall's account, Critical Mass films are intrinsic to the Critical Mass movement, which would not have grown so extensively had it not been for its digital moving images. Critical Mass would have remained local, and not 'local everywhere'. A big obstruction to creating awareness and discussion is the corporate context of the Internet, which, according to Juhasz, limits complexity and discourse. In turn, we are back at the need to apply a political economy in analysing moving images online: 'The ways capitalism works and does not work determine the role of the Internet might play in society. The profit motive, commercialism, public relations, marketing, and advertising – all defining features of contemporary corporate capitalism – are foundational to any assessment of how the Internet has developed and is likely to develop' (McChesney 2013: 13).

The Internet as a capitalist system has shaped and formed its own practice of idealism and activism, which continuously manages to allow access while not threatening the economy that underpins the system. In other words, the intention of the online filmmaker is proving to be both difficult and easy to understand. It is easy to comprehend as a campaigning tool that has the ability to reach huge audiences, but it is more difficult to fathom the consequences of the ephemeral nature of the viewing practice, which leaves the viewer without the opportunity for discussion and without an analogue community.

Conclusion

In the introduction to this chapter, the question was asked whether the activism portrayed is transferred to the film and the viewer of the film. The argument present has been that, since we can classify Critical Mass events as containing Marxist activism, they become the motor of revolution; the films, which are associated with the movement, should therefore also be Marxist activist films. However, this was not the case. It seems that once the activism onscreen goes online, it can so easily evaporate in the process. Furthermore, there is the additional problem of the free-rider perspective in Critical Mass; that the bicycle is closely associated with rebel culture and daringness, which connects Critical Mass to joy riding. In this perspective, individuality is again infused into the bicycle, leaving the collective activist body in its wake. The free-rider and escapist bicyclist question the formation of ecosocialism as being based on class struggle. If the free-wheeling mountain bike rider becomes associated with the 'free rider', he defies the collective eco-machine. This pushes the discussion into the hands of the post-Marxists. In the words of James O'Connor:

> [P]ost-Marxism, influenced by the 'free rider problem' and problems of 'rational choice' and 'social choice' (all problems which presuppose bourgeois individualism), states or implies that struggles over production conditions are different than traditional wage, hours, and working conditions struggles because conditions of production are to a large degree 'commons,' clean air being an obvious example, urban space and educational facilities being somewhat less obvious ones. (O'Connor 1988: 36)

In the same way we can identify the online film viewing within 'bourgeois individualism', as it hides its corporate character while offering consumer 'choice', in that everything is available. It is the ability of the Critical Mass ride to be both an individual tool for activism and a collective eco-machine that can stop progressive productivism, which is also at the heart of the activist filming contradiction – namely, the contradiction between the collective onscreen with the loneliness of watching from home.

Notes

1. In 1990 in Britain, for example, over half of all bicycles sold were mountain bikes (Rosen 2002: 133).
2. The bicycle culture is everyday-like in these cities, i.e. it is simply faster than getting around by car or public transport. Well over half of the trips made within these cities are made by bicycles.
3. This explains why post-Communist cities, such as Yekaterinburg, Budapest and Riga, feature as Critical Mass cities. Communism was, just like Western societies, marked by a drive for automobility. For example, the highest status symbol throughout the Eastern Bloc was to own a car.
4. I deliberately use the words pleasure over pain, as they are similar to the way utilitarians would argue. An action is morally correct if it produces more pleasure and less pain. This has its specific problems, which were highlighted by Bernard Williams (1973). Moral philosopher Peter Singer (2005) rejected Williams' argument, saying that we can still reach a morally right decision that is ethical and beyond intuition.

Reference List

Birchall, D. 2008. 'Online Documentary', in T. Austin and W. de Jong (eds), *Rethinking Documentary: New Perspectives, New Practices*. Maidenhead and New York: Open University Press, pp. 278–83.

Blickstein, S. and S. Hanson. 2001. 'Critical Mass: Forging a Politics of Sustainable Mobility in the Information Age', *Transportation* 28(4): 347–62.

Boal, I.A. 2002. 'The World of the Bicycle', in C. Carlsson (ed.), *Critical Mass: Bicycling's Defiant Celebration*. Edinburgh and Oakland, CA: AK Press, pp. 167–74.

Broeren, J. 2009. 'Digital Attractions: Reloading Early Cinema in Online Video Collections', in P. Snickars and P. Vonderau (eds), *The YouTube Reader*. Stockholm: National Library of Sweden, pp. 154–65.

Carlsson, C. (ed.). 2002. *Critical Mass: Bicycling's Defiant Celebration.* Edinburgh and Oakland, CA: AK Press.
———. 2008. *Nowtopia: How Pirate Programmers, Outlaw Bicyclists, and Vacant-Lot Gardeners Are Inventing the Future.* Edinburgh and Oakland, CA: AK Press.
Culley, T.H. 2002. 'The Power Is Here', in C. Carlsson (ed.), *Critical Mass: Bicycling's Defiant Celebration.* Edinburgh and Oakland, CA: AK Press, pp. 11–17.
Furness, Z. 2005. 'Biketivism and Technology: Historical Reflections and Appropriations, Social Epistemology', *Journal of Knowledge, Culture and Policy* 19(4): 401–17.
Gombrich, E.H. 2006. *The Story of Art.* New York and London: Phaidon.
Herlihy, D.V. 2004. *Bicycle: The History.* New Haven, CT and London: Yale University Press.
Illich, I. 1973. *Tools for Conviviality.* London: Marion Boyars.
Juhasz, A. 2008. 'Documentary on YouTube: The Failure of Direct Cinema of the Slogan', in T. Austin and W. de Jong (eds), *Rethinking Documentary: New Perspectives, New Practices.* Maidenhead and New York: Open University Press, pp. 299–312.
Kemple, T.M. 1995. *Reading Marx Writing: Melodrama, the Market and the 'Grundrisse'.* Stanford, CA: Stanford University Press.
Löwy, M. 2002. 'From Marx to Ecosocialism', *Capitalism Nature Socialism* 13(1): 121–33.
———. 2005. 'What is Ecosocialism?', *Capitalism, Nature, Socialism* 16(2): 15–25.
Madden, R. 2003. 'How Cyclists Around the World Put a Spoke in the Motorist's Wheel', *The Telegraph,* 16 December. Retrieved 30 December 2014 from http://www.telegraph.co.uk/travel/729324/London-How-cyclists-around-the-world-put-a-spoke-in-the-motorists-wheel.html.
Marx, K. 1971. *The Grundrisse,* trans. D. McLellan (ed.). New York and London: Harper and Row.
McChesney, R.W. 2013. *Digital Disconnected: How Capitalism is Turning the Internet against Democracy.* New York and London: The New Press.
Miller, T. 2005. 'Hollywood, Cultural Policy Citadel', in M. Wayne (ed.), *Understanding Film: Marxist Perspectives.* London and Ann Arbor, MI: Pluto Press, pp. 182–93.
———. 2009. 'Cybertarians of the World Unite: You Have Nothing to Lose but Your-Tubes', in P. Snickars and P. Vonderau (eds), *The YouTube Reader.* Stockholm: National Library of Sweden, pp. 424–40.
O'Connor, J. 1988. 'Capitalism, Nature, Socialism: A Theoretical Introduction', *Capitalism Nature Socialism* 1(1): 11–38.
Rosen, P. 2002. *Framing Production: Technology, Culture, and Change in the British Bicycle Industry.* Cambridge, MA and London: The MIT Press.
Sayers, S. 2011. *Marx and Alienation: Essays on Hegelian Themes.* Basingstoke and New York: Palgrave Macmillan.
Singer, P. 2005. 'Intuition and Ethics', *The Journal of Ethics* 9(3/4): 331–52.
Thompson, K. and D. Bordwell. 2010. *Film History: An Introduction.* Boston, MA: McGraw Hill Higher Education.
Virilio, P. 1986. *Speed and Politics.* New York: Semiotext(e).

Vivanco, L.A. 2013. *Reconsidering the Bicycle: An Anthropological Perspective on a New (Old) Thing*. New York and London: Routledge.
Williams, B. and J.J.C. Smart. 1973. *Utilitarianism: For and Against*. Cambridge: Cambridge University Press.
Zimmermann, P.R. 2000. *States of Emergency: Documentaries, Wars, Democracies*. Minneapolis: University of Minnesota Press.

Filmography

The Return of the Scorcher. 1992. Ted White.
We Are Traffic! 1999. Ted White
Still We Ride. 2004. Andrew Lynn, Elizabeth Press and Chris Ryan.
Battleship Potemkin (Bronenosets Potemkin). 1925. Sergei Eisenstein.

CHAPTER 10

Swallowing Time
On the Immaterial Labour of the Video Blogger

Michael Chanan

The explosive development of digital videography is one of the definitive aspects of the new media landscape of twenty-first century mass culture. Back in the 1960s, video recording gear was bulky and only found in television studios, where it was mostly used for taping live programmes. By the 1980s, video had become mobile, replacing the film camera in news reportage, and the first semi-professional and consumer camcorders had arrived, bringing the spread of the skills of videography to new semi-professional and even amateur users. The closing decade of the century brought more miniaturization, convergence with the desktop computer and digitization, and today millions of people carry mobile phones with built-in video cameras and large numbers upload the raw results to platforms like YouTube. It is usual at this point to refer to the thousands of minutes of animals doing funny things, which seem particularly popular, not to mention the volume of pornography, but another major strand is a new mode of reportage, known as citizen journalism, and its cousin, the video blog. All this has occurred so fast, and in such a dispersed fashion, that it isn't easy to comprehend, even for logged-in scholars of the phenomenon, and while plenty of pundits and journalists speculate about what it all means, many aspects of the phenomenon remain unexamined.

YouTube, the leading video streaming platform, was launched in 2005. Eight years later, it boasts of having over eight hundred million unique users visiting the platform each month, watching over four billion hours of video. Some seventy-two hours of video are uploaded every minute, and 70 per cent of the traffic comes from outside the United States.[1] Figures like this not only imply an immense expenditure of what conventional wisdom calls leisure time. The extraordinarily rapid expansion of the web services known as the 'social media' has been possible because these platforms have discovered how to swallow time, not only storing it digitally but crucially inducing users to populate these sites with the products of their own casual and unpaid creative labour, and at their own expense to boot. There is no reliable way to quantify the amount of time that people spend, not in viewing, but in generating the content they upload. Perhaps, if one did a search on Google Scholar (isn't that how we're supposed to do our research nowadays?), one might come across analyses of different types of traffic, or even the proportions of different genres, but that still wouldn't tell you how much creative labour was expended in producing the original videos that form such a large proportion of YouTube content. Short bursts of camera-phone footage may not represent much by way of creative effort — there's even software for amateurs that makes an automatic selection from your footage — but how do you calculate the conscious effort that goes into the range of more sophisticated videos that find their way onto the web, for which people spend time on the editing, sometimes lavishly?

It is tempting to approach this by way of the concept of immaterial labour that emerged from the Italian autonomist tradition, which Michael Hardt and Antonio Negri initially define as 'labor that produces an immaterial good, such as a service, a cultural product, knowledge, or communication' (Hardt and Negri 2000: 290). Following Maurizio Lazzarato, this is 'the activity that produces the "cultural content" of the commodity ... in other words, the kinds of activities involved in defining and fixing cultural and artistic standards, fashions, tastes, consumer norms, and more strategically, public opinion' (1996: 132–46). These activities belong to the culture industry broadly understood, located in what is classed as the service sector of the economy, whose growth in recent decades corresponds to the intensification of the commodification of leisure which is integral to post-industrial capitalism and follows from the introduction of information technology. The web has created a new parallel public sphere, and one of the results is that these functions are now also conducted through the social networks by people who belong to the audience — the fan base, the consumer, the targets of the culture industry — and not those who work within it.

Mere aficionados, who previously produced duplicated fan magazines, can now be found on the web challenging the professionals who earn their income through cultural production — Lazzarato's 'immaterial workers': people 'who work in advertising, fashion, marketing, television, cybernetics, and so forth', all of them producers of subjectivity, and in certain sectors very well paid for it too. In other words, intellectual workers and creatives (as the advertising industry calls them) — copywriters and designers and the like, who have always been the core workers in publicity businesses – these people now have to learn to coexist with the social networks, indeed to find ways of infiltrating them. For many it was not difficult, because they were already adepts of self-promotion.²

The teacher is another kind of immaterial worker, generally less well paid, who produces subjectivity (or helps to shape the subjectivity of the student), and digitization and the web have also started to create radical shifts in education. In all these fields, artistic and practical skills have been retooled, transformed and reshaped by digital technologies, which also render employment more precarious because they make it easy for employers to subcontract their labour needs. The new 'immaterial worker' needs to combine the results of various different kinds of skill: intellectual, technical and aesthetic, along with 'entrepreneurial skills in the management of social relations'. They are a largely atomized work force who often work alone (and sometimes from home), but the sector requires a great deal of highly mediated social cooperation, in which the individual worker is only a remote part. These are also skills, however, that whether part of their job description or not, all sorts of people nowadays exercise in their everyday lives using the same digital tools, at work and away from it, contributing content to the web. From this perspective, Lazzarato's remark that immaterial labour involves doing things that are not normally thought of as 'work' almost appears prophetic of the condition of the social media. Perhaps we could even say that with the appearance of Web 2.0 this kind of labour produces, as Mark Coté and Jennifer Pybus argue, a new version of itself that they call 'immaterial labour 2.0' (Coté and Pybus 2007).

Retooling with new technology often also means deskilling, or the loss of the craftsmanship it replaces. The rise of desktop publishing, for example, threatened the jobs of highly skilled graphic designers (while a spate of ugly and sometimes even unreadable print designs appeared). But the digitized codification of aesthetic techniques – like the automatic exposure and focus of the video camera – have also meant that the new hi-tech gear could discover an enlarged consumer market, where the old categories of amateur and aficionado are transformed, and old dreams about the democratization of the media are revived. Dreams that go back to Vertov in Soviet Russia in the 1920s, conceiving of a network of local cine-amateurs providing a continuous flow of newsreel footage. And then Brecht, writing about radio in 1932 as a medium with the inherent capacity to become 'the finest possible communications apparatus in public life', a vast system of channels of communication, or it could be if it were allowed to transmit as well as receive, 'to let the listener speak as well as hear ... to bring him into a network instead of isolating him' (2000: 42–43). Or Julio García Espinosa in Cuba at the end of the 1960s, who pondered the likely effects on artistic culture 'if the evolution of film technology (there are already signs in evidence) makes it possible that this technology ceases being the privilege of a small few' (1983: 30). For Espinosa, flush with the idealistic current of the Cuban Revolution, the promise of free artistic expression prompts him to remember Marx's dictum that in the future, when communism does away with the rigid division of labour and allows people to fully realise themselves, there will no longer be painters but rather people who, among other things, dedicate themselves to painting. And then again in the 1970s and '80s, the first video activists, working in groupuscules down at community level but imagining a world of community video everywhere. These are all utopian ideas, but as Brecht added, in that case, ask yourself why they're utopian.

Technically speaking, convergence comprises the technical wizardry that allows different devices to 'speak' to each other and data to be transmitted and received, but this also brings the old utopian dreams a step closer. An updated version of Brecht's rider still applies: the communicative utopia of the web is largely channelled through the portals of corporations dedicated to a consumerist ideology, for which participation is little more than a conditioned button-pushing reflex. Nonetheless, what digital convergence produces is not just the instant flow of free expression across borders but also a propensity for causing ideological upset by breaking down social and cultural barriers, and discovering new sociopolitical constituencies. There's a crucial rider, however. If a vocation for free data exchange seems to be built into the fundamental design of the internet and the web that uses its cables, then this apparatus provides a freedom and a chance that comes at a cost, or rather, at costs that cannot be readily calculated. On the one hand, in succumbing to the invitation of the web, its openness, diversity and permissiveness, as worker or as netizen, we provide the apparatus with content, not to mention the metadata that corporations trade in and intelligence agencies seek out. On the other hand, how is one to evaluate the time economy of doing something that has become for so many people as much second nature as reading and writing? What does it mean when this immaterial labour is no longer paid, or even calculated, but simply swallowed up by the corporate websites that constitute the platforms of the social media?

Labour Process

To explain where I'm coming from, this is the account of a participant observer, who joined the ranks of net activists with a series of video blogs posted on the *New Statesman* (NS) in the early months of 2011. The project came about by happy accident. For some years I'd been shooting short video diary pieces whenever a good opportunity arose. In early December 2010 a young friend, a postgrad at a London university, told me of a teach-in against the new Coalition Government's drastic higher education policies due to take place at Tate Britain on the night of the Turner Prize, and we went along together to film it. The event turned out to generate its own drama in front of the camera, and was quick to edit. A chance meeting a few days later resulted in the *New Statesman* inviting me to become their first video blogger, with the brief to report on the developing protest movement.[3]

From the magazine's point of view, the idea of hosting a video blog was a natural enough extension of running a website that expanded what is possible to do in print format. Although the magazine ran on a very tight budget – hence they didn't pay production costs, and this was a zero-budget project – I was told that their publisher was keen on developing the magazine's web presence, and newspapers like *The Guardian* were already engaged in video journalism. Practically the only guideline we agreed on was not to exceed a length of about fifteen minutes at most – and that's already pretty long for watching video on the web. The other main parameter was fast turnover: one or two days' filming, one or two days' editing, so that each blog would be up within a week or less of the events portrayed, rough edges included.

For my part, I was happy with the arrangement for several reasons. Firstly, because posting on the NS gave the videos a different profile from an academic blog: a political identity within the independent left, and a potentially more broad-based audience. Secondly, because the locus of a current affairs magazine also has useful legal implications, since current affairs is legally exempt from certain copyright requirements; in particular, it allows the fair use of footage found on the web taken from sources like television without prior

Figure 10.1. Image from *Chronicle of Protest* (Michael Chanan, 2011), a documentary compiled from the author's video blogs for the *New Statesman*.

clearance. (Of course among video activists it's good practice to make arrangements to share material when you can.) The use of this kind of found material was part of my strategy – and perfectly acceptable to the NS – from the outset, not just to plug narrative gaps but also to contrast the mainstream media representation with what it didn't show. At all events, when the University agreed to pay the costs of the DVD edition, due diligence required that they didn't take the word of their own Professor of Film, but sought legal opinion. The lawyers viewed the film and replied that yes, the film fell under fair dealing, adding, to my amusement, that it would remain so until 'the austerity measures are no longer a matter of public debate'.

Reflecting on the experience raises various questions. For one thing, I call myself a video blogger, but it's a term without a precise meaning. The point of calling something a blog is to flag it as the work of an individual, but like written blogs, video blogs cover a huge range of subjects, styles, genres and purposes. This can also be deceptive. Corporate blogs, for example, unlike press releases, are written in a personal voice, but may actually be produced by professional copywriters (nowadays there are also companies that run Facebook pages) – in short, subcontracted immaterial labour. For present purposes, we can think of the video blog as a form of solo video-journalism, a cross between documentary and citizen reportage, with a mode of address essentially different from conventional television documentary reportage because it escapes a corporate point of view and often instead adopts the partisan stance which is allowed the committed print journalist. Importantly, it is also different in its mode of production: the video blogger doesn't have a budget handed down to them, isn't backed by institutional resources, and doesn't work with a crew (only the help of friends). In a word, it involves a different labour process.

The labour process is a topic almost totally neglected by academic film studies, a field with only limited interest in questions of political economy, despite a number of studies of the economics of production, the economic history of the studios and the like. Largely overlooked is the conflict that arises within the mode of production between the interests of studios, producers, distributors and the capital behind them, and the needs of what Marx understood as aesthetic labour, the creative labour of the artist unhindered by imposed conditions of employment. The film industry introduced new complications in this disjunction precisely by becoming industrialized. Film production stumbled from its initial artisanal mode of production towards its formal division of labour in the studio system from the same two directions that Marx identified in *Capital* as the twofold origin of manufacture. On the one hand, it evolved its own specialized jobs in the areas of its own specific technology – the camera, editing, the laboratory and later, sound; on the other, it brought in workers from different crafts – electricians, carpenters, scene painters, hairdressers, costumiers, etc., and melded them all together into a new hierarchy under the joint authority of the director and the producer. This process was the subject of my own first published work of film scholarship – a history of trade unionism in the British film industry, which appeared in 1976 – and returning to it now half a lifetime later in a new context feels a little like intellectual archaeology.

The question of the labour process was central to New Left-inclined Marxist debate at the time, one of the active topics of theoretical analysis that despite the recent revival of interest in Marx remains forgotten. I well recall listening to discussions on the topic at the CSE (Conference of Socialist Economists) – an event attended by many who were not economists but Marxists in other disciplines, who felt they had to grapple with the subject. Everyone read Harry Braverman's *Labour and Monopoly Capital* (1974), a book by a worker-intellectual about the ways in which capital steals the skills of the worker and takes control of the process out of the worker's hands. When I compared the theory with different types of film crew (I had already accumulated personal experience of features, television documentary, independent documentary and the television studio), I quickly realised that here too the same sort of forces were at work, but with one big difference: film production required the exercise of creative initiative and aesthetic judgement in a collectivized form, which made real controls over the labour process, of the kind exemplified by Henry Ford's production line, impossible. Creative input isn't limited to a few names at the top the credits entitled to receive part of their 'wages' in the form of royalties. As long as an element of judgement is needed on the worker's part, down to the humble makeup artist or the props, then the full resources of real control over the labour process are unworkable. Something, however subtle or slight, escapes mechanization and automation. In short, the film crew is a co-operative team where people do their jobs in turn and wait on others as and when necessary. Nonetheless, the division of labour in film production still needs to be disciplined, and capital therefore has to resort to formal and ideological controls in order to induce a subjective automatism in the worker's exercise of judgement instead.

There are two main aspects to this. At the level of formal controls, conventional wisdom, in taking the hierarchy within the film crew as the natural order, overlooks the convenience of the arrangement from the point of view of capital, and the disadvantage for creative labour, in respect to time economy. The effect is to place producer and director together in the position of agents of capital in the control of the labour process, where one of their essential functions is time management. In the studio system, the director owed their job, beyond whatever creative talent, to their capacity to control the shoot, get the right amount of footage in the can each day and keep within the agreed schedule; but directors were subject to the control exercised by the producer and the studio, which retained the right to final cut (and in certain infamous cases expelled the director from the cutting room).

The second aspect is the very nature of film language, particularly what Noel Burch called the 'institutional mode of representation' (1973) – the codes of shooting and montage that came to govern the construction of the visual narrative according to certain rules of enunciation. Critical film theory has subjected these codes to very extensive semiotic analysis, without always realising their ideological function in containing creative labour within the generic bounds operated by the studios and the distributors. The labour process plays its part in generating genre as a solution to a collective endeavour by providing a series of models or paradigms that tell everyone in the team (behind the camera and in front of it) what they're supposed to be doing (more or less), while also satisfying the requirements of the producers and financiers by enabling them to get what they're expecting (more or less).

In this perspective, documentary was born and remains relatively free. Firstly, it is filmed, as a rule, away from the studio by very small crews on very low budgets. And then its language, its forms of exposition and enunciation, are less constrained by the laws of narrative continuity, working instead through associative, intellectual or poetic montage. The pioneering documentarist Joris Ivens somewhere described it as a creative no-man's-land, an interloper in the genre system. All the same, with the coming of sound, commentary and music would often constrain its power of representation, answering to the requirements of sponsors, while television after the war, and more recently, festivals and distributors, have all impelled documentary to develop its own range of genres and subgenres. Yet the potential to break free remains a powerful factor, and documentary has reinvented itself time and again. In fact it has a tendency to do so every time a technological development provides the chance, and every time it thereby renews both its audience appeal and its capacity to bear witness to the social, anthropological, cultural or political moment. Today is no exception. While the web extends the reach of the kind of long form documentary that returned to cinema screens in the 1990s, perhaps more importantly it also stimulates a plethora of new short forms, styles, genres and subjects.

The Organic Composition of Capital

The concept of immaterial labour evokes Marx's analysis of the difference between productive and unproductive labour. A writer, he says, 'is a productive worker not in so far as he produces ideas, but insofar as he enriches the publisher who publishes his works, or if he is a wage labourer for a capitalist' (Marx 1963: 157–58). Or again, a singer who sings as freely as a bird 'is an unproductive worker. When she sells her song, she is a wage earner or merchant. But the same singer, employed by someone else to give concerts and bring in money, is a productive worker because she directly produces capital' (quoted Attali 1985: 39).

The operative factor here is the idea that productive labour is labour that produces exchange value; if it only produces use values (ideas, songs) it is not productive from the point of view of capital. This distinction goes back to Adam Smith, who spoke in a famous passage from *The Wealth of Nations* about 'perishable services', meaning the type of activity that 'does not fix or realise itself in any permanent subject, or vendible commodity, which endures after the labour is past' (Smith: 1970: 295). Perishable services, like those of both the 'menial servant' and the court musician, do not regenerate the funds that purchase them. The labour of some of the most respectable orders in society, says Smith, as well as some of the most frivolous, is in this respect the same: churchmen, lawyers, physicians and men of letters on the one hand, and on the other, buffoons, musicians, opera singers, opera dancers, etc. Marx commented wryly in *Theories of Surplus Value* on the 'polemical effect' of these arguments. Great numbers of 'so-called "higher grade" workers – such as state officials, military people, artists, doctors, priests, judges, lawyers, etc. – ... found it not at all pleasant', he said, 'to be relegated economically to the same class as clowns and menial servants and to appear merely as ... parasites on the actual producers (or rather agents of production)' (1963: 174–75).

Marx explains in *Theories of Surplus Value* that in order to be economically productive, labour has to reproduce its own value and more: it has to be capable of returning a profit; when performed only as a service, it remains unproductive because it doesn't generate capital, it consumes it. Conversely, even a clown is a productive labourer if he works in the service of a capitalist employer who derives more income from the show than the costs of putting it on, not least the wages. Marx was fifteen years in his grave when a novel invention appeared that rapidly created a new form of exploitation of clownish labour. Cinematography did for the perishable performance of the clown what another new invention, the phonograph, did for the musician: it allowed their immaterial labour to take the commodity form of mechanical reproduction. The exemplary case is Charles Chaplin, a clown quick-witted enough to become the owner of his own immaterial labour power at the inception of Hollywood.

One advantage that Chaplin acquired by becoming his own producer-director was control over the process of production, meaning control over time economy and productivity. In conventional mass commodity production this is achieved through the techniques of scientific management emerging over precisely the same period as the infancy of cinema; indeed cinematography was one of the technologies that the proponents of scientific management employed in their researches.[4] This is ironic, since the kind of labour employed in making films is not mechanical but aesthetic, and thus resists easy measurement. Indeed the reduction of aesthetic labour time to a homogenous standard makes doubtful sense. There is no necessary correlation between the quality of a painting, a symphony or a novel and the amount of time taken to produce them. (Handel famously took ten days to compose *Messiah*, while Brahms tarried over his First Symphony for twelve years.) Artistic work is not standard and uniform but concrete and individual, and subject to psychological variation. Aesthetic labour does not respect utilitarian functions – a kind of magic is also necessary. The threat that hangs over it in the capitalist mode of production is this: that for the purposes of making a profit it will be treated exclusively according to economic criteria, as wage labour measured in the expenditure of time. Who now remembers the 'quota quickies' made in the U.K. in the 1930s at a fixed cost of a pound per minute? Only perhaps in the animation studio can you calculate production costs with some assurance. The history of cinema is littered with productions that have gone over budget because they went beyond the shooting schedule. In short, Marx spoke correctly when he spoke of the hostility of capitalist production to art. This hostility was expressed in the studio system through the imposition of formal and ideological controls over the complex and intricate division of labour, supervised top down by the producer with the director in charge on the studio floor. (The television studio adds to this through the architecture of the channels of communication: the director in the control box can speak to whom they like, but those they talk to cannot answer back.)

Documentary production, while relatively free, does not completely escape these strictures either, especially since it could be brought back under control in the editing phase which necessarily follows shooting. The documentary production units run by John Grierson in the 1930s were in this sense benign dictatorships, where filmmakers enjoyed freedom of aesthetic experiment but were subject to limits in the matter of content, which everyone understood implicitly. As the documentary historian Erik Barnouw saw it, the situation they were in 'kept them sharply aware of the political limits inherent in government sponsorship' (Barnouw 1974: 91). There also emerges the 'industrial' film and the system of commissioning, where content is prescribed and implicit aesthetic rules apply. Conditions after the Second World War were essentially the same as before, but with the addition of new currents in the margins, such as the encouragement of art film documentaries in France.

With the rise of independent documentary in the 1950s and '60s, however, now often supported by public cultural funds, a significant factor ironically drops out of the budget, as the real costs of labour are often discounted. In other words, they are assumed by the filmmaker, who doesn't work by the clock, and may even work around it. On the other hand, television expanded employment and opportunity without fundamentally altering the terms. You were either directly employed by the television station and totally subject to its norms, or you were 'freelance', with prized schedule D tax status – a euphemism for subcontracted labour. Many independent filmmakers typically found employment on other people's films in order to earn a living, and then invested their labour in their own films, especially in developing the idea in the first place. The expansion of production, which accompanied the diversification of television by means of new cable and satellite channels, placed added pressure on the conditions of employment. Working for an independent producer was no better and often worse than working for the channel that commissioned it. I recall an incident from the 1980s when a freelance researcher employed by an independent production company on a commissioned film for Channel Four complained in an open meeting of the exploitive terms of employment, and was told that since he was not employed by the Channel, this was not the Channel's responsibility.

The underlying difficulty is what is known in mainstream (non-Marxian) economics as 'Baumol's cost disease'. The tag gained currency after two Williams, Baumol and Bowen, wrote a study in the 1960s of the ineluctable rise of theatre ticket prices on Broadway, which they then generalized to the world of the performing arts (Baumol and Bowen 1968). The problem was the irreducible cost of artistic labour. The amount of labour required to play a Mozart quartet at Carnegie Hall in New York was the same as at the court of Joseph II two centuries earlier. Productivity in the chamber music sector has been stagnant, while in the manufacturing sector it has rocketed, with a consequent rise in the relative cost of artistic performances. Baumol's 'cost disease' has since been diagnosed in many fields, including education and healthcare. The quality of all such services depends on the quantity of labour invested in them.

It is difficult, says Baumol, to reduce the time needed to perform certain tasks without also reducing the quality of their product. 'If we try to speed up the work of surgeons, teachers, or musicians, we are likely to get shoddy heart surgery, poorly trained students, or a very strange musical performance' (2012). It almost seems we are back in the land of Adam Smith, despite the fact that various artistic services are no longer perishable but have been rendered into vendible commodities by (to invoke Walter Benjamin's term) mechanical reproduction.

Baumol's cost disease is really none other than a form of Marx's organic composition of capital, the ratio of the fixed costs of production (plant, equipment, materials) to the labour power, or variable capital, required. Capitalism advances by introducing technology and increasing productivity to improve this ratio, but there are a whole range of activities – Smith's services, from the law and medicine etc., to clowning, acting and singing – where this is impossible or comes unstuck. Twentieth century technologies make a difference, but in different ways in different service sectors, where the application of technology has different effects. The gramophone created whole new branches of professional popular music, and cinema initially extended musicians' employment opportunities, until conversation to sound threw them out of work. Domestic labour was alleviated by various labour-saving electrical goods, but with the contraction of domestic service, it disappeared into the unpaid labour of the housewife. The photocopier transformed the office; computerization and telecommunications did so even more radically, but often with contradictory effects – the end of the typing pool; deskilling of certain kinds of detail work like design; the rise of the call centre, where workers are not replaced by machines but programmed to act like them.

All this results in what a recent article on the topic describes as 'exactly the opposite of what most people think of as a good service'. Good services, say the authors, are intrinsically expensive because they require a high ratio of labour to product (Skidelsky and Craig 2013). However, the digital office does not increase the productivity of the immaterial labour of intellectual professions like the law or accountancy because their top members provide services to other top people who can afford to pay. When it comes to cultural production and aesthetic labour, another pattern kicks in, for which the film industry serves as a paradigm – because here production depends on irreducible amounts of aesthetic labour, but its economics depend on reaching a mass audience by means of mechanical reproduction. Distribution and exhibition become determinant factors, and after the initial artisanal phase of early cinema these require major investment, but quickly end up in superprofits. Hollywood rose to pre-eminence because it attracted the investment of the New York bankers. Mechanical reproduction creates a mass market, which in turn creates stars able to command huge fees, a monopoly rent payable for their value as cultural properties in a market distorted by the monopoly practices of the majors. Since a hit is never guaranteed, entertainment capital needs to develop its own techniques to protect against risk. These included the star system, the genre system, and various unfair practices, of a kind that Marx already knew about: in the *Grundrisse,* he mentions theatre directors who buy singers for a season not in order to have them sing, but so that they don't sing in a competitor's theatre (1973: 282).

These pressures have a commensurate effect on everyone else's wages, pushing up the cost of variable capital among the leading producers. But this disadvantages the smaller ones. While writing these paragraphs, a case in point is reported in France, where for more than half a century governments left and right have provided the film industry with forms of support designed to help it hold its own in the face of U.S. domination of international distribution. The system has been coming under strain, and the film unions have recently complained that crew members on low-budget films are being forced to take heavy pay cuts while working nights and overtime without due compensation. The government on duty has responded by signing a pact with big producer-distributors and some unions to correct the situation, but independent producers, who account for around 90 per cent of French output, says Angelique Chrisafis, 'have risen up in rebellion, warning that the new deal as it stands would be "disastrous" and a "death warrant" for low-budget arthouse films' (2013). Independent producers, she says, argue that 'risk-taking, quirky auteur films that have helped shape France's reputation for independent cinema would have to be shot abroad or would not be made at all because the new wages would be unaffordable' (ibid.). Meanwhile, according to Vincent Maraval, one of France's leading producers, a small number of French megastar actors are demanding disproportionately huge pay packets because French TV companies, obsessed by competition from the internet, will now only sponsor films which feature the 'bankable names', which supposedly ensure high audience figures (Lichfield 2013).

At the opposite end of the scale, where there are no stars and no unions, digital video dissolves the division of labour. Here it turns out that a video on the web that cost its maker no more than a few pounds can 'go viral' and accumulate millions of viewers without any kind of publicity budget to promote it. But 'viral' is another term without a precise meaning. The concept is relative, with an undefined lower limit. A medical metaphor, the main thing is that its occurrence is unpredictable and uncontrollable. No recipe or formula can tell you how to make a viral video. But if a video blogger normally expects a post to get a few hundred views and it gets a few thousand, then it does so by the same means that produce a viral circulation of millions – by circulation across social platforms. This is the zone of the video activist. But this too is a term with only a loose meaning, since in the scenario being described here, there are clearly numerous different possibilities for intervention, and different levels and kinds of activity.

Don't give up your day job

Looking (on Google Scholar, of course) for any relevant recent writings, I discover a Canadian scholar writing in a new academic journal called Digital Journalism about 'Social Moments in Solo Videojournalism', which sounds promising (Hedley 2012). It turns out that the piece rather misses the point. David Hedley chooses to look at the move from two- or three-person television news crews to 'one-man-band' reportage, using as his model a two-minute award-winning report for KUSA-TV about 'the support offered by a war veteran bikers' group for a dying senior'. The problem is not that his semiotic explication of the report is pretty routine but rather his focus on the professional, because the real impact of solo videography is not to be found in the institutional setting of television. Nor is there anything here to indicate that solo filmmaking has a history that goes back many decades, to the gestation of experimental cinema in the 1920s. Still less is there any notion that the very idea of solo filmmaking contravenes all the norms of industrial and commercial film production, and necessarily raises crucial issues about the labour process and value.

If digital video dissolves the division of labour, then solo videography ditches regular time economy. When you work alone you also tend to work

Figure 10.2. Image from *Chronicle of Protest* (Michael Chanan, 2011), a documentary compiled from the author's video blogs for the *New Statesman*.

unsocial hours and to take as long as it needs to do the job without bothering to count the hours. The regime you work is the epitome of aesthetic labour – not the managerialist notion that workers should look good and behave nicely, but the Marxist concept of free creative labour, which is not subject to the external constraints imposed on regular labour by the conditions of employment, and which Marx held in high esteem, writing in the *Grundrisse* that 'Really free labour, the composing of music for example, is at the same time damned serious and demands the greatest effort' (1973: 124).[5]

Digital videography benefits from this freedom by introducing a rupture in the mode of audio-visual production, not in the commercial market, where its adoption is a matter of necessary technical retooling, but by opening it up to amateurs, aficionados and activists who are thereby no longer excluded from potentially reaching a wide public. The video blog or any form of solo video-journalism takes us outside the world of television, and here, different conditions apply. Freedom from regular time economy means no formal controls over the labour process, which allows a voice free of imposed ideological constraints, a partisan discourse free from institutional doctrines of political balance, and sometimes the space for a different aesthetic. This is the prospect of 'immaterial labour 2.0'. The quid pro quo is that the result is open to the new form of exploitation that is constituted by web 2.0.

The labour process of the individual video blogger contrasts starkly with the conventional mode of documentary production, but it also differs from the egalitarian collective practices of political filmmaking thirty or forty years ago (for example, the workshop movement in the U.K. supported by Channel Four in the 1980s). Both involved small crews and a given, although flexible division of labour, combining specialism with creative collaboration. The video blogger, however, thanks to digital technology, is able to work alone at all stages of production. This gets very close to the concept of the 'caméra-stylo' introduced in the late 1940s by the French avant-garde film-maker Alexandre Astruc, the idea of the camera as a tool to write with – indeed twice over, first when you shoot and then when you write the film on the timeline. But this solitude also becomes a liability, because it deprives the video-author of the creative feedback that goes with the teamwork of a crew. If this is not unconducive to the solo video artist, it's a danger for the video activist, who cannot thrive without the most lively connection to the social, which comprises another aspect of immaterial labour: the work that is put into building relationships which create the vital bond with the subjects of the filming – a far cry from 'entrepreneurial skills in the management of social relations'. People who are actively involved in campaigns are usually readily amenable to participation, since they regard the video as an opportunity, an extension of their own political agency and objectives. Like all documentary filmmaking, however, this is always partly about an instinct for opportunity. My own experience has been that where people identify the videographer as one of themselves, a bond of solidarity is quickly formed that is denied to the institutional camera crew, who are seen as belonging to an alien force. Indeed people will even sometimes volunteer themselves.

The immaterial labour of the video blogger is essentially unquantifiable: there is no rule that says how long it should take to shoot and edit a video, any more than to write a song or a poem. Like the artist who lives from their aesthetic creation, there is no determinable relation to the exchange value, if any, eventually earned by the work. The video activist doesn't even think of earning anything. One may dream of a video going viral, the reality is rather different. The necessary multiplier effect depends on the initial circle of diffusion, and then on random connections with other ever wider circles. There are techniques for getting things out but virtual networks are fickle, in no way as solid and reliable as the social bonds of real old-fashioned physical association.

They are not a replacement for the social solidarity that is still the necessary condition for real political effect. The social media are incomparable at rapid mobilization and the horizontal transmission of solidarity, but remain essentially ephemeral (a strange paradox when everything uploaded remains there in a suspended state forever). Political change needs more concrete forms of social association to gain traction. This, however, need not discourage the video activist. The gap between political aspiration and reality has always been there in all forms of agitational art, and bridging it is the object.

But this, it turns out, is also 'free labour' in a new sense, the donation of those who supply the social media with content, off whose backs, in their millions, enormous profits are made. We should not be surprised by this turn. Another fragment of intellectual archeology flits into my head, a description of the state of music in a pamphlet for the Worker's Music Association at the end of the 1930s, in which the U.S. composer Elie Siegmeister writes that 'capitalism has created the most magnificent apparatus for the production, distribution and consumption of music that the world has ever seen. Yet this apparatus is so riddled with contradictions which are basically economic in origin, that it continually negates its own potentialities' (Siegmeister n.d.). The web, an invention of corporate capitalism in the era of globalization, where I freely upload the oppositional product of my irreducible aesthetic labours, offers a domain of free expression, a potential for human liberation, which in the very same moment is also negated and denied, to leave us perplexed in front of our screens, before the dialectic of the digital.

Notes

1. According to www.youtube.com/yt/press/statistics.html.
2. The question of the traditional critic's role came up as I was completing this essay in the shape of a book by the film critic Mark Kermode, himself an enthusiastic blogger. According to Will Self, reviewing *Hatchet Job* in *The Guardian*, 'His anxiety that in the age of the internet and the worldwide web the role of the serious critic may be becoming otiose speaks to the contemporary condition'. Retrieved from www.theguardian.com/books/2013/oct/09/hatchet-job-mark-kermode-review.
3. The video blogs were subsequently incorporated into a film, *Chronicle of Protest*. Both the film and the original blogs can be found at www.chronicleofprotest-the-film.co.uk.
4. The footage is included in *Clockwork*, Newsreel, 1982.

5. Quoted in Julia Bryan-Wilson, 'Art Versus Work', retrieved from www.artandwork.us/2009/11/art-versus-work.

Reference List

Attali, J. 1985. *Noise*. Minneapolis: University of Minnesota Press.
Barnouw, E. 1974. *Documentary*. Oxford: Oxford University Press.
Baumol, W. 2012. *The Cost Disease*. New Haven, CT: Yale University Press.
Baumol, W. and W. Bowen. 1968. *Performing Arts – The Economic Dilemma*. Cambridge, MA: MIT Press.
Braverman, H. 1974. *Labour and Monopoly Capital*. New York: Monthly Review Press.
Brecht, B. 2000. 'The Radio as a Communications Apparatus', in M. Silberman (ed.), *Brecht on Film and Radio*. London: Methuen.
Burch, N. 1973. *Theory of Film Practice*, trans. H.R. Lane. California: Praeger.
Chanan, M. 1976. *Labour Power in the British Film Industry*. London: BFI.
Chrisafis, A. 2013. 'François Hollande Embroiled in Row over French Film Industry Union Rights', *The Guardian*, 23 August. Retrieved 13 January 2015 from www.theguardian.com/world/2013/aug/23/francois-hollande-french-film-industry-row.
Coté, M. and J. Pybus. 2007. 'Learning to Immaterial Labour 2.0: MySpace and Social Networks', *ephemera* 7(1): 88–106.
Espinosa, J.G. 1983. 'For an Imperfect Cinema', in M. Chanan (ed.), *Twenty-Five Years of the New Latin American Cinema*. London: BFI and Channel Four.
Hardt, M. and A. Negri. 2000. *Empire*. Cambridge, MA: Harvard University Press.
Hedley, D. 2012. 'Social Moments in Solo Videojournalism', *Digital Journalism* 1(1).
Lazzarato, M. 1996. 'Immaterial Labour', trans. P. Colilli and E. Emory, in P. Virno and M. Hardt (eds.), *Radical Thought in Italy*. Minneapolis: University of Minnesota Press.
Lichfield, J. 2013. 'How Bloated Film Stars Ate French Cinema', *Independent*, 5 January. Retrieved 13 January 2015 from www.independent.co.uk/news/world/europe/how-bloated-film-stars-ate-french-cinema-8439082.html.
Marx, K. 1963. *Theories of Surplus Value*. Moscow: Progress Publishers.
———. 1973. *Grundrisse*. London: Penguin.
Siegmeister, E. n.d. *Music and Society*. London: Workers Music Association.
Skidelsky, R. and N. Craig. 2013. 'Press Three if You Wish You were Dead', *New Statesman*, 23–29 August.
Smith, A. 1970. *The Wealth of Nations*. London: Everyman.

Filmography

Chronicle of Protest. 2011. Michael Chanan.

CHAPTER 11
Recovering the Future
Marxism and Film Audiences

Martin Barker

Marxism is a body of theory that developed from and was crafted for social movements.
—Colin Barker, *Marxism and Social Movements*

I don't really understand myself why this film became important to me. I am 48 years old and nothing else has touched me like this one. Maybe it was because it gave me hope for a very gloomy future. Maybe we can triumph over evil. I hope so.
—A response within *The Lord of the Rings* audience research database

In this chapter I draw upon a series of researches into film audiences to ask what might be meant and understood by the idea of a specifically Marxist approach to films. The context for this is my sense that there is a deep-seated malaise in the main tradition of Marxist writings about cinema. I aim to sketch an alternative approach, illustrating this with examples from my audience researches.

The general history of Marxist attitudes to film is pretty well known, with – among other things – its own Wikipedia page and a chapter in the *Oxford Guide to Film Studies* (Kleinham 1998). The story is quite easily told. Lenin declared cinema 'the most important of all arts', and nationalized its production after the Bolshevik Revolution. Many kinds of propaganda films were produced – from the relatively uncontentious (health, food and clothing) to the openly political. Around the latter a series of critical debates grew up between Dziga Vertov, advocating documentary realism, and Lev Kuleshov, promoting constructionist montage. Sergei Eisenstein, surely the most important filmmaker of this period, formally adopted the latter, but arguably shows signs of both within his most famous films. The critical debates and associated productions continued across the 1920s, until the dead – and often murderous – hand of Stalinism imposed the bizarrely misnamed doctrine of 'socialist realism' for three decades. During this period, while still appearing occasionally within the work of independent scholars, Marxist film theory largely went underground – until the late 1960s when, particularly in association with the May '68 events in Paris, a new mode of thinking emerged, first in the film practices of François Truffaut, Jean-Luc Godard and others, then from the pens of a series of thinkers writing about the 'cinematic apparatus' and the need to subvert its 'ideology' (see especially Baudry 1974–75; Comolli 1986). Political film was broadly taken to mean oppositional film, contrasted with 'mainstream' ideological cinema. Alongside these approaches openly influenced by Marxism have run, of course, other interests in political film – social democratic, syndicalist, situationist, anarchist, more recently feminist and queer – all in some sort of dialogue with elements of Marxist theories.

But this history does not really tell us that all that much. It mainly tells us who was and who was not willing in different periods to fly under the banner of Marxism. Perhaps unsurprisingly, these general coverages do not worry themselves too much about who and what ideas might legitimately count themselves as 'Marxist'; leave that to the epigones and the factionalists. Yet in certain respects this surely must matter. For instance, there are many excellent researches into the economic drivers of Hollywood, whose work points to critiques of capitalism (see for instance Garnham 1990), and there are a smaller number of studies of labour processes within the film industry that capture important aspects of the operations of hierarchy, modes of exploitation and the like (see for instance Wasko 1982; Croteau and Hoynes 2005; Blair 2001). There are historical enquiries into collusion between Hollywood and the State Department, the military and other law enforcement agencies, which uncover the power-politics of the business (see for instance Robb 2004). There is a great deal of work on traditions of political filmmaking – that is, films with direct address to political stories and themes (see for instance Koppes and Black 2000). These may not necessarily make formal references to Marx(ism), but they are surely proximate to its interest in capitalist modes of production and the labour process. But just listing these and asking this question points to a puzzle. Oddly, the great bulk of what does pass as 'Marxist theory of film' has been restricted to considerations of the textual nature of films, with the ways in which the film industry may produce 'ideology' as it produces commodities. Whether that is what Marx himself saw as the *point* of cultural critique is arguable. For a start, it appears that it collapses the distinction and tensions that

Marx saw between use-value and exchange-value: to be produced as commodities is not to be counted as simply reproducing capitalism.

And in this respect, when we look more closely at the broader history of Marxist or near-Marxist thought about culture, generally, some further oddities show. Firstly, although cinema was (as is so often cited) claimed by Lenin as the most important of the arts, in truth, Marxist cultural theorists have been much less interested in film and cinema than in literature, drama and music. Trotsky hardly wrote about films, yet produced the series of essays gathered as his *Literature and Revolution*. Georg Lukács' works on the novel are widely known, yet his scattering of writings on film has only recently been published (see Aitken 2012). Members of the Frankfurt School in the main dismissed film as commercial ideology, part of the 'cultural industry' working effectively to trap working people in flaccid entertainment. Lucien Goldmann explored novels, drama and philosophy, but hardly film (1977).[1] Raymond Williams produced one very early small book on film (Orrom and Williams 1954), and then occasionally revisited the topic in the remainder of his life, while writing oodles about drama and literature. And so it goes on. There are of course exceptions or partial differences, but it is only with the 'Althusserian turn' and the rise of those concepts of 'cinematic apparatus' that we get a substantial 'Marxist' address to film and cinema.

But it is not just this absence that is striking, it is that inside such writings appear some worrying, connected tendencies. Firstly, while not quite falling into technological determinism, early Marxist thinkers about film tended to join in the quest for some kind of primordial ontological character to the medium. 'What is film per se?' they asked. And as has been noted, it led several of them – at least for a while – to idealize silent film as the more perfect 'enactment' of film's potentials, even after the arrival of sound. And while Georg Lukács (who did admit that his interest in film was 'incidental') was insisting on the *historical* – therefore *changeable* – character of the novel, he was commenting on cinema in a very different, ahistorical mode.

Secondly, alongside and linked to this is a recurrent trope, which attributes a hypnotized, even childlike, quality to cinema's audiences. Here is Lukács in his first writing about film in 1913: 'The child which inhabits all of us is released and becomes the master of the spectator's psyche' (cited in Levin 1987: 38).[2]

Here is Trotsky, writing in 1923, regretting the lack of serious attention to cinema:

The passion for the cinema is rooted in the desire for distraction, the desire to see something new and improbable, to laugh and to cry, not at your own, but at other people's misfortunes. The cinema satisfies these demands in a very direct, visual, picturesque, and vital way, requiring nothing from the audience; it does not even require them to be literate. That is why the audience bears such a grateful love to the cinema, that inexhaustible fount of impressions and emotions. (1923)[3]

Trotsky 'already knows' who and what cinema is for, although at least he does not condemn it. His ambition in this period was rather to commandeer it for the purposes of socialism – in order, in particular, to provide an alternative attraction to the church, which he saw as offering another kind of 'entertainment', based on rituals and storytelling.

Here too is Theodor Adorno, writing about the exceptional role of music in the pacifist film *No Man's Land* (Trivas 1930), and thus setting out a model of its opposite, mainstream Hollywood:

Music is unveiled as the drug that it is in reality, and its intoxicating, harmfully irrational function becomes transparent. The composition and performance of the music is combined with the picture must demonstrate to the public the distinctive and barbarizing influence of such musical effects. The music must not be continually heroic, else the naïve spectator would become intoxicated by it, like the man portrayed on the screen. Its heroism must appear, as reflected, or to use Brecht's term, 'alienated'. (Adorno and Eisler 1994: 24)

Notice the fear of 'intoxication' as 'irrational', with its implied sharp opposition of intellect and emotion.

Here is Raymond Williams, writing for the first time about film and just at the point where he was moving into his own encounter with Marxism: '[Film] is an immensely powerful medium, and in the darkened auditorium the dominating screen, with its very large, moving figures, its very loud sound, its simultaneous appeal to eye and ear, can, it seems obvious, exercise a kind of "hypnotic" effect which very readily promotes phantasy and easy emotional indulgence' (Orrom and Williams 1954: 12–13).[4] This quote could easily have come from any of the later psychoanalytic theorists of cinema.

By the time film studies openly re-encountered Marxist theory in the 1970s, the language at least had changed. Now, 'the audience' was less infantilized, more an odd combination of 'individualized', as in the persistent reference to 'the spectator' in cinema 'positioning' theories, and 'massified', as in *Jump Cut*'s early 'Editorial' (1974), which, arguing for the reintroduction of Marxist ideas into film studies, talks of the neglected 'mass audience' of existing film theory. Mind, the insistent turn to psychoanalytic modes of reasoning could well be seen as reintroducing the motif of childhood, both in its insistence that 'desire' is broadly a function of stored-up infantile dissatisfactions, and the trope of the cinema space as 'womb-like'. In fact this encounter was not long-lasting, quite quickly shifting to other kinds of critical interest: feminist, 'race', queer and deconstructionist. Where it did stay, it took on coloration from those interests. We might consider, as an example of this, Michael Ryan's contribution to the compendious American tome *Marxism and the Interpretation of Culture* (Nelson 1987). In an essay supposedly about Marxism and film, the greatest space is given over to trying to supplement Marxism with a version of psychoanalysis, without any address to the compatibility of the two. What persist, I would argue, in this current of thinking about film and cinema are two features:

1. An insistent decontextualizing of 'the audience', and an ignoring of the question of how contexts of reception (which could be conceived in very many ways, of course) might shape engagement and response. Yet if Marxism is anything, it is surely an attempt to understand the concrete conditions under which radical, revolutionary movements emerge.
2. Operating within an undeclared model that counterposes 'immersion' (seen as ideologically dangerous) to 'distance' (wherein lie radical political opportunities). Yet surely we must know well enough the long history of reactionary theories of 'the crowd', and of the opposition between intellectual and emotional tendencies, to want to avoid repeating those tropes (for an early critique of this tendency, see Rudé 1964).

To these might be added two others, which become increasingly important as later Marxist work moved from treating the medium ontologically, to addressing particular films:

3. Interrogating films for their 'messages' from the perspective of critics' academic analytic expertise, from which imputations to audience 'effect' are derived. This could of course include the finding of 'good bits' as film scholars seek out 'Marxist elements' in unlikely places. James Kendrik (1999), for example, sought to disclose these within three films by James Cameron. This is surely testament to the heavy influence of literary thinking (the very idea of 'the text') within the rise of film studies.
4. Curiously, proposing an educational role for film, in relation to present and past, but not the future. 'Politics' as a term becomes identified with drawing out the lessons of past and current events, leaving out of consideration the ways in which imagined futures might be important.

This last is at work, for instance, in the wording of one of Lukács' late pronouncements that films only really have value when they are 'making people reflect seriously about a past or present situation' (cited in Levin 1987: 58). It is pronounced as the basis of a focus on ideological readings in Daryl Sparkes' (2006) thesis on Marxism and documentaries: 'All documentary films represent visions of the past'. It is there in one of the most prominent contemporary scholars on Marxism and film, Mike Wayne, for whom political film is effectively film about contemporary politics. But an examination of Wayne's (2001; 2003) books reveals a related and very striking contrast. He evinces an intense interest in the potential political harm that films and other media might do, but has almost nothing to say about possible positives.[5] The emphasis is all on the vulnerability of audiences, as in so much mainstream thinking. So, while conceptions of the audience recur within the tradition, these are worryingly taken for granted, tending even to mirror the rhetorical positions of moralistic campaigns.

If an understanding of audience responses is required as part of rethinking film's relationship with socialism, what is there to call upon to date? The truth is, very little. There is of course work on, for instance, the U.S. working class and Hollywood, but this at best has tended to treat very generally with the role of cinema-going and its representations within working people's lives (see for instance Ross 1999). I know of no attempts to explore how films may relate to (inform, suppress, activate) a class understanding of the world in particular historical moments. Famously, of course, Lev Kuleshov conducted his early experiment in which audiences were shown a montage of shots in which a still, inexpressive actor's face was set, variously, alongside shots of a sleeping baby, a beautiful woman, and a dead body. Kuleshov's claim that his responses showed that audiences attributed different emotions to the actor, according to what his face was linked with, has been widely taken up as grounds for linking Marxism to a montage theory of meaning, and for what I might call an 'enforced criticality' principle – that films are most honest, and radical, when they press gaps, puzzles or disjunctures on us, 'making us think'.[6] But as Prince and Hensley (1992) point out, in their lengthy reconsideration of Kuleshov's work, we know nothing of the circumstances of the experiment (who, where, how many, how introduced to the task, what if any research protocols) (see also Willbrott 1988). Their own attempt to reproduce the experiment in fact produced near-opposite results – although they do admit caution about the implications of this, since it is effectively impossible to reproduce the conditions in which Kuleshov operated (near the birth of cinema, in the midst of revolutionary upheaval, etc.). But this very admission points to a different problem in their attempt. Even here, 'the audience' for Prince and Hensley is a convenience sample (almost inevitably, of U.S. students). It is as if film, still, is being asked to show a generalized influence, irrespective of the makeup, contexts and circumstances of the audience. What is surely needed is research into audiences that is alert to class situation, cultural capital, and local (historical, political) circumstances, at least. That, we simply do not have. In the remainder of this chapter, I want to point to some very small pieces of evidence, which emerged in three bodies of research I have been involved in, over many years, where the signs and fragments of a different account might be seen to begin to emerge.

Middle-earth as Possible-Future Site

From 2003 to 2004 I was one of the coordinators of the huge international project to study the reception of the films of *The Lord of the Rings* (Jackson 2001–3) (see Barker and Mathijs 2008). Bringing together researchers in eighteen countries, and gathering responses in fourteen languages, the project succeeded in gathering just under twenty-five thousand responses to a complex questionnaire combining quantitative with qualitative questions. Many of the broad and major findings of the project have been published, in different places. But there is at least one tendency that we have never fully explored. This shows in the ways in which hundreds of respondents chose to talk about the films in terms of the hopes for the future that they elicited. (See the quotation mastheading this chapter as an example.) Some of these are very short, summarizing the films in terms such as 'Gave me hope for the future', but others begin to spell out what they are seeing, and what they might do with what they have seen:

> *I was totally overwhelmed and deep in thought trying to process what I had just seen. It makes you feel that all is not lost. It gives you hope. The world just needs to have more humility and compassion.*

> *It brought me to a new and magical world where although there was evil, people of different races joined together to bring peace and tolerance among them. Good will overcome evil, and even the smallest person can change the course of the future.*

> *It has changed my ordinary life into something worth thinking about! It has reached out to me and probably thousands of people like me in a way which must be unprecedented. It gives us all an opportunity to get away from the everyday life and be engulfed by another more hopeful world.*

> *Modern life is hard. It often seems hopeless. Heroes are scarce on the ground. There is war, poverty, disease, homelessness, government corruption, pollution of the planet, things most of us feel we can do nothing about. A film like this one lifts us out of the despair that often besets us and makes us feel better, more hopeful.*

A recurrent word in answers of this kind is 'inspire'. The films did more than entertain, or excite. They delivered an energy bolt out of the world of Middle-Earth to offer consolation and hope to a wide range of people who found their world to be oppressive. And it is surely not accidental that these quotes come exclusively from those reporting the highest levels of both pleasure and importance from the films.[7] These shifted, by however small a margin and with of course unknown duration, their capacity to imagine better futures. That 'future' can of course be conceived in innumerable ways, and some respondents did elaborate, at least a little. A few suggest that the films do what the Bible has lost the ability to do. One describes an intense 'patriotism' after watching the films. Several talk of the films helping with recovery from illness, trauma or danger. But in others it is possible to see a wider transference, in which Middle-earth is conceived as a parallel universe to our own, its 'past, present and future' (as several answers strikingly put it), which they visited at the cinema and from which they gleaned moral encouragement. In this account, what *The Lord of the Rings* offered par excellence was an opportunity to observe small, insignificant people facing up to an almost inconceivable challenge, and – despite the best efforts of the films' big, powerful characters – having to take onto themselves the burden of confronting and defeating an apparently insuperable moral evil. The depths of their suffering along the way, their intense self-doubts and – particularly significantly – their *growth* across the narrative allow these kinds of viewers to see inside what it would be like to transform oneself to take on a great challenge.

The general principles we need to extract from this are several. Firstly, this suggests something important about commitment in cinema. It is a point I have made in other contexts (see Barker, Arthurs and Harindranath 2003), that the more committed members of an audience become to engaging with a film (of whatever kind), the more their responses display rich combinations of emotional and intellectual responses, close attention to the detail of the films and, from these, the construction of complex relays between film-worlds and their lived world. This is quite different from the emptied absorption feared by those generations of Marxist critics. It is also different from fandom, at least as traditionally conceived (although not incompatible with fannish delight in the books); it emphasizes an ethical seriousness in responses and a willingness to lose oneself in the films, as a means to obtaining that uplift, that inspiration.

Secondly, it invites us to look to different story genres and traditions than the documentary, the historical, and the realist film. The mechanism of effect is precisely unrestrained emotional participation, leading on to and energizing intellectual self-examination. For perhaps good reasons, in our era precisely those stories that are frequently derided as (or even damned for being) 'escapist' liberate a good many people's imaginative resources, giving them permission to think laterally to our depressing, struggling world – and to find it through surprising aspects of a film.[8] So, science fiction, fantasy and action cinema are the modes of filmmaking to which we might have especially to attend.

Megacity One as Possible-Future Site

This lateralized relationship between films and audience responses was nowhere less expected than in some findings to emerge from earlier research into audiences for the film adaptation *Judge Dredd* (Danny Cameron, 1994) derived from the British comicbook *2001AD*, and set in the dystopian future city 'Megacity One'. This film generically placed itself among comicbook adaptations, science fiction, futuristic law and order, 'action' and, of course, a Sylvester Stallone vehicle (he played its eponymous hero). Our research into responses to the film (undertaken in the U.K. at the tail-end of the Thatcher era) involved a series of focus groups with different kinds of audiences: comicbook fans, action film fans, women, black men, young boys and girls, and retired men (who refused to see it), among others (see Barker and Brooks 1998a; 1998b). A common feature among those who loved this was a pleasure in watching films that 'do something to you'. Commonly associated with special effects, and editing moments that jar the body (an aspect of body genres curiously missing from Linda Williams' otherwise excellent essay [1991], which opened up this topic), what we found in particular cases was that the sought-after 'done-to' effects had a curious complication. Special effects have of course been the topic of a substantial literature, ranging from popular accounts seeing them as one of Hollywood's cheapest entertainment devices, to sophisticated accounts that find a doubling in them between what is seen and how it is seen: seen as drawing attention to the operations of cinema (see for instance LaValley 1985).[9]

But one focus group in particular drew our attention towards a particular version of this. A discussion with young working class boys revealed a structured ambivalence towards films of this kind, focused in and through the same feature: their ability to let you 'see ahead' to what the coming world might be. On the one hand, the promised technologies attracted them mightily (and this was one of the grounds of their love of special effects, generally); on the other, they were aware that they and their kind were going, as ever, to have a hard time. The language in which they expressed this was revealing:

KB: So what sorts of thing do you expect there to be in it…?
John: Violence.

> Turtle: Violence, yeah.
>
> John: Bashing people over the head with a big stick thing ... like, truncheon.
>
> [Mike: Yeah, his truncheon thingy.]
>
> Turtle: And I like, I think I like stuff like bad side of everything, is pretty good, all the baddies and stuff.
>
> John: I like watching futuristic films where you get people's ideas of the future, weapons and stuff.
>
> Turtle: And you get ideas ... of like, what it's gonna be and you think, 'well, can't wait till it gets to be like that year', sort of thing.
>
> KB: Right, em ... what do you think of that view of the future?
>
> John: Well, stuff like the bikes and everything, that was good, but all the lives and everything was tat, I didn't like that.
>
> KB: And what didn't you like about it?
>
> Mike: Well, it was like horrible, wasn't it?
>
> John: You would have thought it would be like really nice where everything was like nice and everything. But it was a state really for the common people.

What struck us forcibly about this, and some equivalent moments of talk, was, firstly, their collectivity. These were boys who talked as a group, completing each others' sentences, re-expressing in front of us a view that they had already talked over among themselves. They only ever disagreed to tease and josh each other, as they moved towards stating an agreed, collective point of view. But their terminology for talking of themselves is oddly old-fashioned and imprecise: 'the common people'. This expression roots back into nineteenth-century discussions of class and culture, and was among a number of potentially dismissive expressions. But around the time of the film a small reclaiming had begun, not least with Pulp's (1995) alternative pop song *Common People*. And it is the same aspects of films of this kind – their envisioning through special effects of a coming world – which simultaneously fascinated them and provided pleasure, and left them feeling outside. This, I would argue, is an emergent class view, thus far unnoticed in the literature on action films (which provide these boys with their most pleasurable moments of this kind), which has been dominated either by discussions about the gender aspects of the films, or by the need to fend off moralizing complaints about the films' 'violence' (see in particular Donovan 2010). Because of its time, and the state of this late-Thatcherite world for many working class people, we should not be surprised at the borrowing from old languages to think through who they are and might be, collectively.

The *Nostromo* as Possible-Future Site

A third project, whose major findings have yet to be published, allows me to draw out some other aspects. In 2012, four of us gathered people's memories of watching Ridley Scott's *Alien* (1979).[10] Our research had several drivers, among them: the opportunity to think about the shape and role of cultural memories, but this time for a quite recent film; and the rather special place this film has in academic writings, having been the topic of over a hundred analyses. Our complex questionnaire managed to recruit 1,127 completions, containing 469,000 words of explanation of people's responses.

In light of those long academic discussions on the meanings or subtexts of the film, we included an open question that asked people: was the film in any sense more than a piece of entertainment for them? This revealed a striking contrast. In the academic literature, well over half of the writings are focused on issues of gender and the body, with a powerfully negative undercurrent, finding particular focus in and through the Lacanian psychoanalytic approach of Barbara Creed (1993), arguing that the film embodies a fear of femininity and motherhood. By contrast, in the overall body of our responses, the predominant issue that emerges is fear of corporate and military power in our world – and where gender and femininity are raised, overwhelmingly the film is seen to be presenting very positive images. But as with *The Lord of the Rings*, isolating those giving the highest valuation to the film ('Masterpiece') reveals a marked tendency to pose this fear in terms of the future (instead of simply seeing the film as a reflection on the present state of the world), and to couple this with wider thoughts about the directions the human race is taking.

Sometimes again these are passing answers, suggesting little substance (for example 'It's hard to say. I think we should be wary of the future'; 'I don't think so, but I like the idea of making us watch a dark future'). But other, longer answers hint towards more elaborated and considered feelings about this:

It certainly expresses our anxiety about human social and economic evolution. Contrasts nicely with Star Trek: evil corporations run the universe, science is subordinated to profit, spaceships are grimy industrial hulks and nobody wears pyjamas to work. In other words, the future is depressingly similar to the present. Only, if anything, it wants you dead even worse. Cheers!

There was a whole political subtext, aside from the feminism (about exploitation, etc.), which I enjoyed. But it was secondary – for me, anyway. Back in 1979, the fact that the movie was very dark and grim, unlike other space movies (e.g. the shiny and white 2001) seemed to chime with the times. I was finishing school, and the future wasn't very bright. Punk had become violent and nasty by that time, and Thatcher was round the corner. Little did we know...

Yes, I even started a blog called Acheron LV-426 to reflect on current developments in terms of our possible biofutures (a dystopia ruled by evil corporations comparable to Weyland Yutani, and the commodification of scientific research and the military). Biology will be THE science of the 21st century in my view, and Alien *anticipates many of these developments.*

Yes, it is definitely more than just 'entertaining'. First of all, to many people who watch it, it isn't very entertaining! Many viewers find it boring and slow while watching it for the first time, which is of course due to the fact that what we expect from films has changed so drastically over the years. Alien *is a movie that you have to 'let in', you have to be able to really be scared and not shut your emotions out. You have to let it affect you all the way. If you do that, you will realize that despite being set in the future and far, far away, the film has a lot to say about us, about people in general, about the way society deals with technology and other things. The film works on many different levels, you probably could just be entertained by it, but it has much more to offer, especially if watched repeatedly.*

In slightly different ways, each of these points to a way in which *Alien* offers images and thereby opens up questions about the world that is, or was then, coming. But the ambivalence implied by that jokey 'Cheers!' – the implication that thinking about these things is faintly uncomfortable, and that is the point – captures something very important. Films of this kind arouse at their best astringent feelings about tendencies in our world, which in an ideal world – which cannot currently be conceived – we would love to challenge. The last answer acknowledges this directly; there might be plenty of reasons for avoiding the experience, but to do so, repeatedly, does not reduce the impact, rather, it complexifies and deepens it.

Conclusion

Conceptions of the future are an important and integral part of how people of all kinds and classes orient to the present. The journal *Futures* has published much of general relevance over its thirty-five-year history (for examples, see *Futures* 39(10), 2007; Davies and Sarpong 2013; Rubin 2013). But a persistent strain in this is a wish for images of the future to be nicer. This trope underlay one of the early major openings of this topic, Frederik Polak's two-volume *The Image of the Future* (1973). Polak despaired at the decline in utopian thinking, seeing it as the end of modernity. This set a pattern for many future studies. In 1974 the futurologist Alvin Toffler conducted an experiment wherein he asked U.S. young people to write essays in which they would conceive how the world might be in thirty years' time. Toffler reported his concern that while they could conceive of changes, his participants mainly detached themselves from these changes, and wrote as though these would simply happen to them: 'It is as though they believed that everything happening outside one's life simply by-passes the individual. The respondents, in short, made no provision for change in themselves, no provision for adaptation to a world exploding with change' (Toffler 1974: 148).[11] Of course the problem here is the notion that conceptions of the future, to be useful, must be attractive and must be somewhere we want to be.

My argument is that we are asking too much, and of the wrong kind, from films – and when they fail to deliver, they are then criticized either as irrelevant or as ideological. The heavily 'teaching', documentary function sought by the dominant tradition of Marxist thinking about film is most relevant to the already persuaded, who are looking to enlarge and deepen their knowledge. But the fact that films are very unlikely to play a direct role in promoting or producing political activism by no means makes them irrelevant. In periods when social movements and class resistance are low and blighted, what films might – in a paradoxical way – do is to re-energise just a little people's capacity to conceive futures. But the last thing these will be is simply nice. Rather, it will likely be through the experiencing of dangers, hardships, struggles and challenges to survive that people are able to look at themselves and their place in the world, and to reassert a sense that it could change.

It is not in the specifics of such imaginings of the future that we should look, but in the tensed relations between our here and now, and those other places. Hence the potential value of those most denigrated genres which deploy stereotyped, simplified conflicts.[12] I am fully aware that in saying this I am setting myself askance a long tradition that has seen nothing but dangers in such conflictful films – not just those who persist with simplistic models of 'copycatting' and 'desensitization', but more thoughtfully those who wish for 'teaching for peace' (see as instances of this Nagler 2001; Hurley 2013.)[13]

How might we advance this approach? It would take, I think, new forms of research encompassing three things: (1) research ideas and implements sophisticated enough to capture the ways people of different classes, and cultural groups, build and make use of ideas about the future; (2) longitudinal studies of people's use of themes and ideas from films over time – life-maps, if you will, precise enough to capture the ways in which ideas from particular films are stored, grasped, aggregated and mobilized in relation to wider beliefs and attitudes; and (3) ways of operationalizing the currently persuasive but too rhetorical notions of 'interpretive community' and 'imagined community'. Above all, however, it will take a step by Marxist cultural critics away from their longstanding assumptions about the incompetent, childlike audience – however theorized – and towards an engagement with the rich findings that have been emerging from audience research over at least the last three decades.

Notes

1. Cinema gets just passing mentions in his *Cultural Creation in Modern Society*, even in his chapter on the role of the mass media – with Godard's *Contempt* (1963) providing one of the few concrete examples, and that is consciously chosen as a 'literary film'.
2. I acknowledge my debt to this essay for almost all my understanding of Lukács' writings on film.

3. The context is striking. This essay considers the dangers posed to the revolution by alcohol, but then by contrast considers the need for 'amusements' and 'play', for which cinema is regarded as the pre-eminent medium.
4. Williams talks further of the 'disproportionately immature' audiences in cinemas in 'The Dramatic Tradition' (Orrom and Williams 1954: 12–13).
5. My comment is based on a simple Index search, totalling page references to two opposite sets of terms: Ideology (99 mentions), Hegemony (24), Reification (23), Abstraction (12), Fetishism (2); as opposed to Audience (0), Imagination (0), Enlightenment (0), Pleasure (0) and Hope (0).
6. This is by no means limited to film, but is generalized across Marxist approaches to other cultural forms. As illustrations, see the emphasis on 'interruption' and 'distanciation' in Slaughter (1980: 186); and on 'disruption' and 'subversion' in Bennett (1981: 153).
7. Our questionnaire asked people to allocate themselves along two dimensions (scaled 1-5): Enjoyment of the films, and the Importance attached to seeing them. Overwhelmingly, those using these languages of 'hope' and 'future' accord the highest ratings to their responses. For a broader discussion of the character of this group's responses, see Barker (2009).
8. I am reminded of Mark Kermode's (2008) surprise, even disappointment and irritation, at many viewers finding an almost spiritual message in *The Shawshank Redemption*. Kermode could not make sense of this kind of intense participation in that film.
9. 'Science fiction and fantasy films hover between being about the world their special effects imply – i.e., about future technology and its extensions – and about special effects and the wizardry of the movies themselves' (LaValley 1985: 144).
10. This research was a collaborative project between myself, Kate Egan, Tom Phillips and Sarah Ralph. I am grateful to my three co-investigators for allowing me to drawn on some emergent elements of our findings in this chapter, ahead of our publishing them more fully and collectively.
11. For an interesting anonymous web essay summarizing much of this history, but in almost despairing tones, see 'Images of the future', retrieved on 20 July 2013 from http://teaching4abetterworld.co.uk/docs/download11.pdf. Strikingly, although this essay reports experiments using student writing and short stories, there is not a single reference to film or cinema in its entirety. The essay very much belongs to the tradition that is only happy when it discovers positivity, and sees in negative images a sign of disaster. I would want at least to qualify this, and argue that negativity can constitute a realistic account – the issue is the degree to which and the available means by which people conceive themselves capable of responding to the bad.
12. I made an argument of this kind many years ago, when considering the ways in which cultural critics turned on 'stereotypes', whose objection regularly was that

group-thinking was bad. Actually, I would want to argue the opposite: that we badly need to be able to see groups, classes, formations. Of course it matters which ones and how conceived, but there is nothing wrong per se with seeing and understanding the world in terms of labels (see chapter six of Barker 1989).

13. Actually, as I showed in relation to another book of this kind (Hutchinson 1996), there can be deep continuities between these books and the standard journalistic approaches – in Hutchinson's case, led by his instant talk of audiences being 'fed a restricted diet', which, he speculates, play on their 'sense of hopelessness' (see Barker and Brooks 1998a: 5–8).

Reference List

Adorno, T. and H. Eisler. 1994. *Composing for the Films*. London: Athlone Press.

Aitken, I. 2012. *Lukácsian Film Theory and Cinema: A Study of Georg Lukács' Writing on Film 1913–1971*. Manchester: Manchester University Press.

Barker, C., et al, eds. 2013. *Marxism and Social Movements*. Leiden: Brill.

Barker, M. 1989. *Comics: Ideology, Power and the Critics*. Manchester: Manchester University Press.

———. 2009. 'Changing Lives, Challenging Concepts: Some Findings and Lessons from the *Lord of the Rings* Project', *International Journal of Cultural Studies* 12(4): 375–94.

Barker, M. and K. Brooks. 1998a. *Knowing Audiences: Judge Dredd, its Friends, Fans and Foes*. Luton: University of Luton Press.

———. 1998b. 'On Looking into Bourdieu's Black Box', in R. Dickinson, O. Linné and R. Harindranath (eds), *Approaches to Audiences*. London: Arnold, pp. 218–32.

Barker, M., J. Arthurs and R. Harindranath. 2003. *The Crash Controversy: Censorship Campaigns and Film Reception*. London: Wallflower Press.

Barker, M. and E. Mathijs, eds. 2008. *Watching The Lord of the Rings: Tolkien's World Audiences*. New York: Peter Lang.

Baudry, J.L. 1974–75. 'Ideological Effects of the Basic Cinematic Apparatus', *Film Quarterly* 28(2): 39–47.

Bennett, T. 1981. 'Marxism and Popular Fiction', *Literature and History* 7(2): 138–56.

Blair, H. 2001. '"You're only as Good as Your Last Job": The Labour Process and Labour Market in the British Film Industry', *Work, Employment and Society* 15(1): 149–69.

Comolli, J.L. 1986. 'Technique and Ideology: Camera, Perspective, Depth of Field', in P. Rosen (ed.), *Narrative, Apparatus, Ideology: A Film Theory Reader*. New York: Columbia University Press, pp. 421–43.

Creed, B. 1993. *The Monstrous-Feminine: Film, Feminism, Psychoanalysis*. London: Routledge.

Croteau, D. and W. Hoynes. 2005. *The Business of Media: Corporate Media and the Public Interest*. Newbury Park, CA: Pine Forge Press.

Davies, C. and D. Sarpong. 2013. 'The Epistemological Relevance of the Arts in Foresight and Future Studies', *Futures* 47: 1–8.

Donovan, B. 2010. *Blood, Guns and Testosterone: Action Films, Audiences, and a Thirst for Violence*. Lanham: Scarecrow Press.

'Futures of Art'. 2007. *Futures* 39(10).

Garnham, N. 1990. *Capitalism and Communication: Global Culture and the Economics of Information*. London: Sage.

Goldmann, L. 1977. *Cultural Creation in Modern Society*. Oxford: Basil Blackwell.

Hurley, K. 2013. 'Envisaging Nonkilling Futures in Film', in J.A. Dator et al. (eds), *Nonkilling Futures*. Honolulu, HI: Centre for Global Nonkilling, pp. 147–64.

Hutchinson, F.P. 1996. *Educating Beyond Violent Futures*. London: Routledge.

Kendrik, J. 1999. 'Marxist Overtones in Three Films by James Cameron', *Journal of Popular Film and Television* 27(3): 36–44.

Kermode, M. 2008. *The Shawshank Redemption*. London: BFI Modern Classics.

Kleinham, C. 1998. 'Marxism and Film', in J. Hill and P. Church Gibson (eds), *The Oxford Guide to Film Studies*. Oxford: Oxford University Press, pp. 106–13.

Koppes, C.R. and G.D. Black. 2000. *Hollywood Goes to War: How Politics, Profits and Propaganda Shaped World War II Movies*. London: Tauris Parke.

LaValley, A. 1985. 'Traditions of Trickery: the Role of Special Effects in the Science Fiction Film', in G. Slusser and E.S. Rabkin (eds), *Shadows of the Magic Lamp: Fantasy and Science Fiction in Film*. Carbondale: Southern Illinois University Press, pp. 141–56.

Levin, T. 1987. 'From Dialectical to Normative Specificity: Reading Lukács on Film', *New German Critique* 40: 35–61.

Nagler, M.N. 2001. *Is There No Other Way? The Search for a Nonviolent Future*. Los Angeles: Berkeley Hills Books.

Nelson, C., ed. 1987. *Marxism and the Interpretation of Culture*. Champaign, IL: University of Illinois Press.

Orrom, M. and R. Williams. 1954. *Preface to Film*. London: Film-Drama.

Polak, F. 1973. *The Image of the Future*, v. 1 and 2. Amsterdam: Elsevier.

Prince, S. and W.E. Hensley. 1992. 'The Kuleshov Effect: Recreating the Classic Experiment', *Cinema Journal* 31(2): 59–75.

Robb, D.L. 2004. *Operation Hollywood: How the Pentagon Shapes and Censors the Movies*. New York: Prometheus Books.

Ross, S.J. 1999. *Working Class Hollywood*. Princeton, NJ: Princeton University Press.

Rubin, A. 2013. 'Hidden, Inconsistent and Influential: Images of the Future in Changing Times', *Futures*, 45: 38–44.

Rudé, G. 1964. *The Crowd in History: Popular Disturbances in France and England, 1730–1848*. New York: John Wiley.

Slaughter, C. 1980. *Marxism, Ideology and Literature*. Basingstoke: Macmillan.
Sparkes, D. 2006. 'Screening Revolution: Constructing a Marxist Theoretical Framework for Social Documentary Film-makers Analysing Class Structure and Class Struggle', Ph.D. thesis. Queensland: Queensland University of Technology.
'The Last Word – Film Studies'. 1974. *Jump Cut* 4: 27–28.
Toffler, A. 1974. *Learning for Tomorrow*. New York: Vintage Books.
Trotsky, L. 1923. 'Vodka, the Church and Cinema', *Pravda*. Retrieved 12 January 2015 from http://www.marxists.org/archive/trotsky/women/life/23_07_12.htm.
Wasko, J. 1982. *Movies and Money: Financing the American Film Industry*. New York: Ablex.
Wayne, M. 2001. *Political Film: The Dialectics of Third Cinema*. London: Pluto Press.
———. 2003. *Marxism and Media Studies: Key Concepts and Contemporary Trends*. London: Pluto Press.
Willbrott, H.G. 1988. 'The Kuleshov Effect', *British Journal of Social Psychology* 27: 357–69.
Williams, L. 1991. 'Film Bodies: Gender, Genre, and Excess', *Film Quarterly* 44(4): 2–13.

Filmography

Alien. 1979. Ridley Scott.
Judge Dredd. 1994. Danny Cameron.
The Lord of the Rings. 2001–2003. Peter Jackson.
No Man's Land. 1930. Victor Trivas.

Contributors

Martin Barker is Emeritus Professor of Film at Aberystwyth University. He has, among several other areas, researched widely on film audiences, ranging from small projects on, for instance, *Being John Malkovich* and *The Usual Suspects*, to the worldwide project on *The Lord of the Rings*, and to sponsored projects on audience responses to sexual violence in films. A good deal of his research has addressed situations where untested claims have been made, by policymakers, moral campaigners or indeed film scholars, about the nature of audience responses. Among his principal audience-focused publications are *Knowing Audiences* (Pluto Press, 1998, with Kate Brooks), *The Crash Controversy* (Wallflower Publications, 2001, with Jane Arthurs and Ramaswami Harindranath), *Watching The Lord of the Rings* (Peter Lang, 2007, edited with Ernest Mathijs) and *Live To Your Local Cinema* (Palgrave, 2012). He is founder and now coeditor of *Participations*, the online journal of audience and reception studies.

Haim Bresheeth is a filmmaker, photographer and film studies scholar, retired professor from the University of East London, now at SOAS. His books include the bestselling *Introduction to the Holocaust* (three reprint since 1997, with Stuart Hood), which has been translated into Turkish, Croatian and Japanese. His edited volumes include *The Gulf War and the New World Order* (Zed Books, 1992, with Nira Yuval-Davis), *Cinema and Memory: Dangerous Liaisons* (Zalman Shazar Centre, Jerusalem, 2004, with S. Sand and M. Zimmerman [Hebrew]) and *The Conflict and Contemporary Visual Culture in Palestine and Israel* (with Haifa Hammami), a special double issue of *Third Text* on Palestinian and Israeli art, literature, architecture and cinema. His films include the widely shown *State of Danger* (BBC2, 1989), a documentary on the first Palestinian intifada. In 2012, he completed the film *London is Burning* on the August 2011 London riots.

William Brown is Senior Lecturer in Film at the University of Roehampton, London. He is the author of *Supercinema: Film-Philosophy for the Digital Age* (Berghahn, 2013) and *Moving People, Moving Images: Cinema and Trafficking in the New Europe* (St Andrews Film Studies, 2010, with Dina Iordanova and

Leshu Torchin). He is the coeditor of *Deleuze and Film* (Edinburgh University Press, 2012, with David Martin-Jones) and of a special issue of *Animation: an Interdisciplinary Journal* on James Cameron's *Avatar* (2012, with Jenna P-S Ng). He has also made several micro-budget feature films, including *En Attendant Godard* (2009), *Afterimages* (2010), *Common Ground* (2012), *China: A User's Manual (Films)* (2012) and *Ur: The End of Civilization in 90 Tableaux* (2014).

Michael Chanan is a seasoned documentarist, writer and Professor of Film and Video at the University of Roehampton, London. His books include studies of the beginnings of cinema, Cuban cinema, the social history of music, the history of recording and the politics of documentary. He made his first films for BBC2 in the early 1970s on avant-garde music, and in the 1980s, directed several documentaries on Latin America, mostly for Channel 4. His more recent films have been either academically funded or zero-budget video blogs, and include *Secret City* (2012) and *Interrupted Memory* (2013). He maintains a website at hhttp://www.mchanan.com and a blog at http://www.putney debater.com.

Jon Kear is a lecturer at the University of Kent in History and Philosophy of Art. He has published widely on various areas of modern visual culture from the nineteenth century to the contemporary period, especially painting, print culture and film, and curated exhibitions of modern and contemporary art. Among his publications are *Cézanne* (forthcoming), *Degas: His Life and Works* (2012), *Portraits and a Dream* (2012), on the artist collective Art & Language, *Impressionism* (2008) and *Sunless* (1998), a study of Chris Marker. He is currently working on a second book on Chris Marker.

Gal Kirn holds a PhD in political philosophy from the University of Nova Gorica. He was a researcher at the Jan van Eyck Academie in Maastricht (2008–09) and a research fellow at Institute of Cultural Inquiry, Berlin (2010–11). He is a coeditor of *Encountering Althusser* (Bloomsbury, 2012, with Peter Thomas, Sara Farris and Katja Diefenbach), *Yugoslav Black Wave Cinema and its Transgressive Moments* (JvE Academie, 2012, with Dubravka Sekulić and Žiga Testen) and *Postfordism and its Discontents* (JvE Academie, B-Books and Mirovni Inštitut, 2010). In his hometown of Ljubljana he is engaged in the Workers and Punks' University, and is also currently a postdoctoral fellow of the Humboldt Foundation (HU, Berlin), where he works on the topics of cinema-train and car-television.

Lars Kristensen is Lecturer in Media, Aesthetics and Narration at the University of Skövde, Sweden. His research focuses on representation in cinema, transnational and postcolonial filmmaking and bicycle cinema. After receiving his doctorate at the University of St Andrews, he has held temporary positions at the University of Central Lancashire and the University of Glasgow. He has published mainly on cross-cultural issues related to Russian cinema and is the editor of *Postcommunist Film: Russia, Eastern Europe and World Culture* (Routledge, 2012) and coeditor of *Postcolonial Approaches to Eastern European Cinema: Portraying Neighbours On-Screen* (I.B.Tauris, 2014, with Eva Näripea and Ewa Mazierska).

Ewa Mazierska is Professor in Film Studies at the School of Journalism and Digital Communication, University of Central Lancashire. She has published nearly twenty monographs and edited collections; they include *Postcolonial Approaches to Eastern European Cinema: Portraying Neighbours On-Screen* (I.B.Tauris, 2014, with Eva Näripea and Lars Kristensen), *Work in Cinema: Labor and Human Condition* (Palgrave Macmillan, 2013), *European Cinema and Intertextuality: History, Memory, Politics* (Palgrave Macmillan, 2011), *Jerzy Skolimowski: The Cinema of a Nonconformist* (Berghahn, 2010), *Masculinities in Polish, Czech and Slovak Cinema* (Berghahn, 2008), *Roman Polanski: The Cinema of a Cultural Traveller* (I.B.Tauris, 2007), *Women in Polish Cinema* (Berghahn, 2006, with Elżbieta Ostrowska), *Crossing New Europe: The European Road Movie* (Wallflower, 2006, with Laura Rascaroli), *Dreams and Diaries: The Cinema of Nanni Moretti* (Wallflower, 2004) and *From Moscow to Madrid: Postmodern Cities, European Cinema* (I.B.Tauris, 2003). Mazierska's work has been translated into over ten languages, including French, Italian, Chinese, Korean, Portuguese, Estonian and Serbian. She is a principal editor of a Routledge journal, *Studies in Eastern European Cinema*.

Steve Presence is a Research Associate in the Centre for Moving Image Research at the University of the West of England (UWE), Bristol. He cofounded the Bristol Radical Film Festival in 2011 and the Radical Film Network in 2013, and is currently working on a book version of his doctoral thesis, *The Political*

Avant-garde: Oppositional Documentary in Britain since 1990. In addition to his work on political cinema, Steve is also working with Professor Andrew Spicer as part of a pan-European research project on critically and commercially successful film and television companies, and with Charlotte Crofts as Associate Editor of *Screenworks,* an online publication of screen-based practice as research in association with the *Journal of Media Practice.*

Manuel Ramos is a Lecturer in Visual Cultures at Goldsmiths, University of London. His current research seeks to generate a critical pedagogy of the image through the examination of militant collective filmmaking. He has published different articles about cinema and the visual arts in peer-reviewed journals such as *Parallax* and *Film-Philosophy,* and in books such as *Theorizing Visual Cultures* and *The Archive.* He is currently working on a book dedicated to the films of Peter Nestler.

Jeremy Spencer is an academic and a writer. He studied Art History at the universities of Leeds and Essex and is currently an Associate Lecturer with the Open University and Camberwell College of Arts, as well as teaching Contextual Studies at the Colchester School of Art. He has written for *Artfractures Quarterly, Rebus* and the *Journal of Visual Art Practice,* and has contributed reviews to *Cassone, Review 31* and the *Marx and Philosophy Review of Books.*

Bruce Williams is Professor and Graduate Director in the Department of Languages and Cultures at the William Paterson University of New Jersey. He has published extensively in the areas of cinema history, film theory, Latin American and European cinemas, and language and cinema. His current research interests include Albanian cinema, cinema as a tool for nation-building in North Korea and Albania, cinematic ties between Brazil and the Soviet Union, and the sociolinguistics of the cinema. His articles have appeared in such journals as *Quarterly Review of Film and Video, New Review of Film and Television, Film History, Canadian Journal of Film Studies, Cinémas* and *Journal of Film and Video.*

Index

¡Cuba Sí! (1961), 82
5 Broken Cameras (2011), 20, 180–181, 183

À bientôt j'espère (1967–68), 83, 85
A Bout de Souffle (1959), 74
A Screaming Man (2010), 20, 145, 149, 151, 155, 160–163
A-Z of Bushcraft (2009), 195
Adair, Alain. 84
Adorno, Theodor, 5–6, 256
Alien (1979), 23, 264–265
Allende, Salvador, 100
Althusser, Louis, 4, 32, 51n12, 65
Arafat, Yasser, 176
Arlorio, Piero, 127
Armes, Roy, 128
Armstrong, Peter, 188
Arthur, Paul, 96
Arvatov, Boris, 68–69
Assad, Hani Abu, 178
Astruc, Alexandre, 250

Bach, Johann Sebastian, 106
Badiou, Alain, 6–9, 107
Balbus, Isaac, 89, 96, 101
Balibar, Etienne, 4
Barker, Colin, 253
Barnard, Timothy, 126
Barnouw, Erik, 244
Barthes, Roland, 4, 72, 75, 226
Battle of Algiers (1966), 62, 133
Battleship Potemkin (1925), 36, 69, 98, 101, 223
Baudry, Jean-Louis, 64, 75
Bauer, Petra, 186
Baumol, William J., 245–246

Bazin, André, 82, 110
Beckett, Colin, 135
Belle de Jour (1967), 59
Benjamin, Walter, 29, 36, 49, 63, 73, 97, 101, 246
Bennett, Naftali, 180
Birchall, Danny, 228–229
Birth of a Nation (1915), 174
Black Gold (2006), 189
Blickstein, Susan, 221
Blow for Blow (1972), 139
Blümlinger, Christa, 38
Bonsaver, Guido, 117
Bordwell, David, 159
Bourdieu, Pierre, 4, 15
Bowen, William G., 245
Braverman, Harry, 240
Brecht, Bertolt, 17, 70–76, 85, 119, 236–237, 256
Breillat, Catherine, 10
Brewer, Anthony, 169
Brik, Osip, 67
British Sounds (1969), 60
Brocka, Lino, 150
Broeren, Joost, 225
Broughton, Zoe, 199
Burch, Noel, 241
Burnat, Emad, 20, 180–182
Burnett, Charles, 157

Cahiers du Cinéma (journal), 18, 61, 66–67, 69, 75, 81, 135
Cameron, James, 13, 258
Campbell, Hamish, 199
Canby, Vincent, 135
Carlsson, Chris, 213, 215

Castro, Fidel, 100
Cébé, Pol, 85
Césaire, Aimé, 162–163
Chahine, Youssef, 150
Chaplin, Charles, 171, 173, 243
Chrisafis, Angelique, 247
Cinéthique (journal), 62–64, 69–70, 74
Classe de Lutte (1968), 86
Cocking, Johnny, 201
Coleman, William D., 136
Conniff, Ray, 130
Corneille, Pierre, 106
Coté, Mark, 236
Creed, Barbara, 264
Creswell, Tim, 213
Cross, James, 136

Dahlgren, Peter, 15
Daly, Macdonald, 4
Davidi, Guy, 20, 180–182
de Andrade, Oswald, 127
de Balzac, Honorè, 12
de Lafuente, Ramiro, 131
de Saussure, Ferdinand, 59
Debord, Guy, 75
Debray, Régis, 100
Deleuze, Gilles, 14, 15, 20, 107, 145–161, 163; and *Cinema 1: The Movement-Image*, 147, 155; and *Cinema 2: The Time-Image*, 148, 160
Derrida, Jacques, 96–97
Deutscher, Isaac, 20, 166
Dey, Shaun, 206
Diamonds are Forever (1971), 133
Dickinson, Margaret, 186
Dimanche à Pékin (1956), 81
Dubosc, Dominique, 139
Dudow, Slatan, 70–71
Duncan, Alan, 189
Duras, Marguerite, 108
Durkheim, Emile, 146

Ďurovičová, Nataša, 139

Eisenstein, Sergei, 34, 36–37, 59, 68–69, 73, 98, 130, 172, 174, 223, 253
Elite Squad (2007), 20, 145, 149, 151, 155–160, 162, 163
Engels, Friedrich, 3–4, 108, 217, 223
Espinosa, Julio García, 237
Esprit (journal), 18, 81
Estevam, Carlos, 127

Fifi, Goffredo, 127
Flaubert, Gustave, 12
Fonda, Jane, 71, 139
Ford, Henry, 241
Foucault, Michel, 6–7, 146
Fowler, Luke, 206
Freud, Sigmund, 89–90, 146
Freyre, Gilberto, 146
Frodon, Jean-Michel, 10
From the Clouds to Resistance (1979), 106
Furness, Zack, 214, 216
Fuzz, Mick, 191, 208n6, 208n7, 208n14

Gardin, Vladimir, 172
Genet, Jean, 175
Getino, Octavio, 14, 19, 124–128, 132–133
Globalisation and the Media (2002), 198
Godard, Jean-Luc, 10, 11–12, 14, 17–18, 19, 50n1, 58–64, 70–75, 82, 84, 85, 125, 135, 137–139, 175, 254, 267n1
Goldmann, Lucian, 4, 255
Gombrich, E.H., 15, 226
Goodman, Nelson, 15
Gorin, Jean-Pierre, 61, 138–139
Gramsci, Antonio, 4
Gregoli, Roberta, 158–159
Grierson, John, 244
Griffith, David W., 174
Grin Without a Cat (1977), 88, 90–91, 93–94, 96, 98, 100–101

Groys, Boris, 30–31, 37–38, 51n7
Guattari, Félix, 120, 146, 149
Guedes, Ann, 186
Guevara, Che, 90, 100–101, 135
Guindine, Mikhail, 40
Güney, Yilmaz, 150

Hall, Stuart, 2, 8, 13
Hamilton-Grant, Iain, 9
Hanson, Susan, 221
Happiness (1935), 83, 86
Hardt, Michael, 22, 105–106, 169, 235
Haroun, Mahomet-Saleh, 20, 145, 163
Harvey, Sylvia, 60
Heartfield, John, 74
Hedley, David, 248
Hensley, Wayne E., 259
Herzl, Theodor, 20, 166–167
Histoire(s) du Cinema (1998), 50n1
Hitler, Adolf, 152
House Beautiful: Bringing the War Home (1967–72)(photomontage), 74
How Do You Live, Comrade Miner? (1932), 46
Howitt, Dylan, 201
Huillet, Danièle, 17, 18–19, 105–113, 115, 118, 120–122

Il ritorno del figlio prodigo – Umiliati (2003), 106
Illich, Ivan, 219
Indymedia European Newsreel (2002), 199
Iven, Joris, 84, 85, 242

J18 (1999), 196–197
Jacir, Anna-Marie, 178
Jameson, Fredric, 18
Johns, Jasper, 59
José Martí, 135
Judge Dredd (1994), 262

Juhasz, Alexandra, 15, 229

Kafka, Franz, 149
Kant, Immanuel, 32
Karamzinsky, Nikolay, 43, 46, 48
Karmitz, Marin, 139
Kautsky, Karl, 4
Kendrik, James, 258
Kennedy, Jackie, 130
Khlebnikov, Velimir, 54n40
Khleifi, Michel, 176, 178, 183
Kidner, Dan, 186
Kinopravda (journal), 83
Klein, Naomi, 169
Klein, William, 84
Korsch, Karl, 4
Kuhle Wampe (1932), 70
Kuleshov, Lev, 34, 69, 172, 253, 258–259

La Chinoise (1967), 59, 63–4, 72–73, 74
La Jetée (1962), 81
La Sixième Face du Pentagone (1968), 94
Lahusen, Thomas, 33
Lang, Fritz, 171
Laporte, Pierre, 136
Lazzarato, Maurizio, 2, 235–236
Le Petit Soldat (1963), 74
Le Tombeau d'Alexandre (1993), 83
Lef (New Lef) (journal), 67–69
Lelouch, Claude, 84
Lenin, Vladimir I., 4, 11, 30, 32, 39, 42, 50n4, 67, 84, 168–169, 171–172, 253, 255
Lerner, Jean-Claude, 84
Lesage, Julia, 138
Letters from Siberia (1957), 81
Level Five (1997), 91, 102
Lévi-Strauss, Claude, 146
Levi, Pavle, 35–36
Liebknecht, Karl, 4
Light, Paul, 200–205, 209n19

Linhart, Robert, 39, 49
Little, Walter, 125
Living in the Future (2006), 195
Loach, Ken, 206
Löwy, Michael, 217
Lukács, Georg, 255, 258, 267n2
Lunch, Chris, 191
Lunch, Nick, 191
Luxemburg, Rosa, 4
Lyotard, Jean-François, 8

MacCabe, Colin, 71–72
Macherey, Pierre, 4, 66
Madame Bovary (1856), 12
Man with a Movie Camera (1929), 83
Mandarini, Matteo, 155
Marcuse, Herbert, 9, 11, 15
Marker, Chris, 10, 17, 18, 39, 41, 61, 81–91, 94–95, 97–102
Marret, Mario, 87
Martin-Jones, David, 151–152, 158–159
Marx, Karl, 1–4, 6, 12, 16, 19, 20, 22, 32, 43, 49, 58–59, 96–97, 105–106, 145–146, 153–155, 169, 187, 217, 219, 223, 237, 240, 242–244, 246–247, 249, 254–255; and 'Theses on Feuerbach', 1; and *The German Ideology*, 1, 43; and *The Communist Manifesto*, 1–2, 3, 60; and *Das Kapital*, 3, 240; and *The Eighteenth Brumaire of Louis Bonaparte*, 58, 105; and *Grundrisse*, 219, 247, 249; and *Theories of Surplus Value*, 243
Masharawi, Rashid, 178
Massad, Joseph, 178
Mathy, Jean-Phillipe, 93
Mattelart, Armand, 87
Mayakovsky, Vladimir, 67, 172
Mayoux, Valérie, 84, 87, 94
McCarthy, Joseph, 171
McGuire, James W., 125

McKay, George, 203, 208n13
Medvedkin, Aleksandr, 11–12, 17, 18, 31, 34, 37–44, 46, 49, 51n8, 52n17, 53n30, 83–84
Meppiel, Jacqueline, 87
Metropolis (1927), 171
Miller, Toby, 228
Minnelli, Vincente, 151–152
Modern Times (1936), 171
Monet, Suzanne, 138
Montand, Yves, 71, 139
Moreh, Dror, 180
Moses and Aron (1974)
Mullarkey, John, 153–154
Murillo, María Victoria, 125

Negri, Antonio, 7, 22, 105–106, 169, 235
New Statesman (magazine), 22, 238–239
Nietzsche, Friedrich, 146

O'Connor, James, 215, 217–218, 230
O'Connor, Paul, 194, 196–199, 209n19
Ocampo, Gilberto Gómez, 132
October (1928), 36
Okhlopov, Nikolay, 44
On the Push (2009), 195
Onganía, Juan Carlos, 126
Othon (1970)
Ozu, Yasujiro, 150

Padilha José, 20, 145
Panos, David, 206
Paradise Now (2005), 181
Paranagua, Paulo Antonio, 137
Paul II, John Pope, 146
Pavese, Cesare, 108
Penley, Constance, 213
Perón, Eva, 130
Perón, Juan, 19, 124–125, 130, 133, 135–136
Persona (1966), 59
Pick, Zuzana, 136–137

Pierrot le fou (1965), 73
Pilger, John, 206
Pisters, Patricia, 152, 158
Pleynet, Marcelin, 62, 64, 75
Polak, Frederik, 266
Pravda (1969), 61
Prince, Stephen, 259
Pudovkin, Vsevolod, 34, 69, 172
Pybus, Jennifer, 236

Rancière, Jacques, 12–13, 18, 23, 29, 35, 51n6, 58, 72–77, 86, 107, 109–110, 112, 116, 119, 153
Rauschenberg, Robert, 59
Resnais, Alain, 61, 84
Revolting in Prague (2000), 198, 208n14
Riots Reframed (2013), 206
Rizzo, Teresa, 159
Rocha, Glauber, 127, 149–150, 157, 159
Roger, Jean-Henri, 61
Rogue Reels (1999), 186
Rohmer, Eric, 116
Rosen, Paul, 220
Rosenberg, Harold, 58
Rosler, Martha, 74
Ross, Andrew, 213
Ross, Kristin, 91–92
Rossellini, Roberto, 110
Rothschild, Mayer, 166
Route 181 (2003), 183
Rushton, Richard, 151–152, 155
Ryan, Michael, 257

Sans Soleil (1983), 83, 88–91, 94–95
Saraceni, Paulo Cesar, 127
Sartre, Jean-Paul, 4
Sayers, Sean, 219
SchNEWS at Ten (2005), 202, 204
Scott, Ridley, 264
Secret City (2012), 206
Sembène, Ousmane, 149–150, 157

Shaked, Ayelet, 180
Shohat, Ella, 128, 150
Shub, Esfir, 69
Sicily! (1999), 106
Siegmeister, Elie, 251
Sivan, Eyal, 183
Smith, Adam, 146, 243, 246
Sokolov, Ippolit, 172–173
Solanas, Fernando, 14, 19, 124–128, 132–135, 138
Sparkes, Daryl, 258
Stalin, Josef, 38, 47–48, 82
Stallone, Sylvester, 262
Stam, Robert, 128, 130, 150
Star Trek (1966–1969), 265
Still We Ride (2004), 222
Straub, Jean-Marie, 17, 18–19, 105–113, 115, 118, 120–122
Suleiman, Elia, 178–179

Taylor, Richard, 171
Thatcher, Margaret, 265
The Challenge (1965), 127
The Chronicle of Anna Magdalena Bach (1967), 106
The Confession (1970), 62–63
The End of the Line (2009), 189
The Gatekeepers (2012), 180
The Godfather (1972), 133
The Hours of Furnaces (1968), 14, 19, 124–125, 127–128, 131–140
The Last Bolshevik (1993), 18, 39
The LIP Conflict (1973–74), 139
The Lord of the Rings (2001), 253, 259–261, 264
The Matrix, 10
The Meaning of the Hitler Salute: Little man asks for big gifts. Motto: Millions Stand Behind Me! (1932), 74
The Return of the Scorcher (1992), 213
The Return to Haifa (1982), 175

The Spiral (1975), 87
The Time that Remains (2009), 179
The Train Rolls On (1971), 41, 83, 86
Titans of the Ring (1973), 133
Toffler, Alvin, 266
Tooker, John, 84
Torchin, Leshu, 16
Torre, Juan Carlos, 126
Torri, Gianfranco, 127
Tout va bien (1972), 71, 139
Travail et Culture (journal), 18, 81
Tretyakov, Sergei, 68
Trevelyan, Humphry, 186
Triple Agent (2004), 116
Trotsky, Leon, 33, 50n4, 52n14, 255–256
Truffaut, François, 254
Two or Three Things I Know About Her (1967), 71–72

Undercurrents 10¾ (2002), 197
Undercurrents News Network (2004), 199

Valéry, Paul, 120–121
Varda, Agnès, 84
Vertov, Dziga, 10, 11–12, 14, 17, 34, 37, 52n24, 60–61, 68–69, 83, 236, 253
Vincent, Maraval, 247
Virilio, Paul, 216, 229
Vittachi, Anuradha, 188
Vittorini, Elio, 108–109, 111, 113, 117–118
Vivanco, Luis A., 215–216
Vivre sa vie (1962), 74

Vlady, Marina, 71
Volpi, Gianni, 127
von Harbou, Thea, 171
von Hirsch, Maurice, 166

Wachowski, Andy and Lana, 13
Warren, Bill, 168–169
Watkins, Peter, 12
Wayne, Mike, 258
Weber, Max, 146
Wedding in Galilee (1988), 176
Weizmann, Chaim, 167
White, Ted, 213, 222
Who Polices the Police? (2012), 206
Williams, Linda, 262
Williams, Raymond, 255–256
Wind from the East (1970), 138–139
Winstanley, Asa, 182
Wollen, Peter, 18, 61–62
Women of Messina (novel) (1949), 108–109, 111–112, 117–118
Workers, Peasants (2000), 19, 105–122
Working Together (2013), 186

Young, Zoe, 191, 203, 208n6, 208n14, 209n17

Z (1969), 62
Zimmerman, Patricia R., 213
Zindeeq (2011), 178–179
Žižek, Slavoj, 6, 30, 32, 53n28
Zobel, Gibby, 201

www.ingramcontent.com/pod-product-compliance
Lightning Source LLC
Chambersburg PA
CBHW072147100526
44589CB00015B/2122